DEVELOPING FACULTY MENTORING PROGRAMS

A COMPREHENSIVE HANDBOOK

DAVID KIEL

ACADEMIC IMPRESSIONS | 2019
DENVER, CO

Published by Academic Impressions.

CR Mrig Company. 4601 DTC Blvd., Suite 800, Denver, CO 80237.

Copyright © 2019 David Kiel.

Cover design by Brady Stanton.

All rights reserved.

No part of this book may be reproduced, or stored in a retrieval system, or transmitted in any form or by any means, electronic, mechanical, photocopying, recording, or otherwise, without express written permission of the publisher.

For reproduction, distribution, or copy permissions, or to order additional copies, please contact the Academic Impressions office at 720.488.6800 or visit:

http://bit.ly/2qbHuLr

Academic Impressions

ISBN: 978-1-948658-08-9

Printed in the United States of America.

ANOTHER BOOK YOU MAY ENJOY

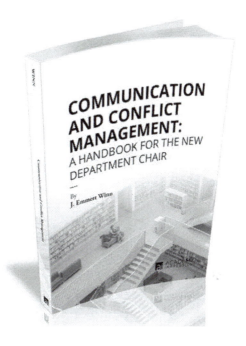

Effective communication will make or break a department chair. Get a primer on the essential communication and conflict management skills that every department chair needs.

Explore the book at:
https://www.academicimpressions.com/product/communication-conflict-management-handbook-new-department-chair/

DAVID KIEL

CONTENTS

1   OVERVIEW

1   Introduction

2   7 Ways to Use This Book

5   5 Reasons Why Well-Defined Faculty Mentoring Programs Are Essential

9   What Do We Mean by Well-Defined Faculty Mentoring?

12   The Qualities of a Good Mentoring Relationship

13   How Program Design Can Foster Good Mentoring

13   Inclusion and Diversity

15   Mentoring and Faculty Development: Not Just for Tenured and Tenure-Track

16   Conclusion: Making the Case

21   CHAPTER 1:
DESIGN THE MENTORING PROGRAM
YOUR ACADEMIC UNIT REALLY NEEDS

22   2 Key Elements of any Well-Defined Mentoring Program

33   4 Important Design Criteria for Your Mentoring Program

41   6 Essential Decisions in Defining the Mentoring Program

58   Making Mentoring Work: 7 Operational Decisions

72   9 Factors That Influence Program Design

79   Concluding Thoughts

95   CHAPTER 2:
WHAT MENTORING SERVICES ARE
NEEDED TO SUPPORT EARLY CAREER
FACULTY ON YOUR CAMPUS?

99   Helping Early Career Faculty Understand and Prepare for Tenure and Promotion

118 Supporting the Development of Teaching Skills for Early Career Faculty

121 Supporting the Development of Research and Writing Skills for Early Career Faculty

129 Providing Effective Professional Development Services for Early Career Faculty

132 Providing Effective Mentoring and Faculty Development Services for Women and Under-Represented Minority Faculty Members

148 Conclusion: How to Get Started

160 CHAPTER 3:
DESIGNING AND IMPLEMENTING MID-CAREER MENTORING AND FACULTY DEVELOPMENT PROGRAMS

161 Sometimes Promotion Can Be a Career Crisis

165 Additional Consequences of the Mid-Career Crisis

169 Creative Responses to the Mid-Career Faculty Crisis at the Unit Level

209 CHAPTER 4:
DEVELOPING SENIOR FACULTY: GUIDANCE FOR CHAIRS, DEANS, AND OTHER ACADEMIC LEADERS

211 The Case for Senior Faculty Development

212 Key Considerations to Guide the Creation of SFD Programs

215 Specific Programs to Support Senior Faculty at the Individual Level

223 Specific Programs to Support Senior Faculty at the Functional Level

232 Specific Programs to Support Senior Faculty at the Institutional Level

248 Summary

261 CHAPTER 5:
TO GET STARTED AND KEEP GOING: 10
EFFECTIVE PRACTICES

263 1. Be Mindful of Existing Policies and Directives

264 2. Assess Current Practices and Existing Resources—Build from What You Have in Place

275 3. Set Priorities Based on Peer Research Relative to Faculty Recruitment and Retention

277 4. Involve Faculty in the Planning

280 5. Establish Policies That Produce Action at Your Level

284 6. Provide Support for Implementation

287 7. Centralize or De-centralize Mentoring Services (to Fit Your Situation)

288 8. Address the Needs of Smaller Units

292 9. Invest in Faculty and Staff Time to Implement Mentoring Activities

294 10. Follow Through

302 Conclusion—Implementation is a Team Effort

APPENDICES

307 APPENDIX A:
MENTORING AND SUPPORT FOR FULL-
TIME, NON-TENURE-TRACK FACULTY

309 Defining FTF Needs and Identifying Directions for Improvement of Jobs and Working Conditions

314 Case Studies: Improving FTF Jobs at Research Universities

320 Conclusion: Charting a Way Forward for FTF

327 APPENDIX B: WORKBOOK

549 APPENDIX C: BIBLIOGRAPHY

DAVID KIEL

DEDICATION AND ACKNOWLEDGMENTS

This book is about mentoring, so it is only fitting that I dedicate it to my own mentor Rolf Lynton, author of many books, founder of innovative institutions on four continents, a former dean, and change agent extraordinaire. At 95 years of age, Rolf is still making discoveries about how to foster innovation and writing about them for a global audience.

I was fortunate to have Rolf as a role model and mentor, and, for the last twenty-five years, a colleague and friend. Ours has been one of those traditional mentoring relationships where a life-long bond is established that continues to foster mutual creativity.

But, as you will see in the pages of this book, it also makes sense to have a network of mentors as well as one touchstone. I was fortunate to have other people who helped me along the way, taught me valuable skills and lessons, and even came to rescue my career and sanity at various points. In this company, I must name Doug Champion, David Hawkins, Bert Kaplan, Ken Lessler, Jean McLendon, Terry Miller, Bill Peck, Marian Smallegan, Terry Vance, Bob Vaillancourt, and Bill Woodward. Where I would have been without them is anybody's guess.

I also want to dedicate this book to Professor Ruel Tyson, former Chair of Religious Studies at UNC-CH, and founding and long-time Director of the Institute for the Arts and Humanities (IAH). The IAH has provided a semester research leave for over 500 scholars in the arts, humanities, and qualitative social sciences and it has been a trailblazer for faculty development efforts on the Carolina campus. An intellectual's intellectual, Ruel seemed an unlikely choice for a salesman of the Arts and Humanities to the broader worlds of business and philanthropy. Yet over a 25-year period, he and his team, and successors, starting with a $5000 stake from a hopeful dean, managed to raise over $50,000,000 and counting for faculty development at UNC-CH. For Ruel, evidently, "the miracle of the loaves and the fishes," as recounted in the New Testament, was more than a parable. It was Ruel who also took a chance on me in 2001 and gave me the opportunity to work at the IAH, and that led to a second career in faculty development. In essence, Rolf Lynton and my other mentors showed me what to do, and Ruel Tyson gave me the opportunity to do it, hence this book and all it represents.

I also had helpers in creating this book. My former boss at the Center for Faculty Excellence, Todd Zakrajsek, introduced me to the world of faculty development. MSU Associate Provost Deb DeZure first introduced me to the literature on mentoring in the academy. They were kind enough to look over draft chapters and encouraged me to continue with the project as did my colleague Rob Kramer, an academic leadership and coaching expert. This book has also benefitted greatly from the suggestions and comments of AI Director of Publications Daniel Fusch and AI Senior Program Manager Tunde Brimah. Amit Mrig, AI's President, is herewith publicly accused of putting the idea to write a book for AI into my head in the first place.

OVERVIEW

NOTE TO THE READER

If you are already convinced that your campus or unit needs to formalize, extend, and improve its mentoring programs, read the first two sections of this introduction and then go straight to Chapter 1.

If you want to review the case for why well-defined mentoring programs should replace current informal or ad hoc arrangements, continue to the end of the Overview.

Introduction

In 2010, Bruce Carney, the Provost at the University of North Carolina at Chapel Hill, endorsed the following report from a faculty task force he had appointed the year before.

> Mentoring is central to both individual and institutional success. Good mentorship is a hallmark of successful academic units. The department chair or school dean is responsible for ensuring mentoring is available and for establishing an environment conducive to and supportive of mentorship. Senior faculty members have a responsibility to support and advise their junior colleagues. Early career faculty should be proactive in developing mentoring relationships and are responsible for taking advantage of the mentorship opportunities available to them. (1)

He said the provost's office would now look at the polices and programs each unit had in place for faculty mentoring as a part of the five year review conducted by the graduate school. Deans took notice. Chairs began to conduct their own reviews, and chairs were asked about the mentoring services their departments provided.

I had just been hired into a job that focused on building support programs for faculty leaders across the campus. As often happens in organizations, people get assigned new tasks without much preparation. I was now asked, in addition, to create programs and activities designed to help chairs and deans implement mentoring programs. I needed to get up to speed very fast on the whys, wherefores, and hows of faculty mentoring.

It took me seven years of study, action, and review to accumulate the information contained in this handbook that I now share with you.

The chapters, supplement, and appendices that follow this Overview are designed to constitute a rich information resource for your campus.

7 Ways to Use This Book

Here are seven ways to use this book to help your campus strengthen mentoring and faculty development services for faculty throughout the career cycle.

1. Get your leadership on the same page

This book brings together in one place the information academic leaders need to create or strengthen faculty mentoring and faculty development on their campuses. It is designed to help you plan and take effective action to improve mentoring and faculty development services. By purchasing multiple copies for use by a planning committee or simply providing copies to the chairs and deans, you can assure access to the needed information in one volume.

2. Understand the *whys* of mentoring

The rest of this Overview describes why well-defined, comprehensive faculty mentoring and development programs are needed now more than ever. I will also discuss why they are necessary, not only for enhancing the productivity and retention of academic talent, but also for realizing the values of equity, inclusion, and diversity.

3. Support early career faculty

In Chapters 1-2, you receive a comprehensive guide to methods and approaches for improving mentoring programs and faculty development services for tenure track and non-tenure-track early career faculty. I will provide information about the design and implementation of mentoring programs in granular detail not usually seen in discussions of mentoring. I will also share examples of many effective practices that you can adapt to the situation of your department, school, or campus whether you are at a university, a liberal arts college, or two-year institution.

4. Extend mentoring to mid/late-career

Chapter 3 extends the discussion to supporting faculty members through the crisis of the mid-career. Chapter 4 shows how all the good work in faculty development may culminate in support for senior faculty during what should be the most productive time in their career. Throughout, I will provide examples of policy statements, program descriptions, and case studies that can be adapted for local use.

5. Get it done

Chapter 5 provides detailed guidance for chairs, deans, and senior leaders on implementation for the campus, school and department level.

6. Provide tools for training

In the text and appendices that follow, I will provide easily adaptable tools, tips, and checklists that have been used for orienting and training mentors and mentees. In addition, there are materials for guiding and assisting faculty leaders who are tasked with designing programs of mentoring and faculty development.

7. Get a portal to additional resources

I will try not to burden the reader with copious academic references in the text, but footnotes at the end of each chapter provide readers with access to original sources so readers can follow up on their own and extend their inquiries as needed. (The URLs included in these notes were accurate as of January 29, 2019.) I have searched for good examples of what institutions of higher education are doing to support mentoring at all career stages. Another helpful feature of the book is a selected annotated bibliography of resources including books, websites, and organizations. Once your team has this book they should have access to the information they need to strengthen faculty mentoring and faculty development services at your college or university.

Finally, the book also contains a supplement that addresses the special needs of non-tenure-track, full-time faculty. Throughout the book, I will suggest mentoring options for this group. This is a growing proportion of the faculty at many institutions, but this supplement is a recognition of the fact that on many campuses they will need significant improvement of their jobs before mentoring and faculty development services can have the desired effect.

5 Reasons Why Well-Defined Faculty Mentoring Programs Are Essential

Here are five reasons why well-defined faculty mentoring programs are a "must have feature" of campus life.

1. Increased diversity

Increasing diversity has added to the need for well-structured mentoring. For most of its history, the students and faculty of US colleges and universities have been predominantly male and white and served a small proportion of the population. After WWII and the passage of the GI Bill, the US became the first country to move toward a mass system of higher education. Institutions of higher education began to attract and accept many more white males from families whose parents never attended college.

After the passage of the Higher Education Act of 1965, the increasing enforcement of civil rights laws, and the

1972 adoption of Title IX (that promoted equal opportunities for women) greater numbers of women and people of color also began to enroll in the previously white male-oriented institutions across the country. Increased federal aid to students also fueled this expansion. In addition, enrollment in two-year community colleges greatly increased. (2)

Partly as a response to these events, demands for the faculty to diversify as well became ever more insistent. As more women and faculty members of color were hired beginning in the late 1960s and early 1970s, it eventually became clear that the informal mentoring system and the established norms of promotion and tenure were not going to work for all. White men who had informal mentors would get information and assistance that women and faculty members of color did not have access to. There was little appreciation for the demands of child-rearing facing young mothers on the tenure track. There was evidence of implicit bias and evident gender, race, and other biases in selection and promotion. (3)

Generational differences have come into play as well. Younger baby boomers and Gen X faculty "have been vocal about wanting...more transparency and processes, more welcoming and supportive processes, more welcoming and supportive workplace/department, and more frequent and helpful feedback about progress." (4)

Also, as faculty from other nations became US faculty members, it became clear that the styles of teaching, research, and student-faculty interactions they learned might not fit with preferred US approaches. New concerns about gender identity and sexual orientation add other areas of complexity. As diversity increases, the university becomes more "a low context culture" where cues on how to succeed are less easily acquired from normal interactions and observations and so faculty need help in navigating that culture successfully. (5)

2. Social barriers

Social dynamics can be a barrier to getting help for new faculty members. From my discussions with chairs, I know that personality and patterns of senior/early career faculty interaction are also factors in skewing who gets help in departments. Some talented people might derail in informal or poorly structured mentoring programs because they fail to seek help when they need it, in the mistaken view this will compromise their independence. They may also fear to seek help from the senior faculty who they think might evaluate or constrain them. On the other hand potential mentors may be too busy with their own work to reach out to younger faculty and may not see that as their role or obligation. Or they may fear that their offers will be seen as interference. They may not have had effective mentors and may be unsure how to perform the role.

If you are a new minority faculty member, or a new female faculty member in an overwhelmingly male department, there is a chance you might feel quite isolated if someone did not reach out to you and help you become part of the group – and guide you through the tenure process. On the other hand, white male faculty may be uncomfortable in reaching out, because they don't want to emphasize differences. So, there may be many factors that confound the informal mentoring system.

3. Increased standards for productivity

Increasing standards for productivity also adds to the need for structured mentoring. Furthermore, as expectations for faculty grow ever higher, young faculty members, male and female, white and of color, became more anxious about what is going to be demanded of them. National surveys show that early career faculty members are looking for more clarity, guidance, and collegiality. In the competition for the best talent, having a reputation as a place where young faculty members "sink or swim" on their own is not a selling point.

4. Mentor non-tenure-track faculty

Adding more non-tenure-track faculty also increases the need for mentoring programs. In addition, as long-serving fixed-term full-time faculty members become more prominent in the academy, they are playing increasingly important roles. They have not typically had focused career development or mentoring support so there is a gap that becomes more obvious as formal programs are being put in place for the tenure track. More and more frequently full-time non-tenure-track faculty are successfully making the claim they should be integrated into the regular faculty and have clear paths for advancement supported by mentoring and faculty development opportunities. (6)

5. Growing recognition of the need for mentoring programs beyond early career

There is a new recognition of the need for mentoring for mid-career and beyond. Once early career faculty members are promoted (either on the tenure or non-tenure track) there is often a drop off in motivation and careers can become stalled. Increasingly, academic leaders are looking to mentoring and faculty development programs to forestall this "post-tenure slump" or to accelerate the way back to higher morale and productivity.

So for at least these five reasons, institutions of higher education (IHEs) have increasingly come to the conclusion that purely informal systems of mentoring are inherently unfair and ineffective. Some talented early career faculty will lose out, the department will be subjected to costly unwanted turnover, and the reputation and morale of the unit could be damaged.

As a result of these and other considerations, good support and guidance for new faculty, especially those on the tenure track, have become an expectation for leading universities and colleges. Academic leaders are becoming convinced "it's the right thing to do." More clearly defined mentoring systems are seen as ways of leveling the playing field and providing guidance and support for early-career faculty members and also, increasingly, mid-career and late-career faculty members who are the role models and gate keepers for others. Universities increasingly want to be known as a university that hires talented faculty and helps them become our next generation of leading scholars.

Many studies are now showing that faculty mentoring programs are helpful to new faculty and to IHEs in various ways. Benefits include recruiting, retention and advancement, socialization, relationship building, productivity, and professional growth. (7)

What Do We Mean by Well-Defined Faculty Mentoring?

What do we mean by well-defined faculty mentoring and how is it important in the context of faculty development?

I have argued that more formal faculty mentoring programs are becoming more standard across the academy. Since I have made this case so strongly, it is incumbent upon me to better define our terms so actions can be well directed. Mentoring is a common term and the traditional meanings may not always fit the current context.

The *traditional* concept of mentoring involves a life changing and often career-long relationship between an older, knowledgeable individual and a younger person coming along in the same field. The relationship evolves informally and is sustained by the satisfaction and benefits that both parties experience. There is nothing wrong with this concept of mentoring. The only thing is that this traditional sense of the relationship cannot be programmed; it happens naturally when there is good chemistry between a younger person who wants mentoring and an older person who wants to provide it. (8)

As I have previously said, there are many barriers to this kind of mentoring relationship occurring across lines of gender, class, nationality, and race. So, if conditions are making mentoring more crucial, but less "naturally" available because of the increasing pressure on everyone's time, it then becomes necessary to formally structure well-defined programs of mentoring that will better serve faculty and our IHEs. These well-defined mentoring programs cannot assure that "traditional" mentoring occurs in terms of lifelong deep, mutual relationships, but they can greatly increase the chances that the new or younger faculty member will get the help he or she needs to be successful in terms of promotion and professional development.

Formal or well-defined mentoring programs achieve this result by structuring the mentoring role in terms of behavioral expectations rather than the expectation of a particular kind of a relationship. Since each unit will create a specific role for mentors that help the unit implement its particular mentoring and faculty development goals, the prescribed mentoring role will differ a bit in each department or school. Despite wide variation in how the mentoring role is carried out, there are some common elements. The mentor role most often includes the following: providing guidance about promotion standards and procedures, feedback about the candidate's progress relative to those standards, and substantive advice in terms of strengthening teaching and scholarship so as to meet unit productivity standards. Within that context a lasting relationship may or may not evolve but at least the mentees will get the basic information they need to be successful in the department or school that employs them.

Faculty development is a broader term than *mentoring*, but arguably mentoring is the core faculty development service especially in the early years. Faculty development may be comprised of other activities besides one-on-one mentoring. These include: attending workshops on teaching practices or research methods, participating in peer support groups, grant support for attending conferences, starting research, or taking time off to develop a course. These also include leadership practices that recognize important transitions and achievement and are inclusive and welcoming, and, in general, create a motivating climate that fosters faculty success throughout the length of the career.

In this book, I will focus on the establishment of well-defined faculty mentoring programs in the early chapters, but also expand our perspective to other forms of faculty development once that basic function is clarified and fully explicated.

The Qualities of a Good Mentoring Relationship

The well-defined mentoring relationship, however structured, has a specific job to do (e.g., impart essential knowledge about promotion processes, assure good teaching, and guide scholarship). So, the first requirement is that the mentor or mentors assigned have the knowledge, ability, and motivation to do this job. However, the relational part of the mentor-mentor connection is also critical. It is important to demonstrate to the mentee that the mentor(s) have the best interests of the mentee at heart, that the mentor(s) can be trusted, that they will make time for the mentee, and they will do their jobs in the mentoring context. Any relationship is a two-way street so the mentee must demonstrate commitment, responsibility, and initiative as well.

In any human relationship, there are differing degrees of control, closeness, and affection that are extended by one and desired by the other. Hopefully, there is a good fit on these dimensions, but if the fit is a big problem for one or both parties, there needs to be a mechanism in place to adjust the relationship or find a new mentor. While the academic unit can control the structure and expectations of any mentoring system, there will be considerable variability that can only be chalked up to "human nature." You can create good mentoring processes and programs, but you cannot mandate good mentoring relationships. (9)

How Program Design Can Foster Good Mentoring

You cannot assure that a mentoring relationship will be of the classical life-long, career informing, and deep intellectual connection variety, or that it be a perfect fit for both the mentors and the mentees. However, you can work to assure the relationship gets off to a good start and has a decent chance of succeeding. You can ensure the overall program goals are clear and relevant to the needs of the unit and the mentee, that the role of the mentor and mentees are well defined, that pairing of mentors and mentees is the result of a thoughtful process, that required and elective activities are specified, that there is effective communication about the program, that there are adequate resources for program administration, and, finally, that you check from time to time to see how each relationship and the overall program is working. Attention to these issues helps prevent problems born of misunderstanding that can be damaging to a new faculty member who is in a vulnerable state and also damage the reputation and morale of faculty members in the unit who may feel responsible for whatever problems arise. (10)

Inclusion and Diversity

Here I refer to mentoring that works across lines of gender, color, and other flashpoints of difference. I started this introduction by saying that part of the original impetus toward more formal mentoring programs had to do with accommodating faculty members who were neither male nor white and with providing a basic level of support and guidance for all early career faculty. Now I have to say, sadly, in addition, that a well-structured mentoring program does not inoculate against these problems with respect to gender or race or other issues related to difference. I will have a lot to say about how to address the endemic challenges that face under-represented minority faculty members throughout this book, but I will start with the suggestion that awareness is key.

If you are a chair or dean or mentoring program head, you should work to acquaint yourself with the issues that may arise and options for handling these issues. If a faculty member senses that she is the victim of prejudice or neglect, hopefully she will come talk with you about it. The worst-case scenario is when you find out you have lost a promising faculty member because you were unaware of the problems—or find out when a grievance or OEO complaint is filed.

In addition to a heightened awareness of these types of problems, it makes sense for chairs and deans to assure that faculty members who have concerns related to any issue of difference have access to talk with someone outside the mentoring committee or even the department or school. Ideally, the chair or head of the unit mentoring effort will build in safeguards such as making sure the mentees know where they can go to have confidential conversations elsewhere on campus that ultimately can lead to surfacing and addressing any problems. (11) Some universities have ombuds programs that serve this function. (12)

Mentoring and Faculty Development: Not Just for Tenured and Tenure-Track

Another guiding principle of this handbook is that mentoring and faculty development are not just for tenured and tenure track faculty. Actually we still have a long way to go to make sure that the programs that support tenure and tenure track faculty are what they need to be. However, we have even more to do to see that mentoring and faculty development services are extended to full-time, non-tenure-track faculty. In universities and colleges, it is actually these faculty members who do the bulk of the teaching in language instruction, introductory STEM courses, music performance and creative writing instruction, teacher education, and many business courses. In research universities, fixed-term faculty members may also be found in full-time research roles or in the health professions in clinical and teaching roles. More and more IHEs are creating career paths with promotional standards and junior, mid-level, and senior rank designations for non-tenure-track faculty. In this book, I provide guidance for how mentoring and faculty development services can also become available for fixed-term full-time faculty as well. In Appendix A, I discuss the special concerns that might affect fixed-term full-time faculty and how these should be addressed before you can expect mentoring and faculty development services to produce the desired results for this group.

In an ideal world, mentoring and faculty development services would be extended to adjunct or part-time faculty as well, and where it's practical I recommend that. However, a review of the literature on adjunct and part-time faculty shows that so many issues exist in making existing part-time faculty jobs achieve even minimally accepted standards for this large group of US faculty members that the mentoring and faculty development discussion for this group may be premature, pending other types of job improvements that are more basic. (13)

Conclusion: Making the Case

Since I will spend the rest of this book discussing how best to design and implement effective faculty development programs for your faculty, it makes sense to conclude this introduction and overview by summarizing the main reasons it's worth the considerable investment in time and energy such an effort entails.

Here is the case for investing in stronger mentoring and faculty development programs. The main reasons include:

- Faculty need more support because of the increasing demands and expectations in terms of teaching, research, and service.

- Informal mentoring arrangements are likely to let some faculty fall between the cracks, and under-represented minority faculty—those that most departments are trying so hard to recruit and retain—are most at risk.

- Late Gen X and Gen Y faculty have higher expectations for transparency, support, and collegiality than the older "boomers" and their predecessors.

- There are increasing expectations that full-time, non-tenure-track faculty should have promotional paths, mentoring, and development opportunities.

- Failure to meet rising expectation for effective mentoring and support could result in costly faculty turnover.

- As institutions work to upgrade their mentoring and faculty development systems, IHEs who are lagging may be at a competitive disadvantage in recruitment.

- Research shows that faculty mentoring improves faculty satisfaction, retention, and productivity.

Now, read the rest of this book and find out the best ways to strengthen mentoring and faculty development on your campuses and reap the benefits of a productive and satisfied faculty group.

Notes

1. See "The Report of the UNC Task Force on Future Promotion and Tenure Policies and Practices." May 2009.

   https://provost.unc.edu/taskforce-future-promotion-tenure-policies-practices/

2. For a good brief overview of the history of changes in US college and university enrollment, see Louis Menand's "College: The End of the

Golden Age" in *The New York Review of Books*, Oct. 2001 Issue. Access at:

http://www.nybooks.com/articles/2001/10/18/college-the-end-of-the-golden-age/

3. I think it's fair to say this historical narrative is generally accepted. For research documenting the particular difficulties that women and faculty of color face, see Carnegie Mellon's "Fostering a Mentoring Culture: A Guide for Department Heads," Mark Kamlet Provost, Revised 2002. p.2. https://www.cmu.edu/teaching/resources/MentoringFaculty/MentoringGuideDepartmentHeads.pdf and Rachel Thomas' "Exemplary Junior Faculty Mentoring Programs, WFF-Yale University, 2005, p. 15, citing documented issues at the University of Wisconsin:

https://cpb-us-e1.wpmucdn.com/blogs.cornell.edu/dist/8/6767/files/2016/01/Exemplary-Junior-Faculty-Mentoring-Programs-105ab08.pdf

4. Cathy Ann Trower, *Success on the Tenure Track: Five keys to Faculty Job Satisfaction*, Johns Hopkins University Press, Baltimore, p. 23.

5. There is more on this in Walter H. Gmelch and Jeffrey L. Buller's *Building Academic Leadership Capacity: A Guide to Best Practices*, Jossey Bass, 2015, p. 159.

6. For one example of advocacy in this regard see "The Imperative for Change: Understanding the Necessity of Changing Non-Tenure-Track Faculty

Policies and Practices" by Adrianna Kezar, Daniel Maxey, and Lara Badke. This is a White Paper prepared as part of the Delphi Project, 2014. The Delphi Project is housed in the Pullias School of Education at the University of Southern California: https://pullias.usc.edu/delphi/

7. Joselynn Fountain and Kathyrin E. Newcomer summarize the literature through 2012 in their 2016 article "Developing and Sustaining Effective Faculty Mentoring Programs, *Journal of Public Affairs Education, JPAE 22* (4), 483– 506.

8. See the discussion of traditional mentoring in the *VCU School of Medicine Faculty Mentoring Guide*, Revised March 2002, by Dean Heber H. Newsome, and Associate Dean Carol H. Hampton, p 1-2.

    https://medschool.vcu.edu/media/medschool/documents/fmguide.pdf

9. What constitutes a good mentoring relationship in a classic sense is discussed in the book *Good Mentoring: Fostering Excellent Practice in Higher Education*, by Jeanne Nakamura and David J. Shernoff, Jossey Bass, John Wiley and Sons, 2009. See especially pages 219-265.

10. The research basis for determining the characteristics of well-structured mentoring programs is identified by Fountain and Newcomer in the article cited in note 7, p. 485 & p. 492.

11. Kerry Ann Rokquemore provides a good primer for chairs on the issues that might arise for under-

represented minority faculty in *Inside Higher Ed*: https://www.insidehighered.com/users/kerry-ann-rockquemore. See her essays:

- "Advice for Mentoring Underrepresented Senior Faculty Members." *Inside Higher Ed,* 3/02/16.

- "Advice to a White Professor About Mentoring Scholars of Color." *Inside Higher Ed,* 2/17/16.

- "How to Follow up with Underrepresented Faculty Who Decide to Leave Your Institution." *Inside Higher Ed,* 2/20/16.

- "How to Retain a Diverse Faculty." *Inside Higher Ed,* 1/06/16.

12. Many universities currently have such programs, including Columbia, Kentucky, Stanford, Oregon State, Vanderbilt, and UNC. For more information on these types of programs, see:

http://www.ombudsassociation.org/About-Us.aspx

Also see "One Faculty Serving All Students," Coalition on the Academic Workforce, February, 2010 Issue Brief:

http://www.academicworkforce.org/Research_reports.html

CHAPTER 1
DESIGN THE MENTORING PROGRAM YOUR ACADEMIC UNIT REALLY NEEDS

"A formal intentional approach to the mentoring experience is most likely to succeed … one in which mentor/mentee interactions are deliberate, structured, and goal oriented."

(Bland, Taylor, et al., *Faculty Success Through Mentoring, A Guide for Mentors, Mentees and Leaders*. ACE Series on Higher Education. Roman and Littlefield, 2009.)

This chapter is for chairs, deans, and other academic leaders who are working to design or improve a mentoring program for their unit. In this chapter, you will see how thoughtful upfront design of mentoring programs is really important and why one size does not fit all. In the material that follows, I will examine the key design elements of mentoring programs in logical order:

1. Understand the two key functions of a well-defined mentoring program.

2. Review four important design criteria for choosing the form of your mentoring program.

3. Make six essential decisions for defining the mentoring program.

4. Clarify seven operational choices that are necessary for implementation.

5. Identify nine issues faculty will need to discuss to prepare the ground for your mentoring program.

By the end of this chapter, if you read with your specific situation in mind, you will be fully prepared to create the mentoring program your academic unit needs or to revise the one you have so it better fits your situation.

ADDITIONAL ADVICE TO THE READER

To use this handbook to greatest advantage, complete the assessments that accompany each chapter. You will find these in **Appendix B**.

In developing this framework, I draw directly on my 15 years of faculty development experience, and I have reviewed much of the current research and writing on mentoring and faculty development.

2 Key Elements of any Well-Defined Mentoring Program

The two key elements of well-defined mentoring programs (1) are simple:

1. First, putting mentors and mentees together.

2. Second, ensuring that the mentoring relationships are working as planned.

These two key elements are common for many of the types of programs I will discuss: mentoring committees, one-on-one mentoring, group programs, and mentoring network designs. Someone needs to make sure the mentors and the mentees find each other, form relationships, and perform the mentoring tasks, however these are defined. Linking and monitoring are the two functions that differentiate the loosely structured and informal programs that have existed in the past with the well-defined and more structured programs that are becoming the norm.

1. Facilitating access to mentors: Someone needs to be on point for this

This is the most basic feature of any mentoring initiative: putting mentors and mentees together. In formal mentoring programs, this responsibility often falls to the chair of the unit or the chair of the mentoring program in the unit or, in the case of a school, the dean or an associate dean. In large units like a medical school, this function may be overseen by division heads who report to the chair of a large department. In the case of group mentoring models, there is an associate dean or vice chair for faculty development who mentors a group of new faculty. In the case of peer mentoring models, there may a team of specially trained faculty co-leaders. But the first point here is that *someone* must have formal responsibility to link the mentor to the mentee and get the mentoring process started.

By way of contrast, in informal mentoring programs, the chair or other designated leader suggests to the new faculty member that he or she seek out a mentor on their own, and may provide some guidance with that. While faculty may even discuss among themselves their obligation to mentor, this is not codified nor, as a consequence, is it certain that each faculty member receives mentoring services.

Sometimes (because of interdisciplinary interests) there may not be an appropriate mentor in the department, or what the department can provide will need to be supplemented. The person in charge of linking the mentor to the mentee will need to be able to negotiate the cross-departmental relationships to facilitate the needed connection with the new faculty. Sometimes an interdisciplinary unit (i.e., Humanities Center, Center for Population Studies, Center for Translational Medical Research, etc.) will be in a position to locate a faculty member with the specialty knowledge that is relevant to the needs of a new assistant professor.

Picking the right mentor for a new faculty member is a process that ideally should begin during recruitment. The "linker" should work on identifying the mentor or mentor team once the recruitment process begins to narrow. Once a new faculty member is recruited, it is possible to start connecting the new faculty to a potential mentor even before he or she comes to campus. It is often the case there is a strong advocate for the new faculty member in the selection process. In that case, it is obvious to consider that person as one of the mentors for the new faculty members. However, it is very important to check this assumption with both parties before making an assignment, just to make sure there are no unforeseen barriers to the relationship. As you will see, there are many different types of effective mentoring programs, and mentor roles may be extensive or minimalist, solitary or group focused, but they all start with the first connection of mentor to mentee.

Often the department chair is the "matchmaker" between the mentor and the mentee. The chair may consult the faculty about who would be the best mentor for the new faculty member on the basis of shared interest. The chair may also ask the new faculty members who they think would be the most helpful to them and on that basis make an assignment, talking with both parties in advance or even brokering a first meeting. Some units put the onus of choosing a faculty mentor on the mentee, but if so, then the "linker" (chair or mentoring program head) needs to be proactive in facilitating the connection, or coaching the new faculty member on how to go about this. The linker then should follow up to make sure a good connection is made and a mentoring relationship is, in fact, established. The criteria for selecting a good mentor includes both positive criteria and negative criteria. See Exhibit 1.1 on the next page. (2)

Some units offer a provisional mentor for the first six months or a year with the understanding that the new faculty member will choose their own group of mentors once they get to know people better. Some units have highly structured mentoring committees for each new faculty member and fitting into that structure is part of the job of the new faculty member. In some units an associate chair or dean is the group mentor and operates a cluster of support services for new faculty. However the unit makes this happen, it is basic for a process to be in place by which mentors and mentees are seeking each other from the very start.

For programs that are not departmentally-based but campus-based, some campuses or schools have been successful in recruiting a cadre of mentors by issuing a call for participation. In the spring, the call is issued; mentors are vetted and selected, trained, and assigned mentees. Often the group issuing the call is a specialized unit such as a teaching and learning center, or a faculty development officer who is an associate dean of a large school or in the office of the provost. (3)

EXHIBIT 1.1: CRITERIA FOR CHOOSING A MENTOR FOR A NEW FACULTY MEMBER

Positive Criteria

- Listening ability

- Knowledge base

- Helpful attitude

- Willingness and ability to make time

- A sense that the mentor will enjoy and benefit also from the process

- Shared interests

Negative Criteria

- Not identified with a strong faction in a contentious situation

- Not known to be gender or race biased

- Not negative towards the mentee's research or teaching interests

- Not known to be excessively dogmatic or critical

- Not hostile to the philosophy of the mentoring program

---

2. Ensuring that the mentoring relationship is working correctly: Do not leave this to chance

Each mentoring program needs at least two checkpoints:

1. One checkpoint **early on** is to confirm with both parties that the contact has been made and the process of forming the mentoring relationships has begun, and

2. One checkpoint **at the end of the year** is to make sure that the mentoring relationship is working well enough to continue.

In my discussions with chairs and deans I have found that some new faculty members will definitely let the chair or mentoring program head know if there is a problem, but some will not, for whatever reason. Sometimes there is a failure of a mentor to reach out because of stress or overload, or because the mentor does not know how. Most mentees want help or guidance, but a few may consider mentoring an infringement on their autonomy.

The person who is responsible for overseeing the quality of mentoring relationships needs a strategy for checking in with mentors and mentees. It can be informal (checking in with the new mentees from time to time), or it can be formal: sending an email with pointed questions (say, 6 weeks into the semester), followed by an end of the year survey. For sample check-in emails, see Exhibits 1.2 and 1.3 on the following pages.

Such a check-in can be built into regular processes. In some units, the chair has an end-of-year interview with each new faculty member and gives a formal review of progress. This is an excellent opportunity for the chair to probe how the mentoring relationship is going. To be effective, chairs need to have a protocol for this type of questioning and to be consistent and systematic in their interviews with new faculty members.

EXHIBIT 1.2: SAMPLE EMAIL CHECKING IN WITH THE MENTOR ON THE STATUS OF THE MENTORSHIP

From: Vice Chair for Faculty Development

To: Faculty Mentors

Date: November 1

As you may recall when we discussed your mentoring assignment, I mentioned that part of my role in the program would be to check in at least once a semester on a formal basis as to whether you were able to schedule at least one meeting with your mentee and how that went. Please confirm by November 15 that you were able to meet with your mentee.

If you would like to discuss any matter related to the mentee or the mentoring program, I am certainly available. Thanks so much for your participation as a mentor-- it means so much to the department and to our early career faculty!

Sincerely, Sally Smith, Ph. D.

Vice Chair for Faculty Development

EXHIBIT 1.3: SAMPLE EMAIL CHECKING IN WITH THE MENTEE TO ESTABLISH A TIME FOR REVIEWING THE MENTORING RELATIONSHIP

Dear Professor Green,

I am looking forward to our annual meeting to discuss your progress towards renewal. This year's meeting is scheduled for Mar 20 at 3:00 p.m. in my office. In advance of the meeting, please complete the attached questionnaire about your work this year and submit an updated resume with all current publications, teaching, presentations, etc.

In addition, I would like to discuss with you your mentoring experience so far this year. I would like to know if you have met with your mentors, how frequently, and how they have been helpful to you in the light of your goals and issues that may have arisen this year. If you have any concerns or questions, please let me know. If problems have arisen of any kind we can try to improve your mentoring situation. We are invested in your success.

Best wishes,

Bill Black,

Department Chair

In some mentoring programs there is a requirement that mentors and mentees have a formal meeting at least once a semester. Checking on whether these meetings were held and if they were effective seems like a minimal baseline assessment. Ideally, this check-in will go deeper and assess the progress and quality of the relationship. In my interviews with chairs and work with faculty members I ran into accounts of problems that were caught by alert mentors, chairs, and mentoring program directors that were identified and corrected. Here are some examples:

- One very promising science faculty member was reportedly very critical and demanding with graduate students in her laboratory. Some left her after a short period. Her mentor caught this, conferred with the chair, and got her a coach who helped her rectify this situation which could have been career-threatening.

- One young faculty member from another country got terrible reviews from her students in the first semester. Her chair, who was paying attention, got one of the strong teachers in the department to talk with her. It turns out the teaching style expected in her country was diametrically opposed to what was expected by students here. The assigned mentor helped her make an adjustment in how she approached her classes, and she was fine from then on.

- In a clinical department, a young research professor was given more clinical hours than had been agreed on in her original appointment. She complained to her mentor, who, fortunately, was a distinguished member of the department and the discipline, and her mentor went to the Division Chief and got the problem fixed. The young faculty member later rose to be the head of the Division herself. However, they could have lost her had they thwarted her research career.

I have also run into situations in which problems surfaced too late to take action.

- An African American faculty member was recruited into a predominantly white department. To everyone's delight, she did great. In fact, she seemed to be twice as productive as any other faculty member. Then they were stunned when she suddenly announced she was leaving the department for a less demanding job at a contract research unit. It turned out that working twice as hard as necessary was what she thought she had to do, and since she was a mother with two small children, she thought it was unsustainable. Evidently, her mentors were not really in touch with how she was thinking and feeling.

- One arts department that had a tradition that faculty members would be equally balanced between practice, teaching, and scholarship decided (after some contention) that they would recruit some faculty members who were primarily scholars and change the mix. One new faculty member was hired under this premise, but her mentor apparently did not get the memo about this. He was pushing her into taking on responsibilities that the faculty member thought was going to take time from her research. A row ensued, and a dean had to mediate.

While there is overwhelming evidence that faculty mentoring is a "must-have" practice that benefits the institution, the mentor, and the mentee, things can go wrong. A study of successful and failed mentoring relationships in Academic Medicine identified the following types of problems that can occur. These included:

- Lack of communication.

- Lack of experienced and knowledgeable mentors.

- Lack of commitment to the relationship.

- Competition between mentors and mentees.

- An exploitative relationship where either owner-ship of intellectual property was not clear, or where the mentor and mentee had competing interests.

The authors of the study concluded, "Of particular concern is how common the participants in our study perceived these toxic relationships to be, especially given that mentors often serve as role models for their mentees." (4)

Sometimes—too often—new faculty members get off on the wrong foot. It is so much better to catch that early when it can be corrected, rather than late when there can be serious problems in the making. Having a working mentoring relationship is a fail-safe for the faculty member and the academic unit. So, defining how you will check-in on "how it's going" is worth your attention, as it's an important part of mentoring program design.

QUESTIONS FOR THE READER

Who is "on point" to make sure that there are mentors for every mentee in your department? What provisions are in place to check in with mentors and mentees to see whether the relationship is working well?

4 Important Design Criteria for Your Mentoring Program

These are criteria to review when choosing the form your mentoring program will take. A shorthand way of summarizing these criteria would be:

Numbers

Specialty

History

Culture

In this section, you will get specific examples that illustrate the importance of these four factors for designing your mentoring effort.

Why numbers at various faculty ranks is an important design factor

In large (i.e., over 100 faculty members), established departments of a medical school (e.g., Pediatrics or Psychiatry) that have a high ratio of senior to early career faculty, I have observed highly structured mentoring committees with 3 to 5 mentors. Units this size can afford a high level of structure, and this is more the norm in the medical world than, for example, in humanities departments. Because there is a high ratio of senior to early career faculty, it is possible to have multiple mentors for each early career faculty member. This also engages more people in the mentoring effort and multiplies the resources available to the mentee.

To organize such an effort, there may be a department-wide steering committee for the mentoring program with a chair who may be an associate chair of the department. They set out guidelines for forming a mentoring committee. Each assistant professor forms a 3-person committee, and a chair is appointed. In one such department, the committee meets twice a year and the mentee is responsible for putting forward an approved plan for the year and mentors are responsible for assisting. In the most structured approach that I observed, the plans are reported to the steering committee chair who monitors the work of each committee. Both tenure track and fixed-term faculty participate.

Where the ratio of senior to early career faculty is reversed, i.e., when there are few mentors and many potential mentees, another approach is needed. In a department of area and language studies that I worked with, where multiple separate languages are taught, about half the faculty are fixed-term, and half are tenure track. The latter have research as well as teaching roles and the former are language instructors. The department had a one-to-one mentoring arrangement for the new tenure track faculty members who were researchers, but they had no program to support the full-time fixed-term faculty members. A new chair perceived the lack of mentoring support for language instructors as a problem. With support from her dean, she gave one of the more senior language instructors a course release and made her a mentor for the more junior fixed-term faculty, using a group model. The mentor's role was helping them develop their pedagogy and coaching them through the newly developed promotion process for the full-time, fixed-term faculty whose jobs were primarily or exclusively language instruction.

In the case of a small and slowly growing young humanities department where there might be as few as 6 faculty members, and only one new faculty member joins the department every several years, the one-on-one mentoring model is more practical. The chair assigns one faculty member to be a formal mentor to the new faculty member as a go-to-person for questions, but the entire faculty of the unit is enjoined to make themselves available as needed, and the mentee is encouraged and guided to seek out resources inside and outside the university as needed.

In a rapidly growing but relatively new multidisciplinary social science department that I worked with, there were almost as many early career faculty as senior faculty. In this situation, one faculty member was appointed as the mentor for the cohort of early career faculty members, and she held monthly mentoring meetings of the cohort to answer questions. In this setup, quite a bit of mentoring of the newest faculty comes from the early career faculty who are farther along, if only one or two years. The appointed formal mentor is mostly responsible for making sure the early career faculty members understand the promotion and/or tenure processes, and counseling them about where to get the help they need elsewhere in the department or university.

These examples illustrate how mentoring programs may be designed in established and emerging units and in large and small departments where the ratio of senior to early career faculty may be either high or low. Units in both situations can have sustainable programs that help their early career faculty, but they must take into account the resources available and design accordingly.

In schools where departments are small or have few resources, it may be more practical to operate a mentoring program using an interdisciplinary group-mentoring model. In this model, a couple of faculty or staff members are specially trained as mentors and operate a year-long program for faculty in their first and maybe subsequent years. Departments refer new faculty members to this program who get an orientation to the campus and then get mentoring from the group and leaders if problems arise. Such a program may be operated out of the provost's office or an interdisciplinary center (e.g., Center for Teaching and Learning or Faculty Development.)

To summarize, if the ratio of needed mentors to potential mentees is high, then a committee model may be possible, and the mentoring committee can perform multiple functions for the mentee. If that ratio is lower and there is a good fit between mentor and mentee's interest, then a one-to-one model may make the most sense. If the ratio of mentees to potential mentors is high, then a group model may make the most sense. In all cases, the mentee should be encouraged to supplement formal mentoring structures with a broader networking effort. It is unlikely that a single mentor or even a mentoring committee can meet a new faculty's need for guidance, advice, and social support, and counseling when problems arise.

QUESTIONS FOR THE READER

Will your mentoring program need to accommodate one or more new faculty members a year?

How many will be tenure track? How many will be fixed-term/contingent?

What is the ratio of potential mentors to mentees based on the size of your unit?

How many faculty members have the ability and willingness to be good mentors?

Why disciplinary specialty makes a difference

It's important to make sure the standards for promotion and/or tenure fit the kind of scholarly activity required of that specialty.

In a Journalism school where faculty members teach either in an academic track or a professional track, there are different standards for scholarly products required for promotion and tenure. The school's expectations for academic scholarship are largely similar to expectations for faculty in the humanities or social sciences across the campus. In the professional track, in contrast, faculty members are expected to produce exemplary journalistic products (e.g., articles, videos, blogs, etc.) and studies relevant to current trends in the profession. In Departments of Anthropology and Classics where Archaeology is often a sub-specialty, the different research methods of the Archaeologist require mentoring approaches that are different from both the Humanities-oriented research of the Classicist and the participant-observer methods of the Cultural Anthropologist.

QUESTIONS FOR THE READER

How important is it to match a mentee with a person of the same specialty to meet the new faculty's needs for advancement and development?

If the mentoring is mostly about *process* issues for promotion or tenure, then can any knowledgeable person serve?

If not, what process is in place to help early career faculty get specialty-related mentoring?

Pharmacy faculty who are in units that focus on drug development have standards that resemble applied and basic science programs, but units that focus on drug policy may operate with more social science-oriented methods. In these and many other situations (e.g., Studio Art and Art History; English and Creative Writing), the mentoring standards and activities will need to fit the sub-discipline.

Why the history of institutional priorities and unmet needs may help determine the form of the mentoring initiative

A freestanding institute on a university campus with over 60 investigators and $30 million in annual research revenues identified a problem in junior researchers achieving the skills they needed to become independent researchers and win awards. This was critical to the institute, which was almost entirely funded on soft money. Typically each investigator in the institute needed to have 100% of salaries covered by grants. To solve the problem, the institute set up a mentoring approach that focused on research skills development. Nine junior investigators had 5% of their time paid for by internal funds so they could engage in development activities to accelerate their research careers. Each was paired with a senior investigator to develop research proposals and programs. The Associate Director for Research managed the whole program. The idea behind this approach was that the long-term wellbeing of the Institute depended on the success of the next generation of junior investigators and therefore their mentoring and professional develop-ment was a "must have" priority rather than a "nice to have" priority.

This program had a clear measure of success: decreasing the length of time it took a researcher to become independent and develop her own program of funded research. Other targeted goals of mentoring programs I have worked with include: ability to do a specific type of evaluation research; ability to make contact with industry for research projects; ability to use "flipped classroom" methods; and ability to publish based on extension service experiences.

> ## QUESTIONS FOR THE READER
>
> Is your mentoring program expected to deliver some specific benefit to the unit, and if so, is the program designed effectively to achieve that goal?

Why organizational culture and structure may be a factor

For example, whether the department or school has a culture that emphasizes hierarchy or collegiality could factor into design decisions. Collegial departments may prefer some version of an "on-call mentoring group" or cohort mentoring program or services. A hierarchical department may be more comfortable with a single mentor approach or a mentoring committee with designated chair. Some science departments may recruit faculty members to be in specific laboratories or institutes and their mentoring comes as being part of that lab or research center. In some fields, though, the mentoring may be very focused on developing the individual as an independent scholar. Collegial units tend to place some priority on making sure the new faculty member has a lot of agency in his or her mentoring process. On the other hand, hierarchical units may expect the new faculty member to conform to an established process that has helped faculty succeed in the past.

A very collegial law school developed an all-to-all mentoring committee approach. They did not want a traditional mentoring approach because they had such a strong value that scholars should find their own way and not serve an "apprenticeship" which rightly or wrongly they associated with the one-to-one mentoring approach. Yet they wanted to help their early career faculty succeed. The solution they evolved is as follows: a series of faculty are formally designated at-large mentors and new faculty members are encouraged to approach them with questions and concerns. There is an Associate Dean for Faculty Development who provides detailed guidance on processes and procedures leading to tenure and promotion. In addition, the school has a number of programs and services it provides to all new faculty to assist them in teaching and research, but there are no designated mentors and mentee pairs.

A small department of Urology (about a dozen faculty members) designed a mentoring program to supplement their annual goal-setting sessions. The department chair meets annually with each faculty member to determine specific assignments and productivity goals. The department is financially driven and must pay for itself within the Medical School through research funding and clinical revenues. However, to create a mentoring program that fit this organization's culture and situation, the associate chair set up a mid-year structured meeting with each early career faculty member to discuss their long-term career plan and provide guidance and assistance. The faculty member's goals would then get factored into the assignment meeting with the chair over the next year. So for example, if a faculty member wants to move in a more research direction, an accommodation can be made in the clinical expectations, assuming there is a source of research funds to make up the loss of clinical revenue.

Questions for the Reader

Is there something special about your unit's culture, structure, funding, or history that should shape the choice of a mentoring model for the unit?

6 Essential Decisions in Defining the Mentoring Program

Given the wide variety of mentoring arrangements that are needed to respond to the special requirements and diverse cultures on each campus, it is not an easy matter to design the right mentoring arrangement. In fact, there are about half a dozen program design decisions each unit needs to make.

While understanding that it is not always possible to follow pure logic, I will present these decisions in a sequence that makes the most logical sense for planners:

1. Broad goals.

2. What services are provided.

3. Who is served.

4. Who mentors.

5. The program format.

6. The specific activities that define the needed services.

1. Determine the program goals

What are the two or three most important goals the mentoring program is designed to achieve? Pick one or two to optimize in program design for the next several years.

Typical goals include:

- Increasing transparency and clarity about tenure and/or applicable promotion standards and processes for fixed-term and/or tenure track faculty members.

- Better preparing candidates for the tenure/promotion process by providing regular feedback on progress.

- Making sure that the unit's program meets campus-wide standards and policies.

- Assuring that mentees have a point-person they can go to with questions.

- Promoting improvement of teaching skills and performance.

- Increasing research skills and productivity.

- Increasing clinical, public service, or administrative skills and performance.

- Deepening the engagement with the discipline.

- Building connections with industry or relevant agencies.

- Strengthening engagement on the campus or in the unit.

- Bringing the unit into compliance with new standards for mentoring.

- Providing support for faculty members who may experience stress or conflict.

- Extending mentoring services to fixed-term faculty on a promotion track.

- Extending mentoring services to mid-career.

- Extending mentoring services to late-career.

In my surveys of department chairs and deans, I sometimes found that the origin of the mentoring program is an attempt to fix a problem in the recent past. This may become the driving force for design of the new program. So, for example, if a tenure portfolio comes to the interdepartmental review committee or to the dean that is poorly prepared, this suggests there is a problem in mentoring about process.

If a tenure application is turned down at a higher level, it implies internal standards are not high enough. If women and minority candidates seem to be struggling more than others with promotion issues, this suggests that some change is needed in the way the mentoring program is structured and implemented, and perhaps a need to examine whether the unit's promotion process is biased in some way.

Where there are no observed problems, the program goal could also be as simple as ensuring compliance with newly developed campus standards. Some units see the mentoring process as a way to raise its research standing; another might be reacting to a drop in ratings by students on course evaluations. In these cases, the mentoring process will be focused on skill acquisition.

NOTE TO THE READER

A dean or chair or committee head should be as clear as possible about the primary problems he or she is trying to solve or the primary advantages they are trying to achieve and set the goals accordingly. Not all goals can be optimized at the same time, so it is important to be clear about the hierarchy of goals in designing the program. If program goals are clear, then indicators of success can be more easily formulated and monitored.

In still other units, there may be a goal to extend mentoring to additional ranks and statuses of faculty if one group is already being served. So, a department may have a working process in place for the tenure track but not for the fixed-term faculty, or for early career faculty but not mid-career faculty. As a consequence, they need to extend mentoring services to a new group. In designing the extension they will have to take into account the demands on faculty that derive from the programs that are already in place and also what will be required to address the mentoring goals for the new group of mentees.

2. Decide what services to provide to early career faculty

All mentoring programs at the junior level have the general goal of helping faculty members be successful and move to the next rank based on demonstrated accomplishments and increased capacity. The key question is: what services will be most valuable to provide as part of a mentoring or faculty development program?

If faculty members who are redesigning their units' mentoring efforts can have a good discussion about which goals are primary and which goals are secondary for their units, then they are in a good position to decide what services will most help them reach those goals. Services should fit goals.

I will deal with this much more extensively in Chapter 2, but in brief, mentoring programs typically provide four "clusters" of assistance:

a) Clarifying promotion and tenure process, providing mentees feedback as to progress, and identifying areas of skill and achievement required for further advancement.

b) Strengthening skills in teaching and working with students.

c) Improving research methods and capabilities.

d) Enhancing disciplinary identity, professional engagement, departmental citizenship, and campus engagement.

NOTE TO THE READER

You can clarify the goals of your mentoring program by allocating the proportion of effort you think the mentoring program should deliver in the four above areas. So: allocate 25% to each area, or make one area more important than all the others?

A refinement of this process would be to perform this exercise for each year the young faculty member is on the tenure track or is a candidate for promotion as a fixed-term contract faculty member. That is, what % of time should the faculty member allocate to make progress on the most important priorities for this year?

---

3. Decide who is mentored

Who is being mentored? Tenure track faculty? Fixed-term faculty? Faculty from all sub-disciplines in the unit or just those with defined issues or concerns?

If the main goal is to provide more feedback for tenure track faculty, then the question of who is mentored is answered. Similarly if the goal is to extend mentoring services to previously under-served (e.g. fixed-term faculty) the answer to who is mentored also becomes clear. This is an important question to answer because one mentoring design will not necessarily address the needs of, or be practical for, all ranks and career levels of faculty. It may be that as new categories of faculty are added as mentees, the planners may need to review the program and to see if they need also to add new categories of services. So, in the case of adding a mentoring program for new language instruction faculty that I mentioned above, the emphasis may be more intensive on teaching and student coaching than on research, while for the tenure track faculty the mentoring improvement activity may shift toward research skills and productivity.

It may be that the current mentoring program for studio artists is going just fine, but the art historians are having a problem that needs to be addressed by improved mentoring effort and so on. If there are multiple needs, leaders should not be afraid to prioritize them and create a multi-phased implementation process instead of trying to meet all needs simultaneously. Rome was not built in a day; sometimes steady, incremental change brings more lasting results than episodic revolution.

4. Decide who the mentors are

Are the mentors department faculty only? Faculty in the sub-specialty only? Are outside-the-department/special mentors permitted or required? Can all ranks have a role or just senior faculty? Is everyone required to mentor or only those who have the interest and skill?

These decisions are necessary whether there is a one-on-one or group model. In making this decision, I would argue again that "form follows function," i.e., base decisions on the realities of the current situation and what is sustainable and positive. In the following examples, you will be able to consider some of the reasons it may be necessary to specify who should or may not serve as a mentor.

Same specialty or not?

One Chemistry Department had grown from a unit of 15 people to over 50 with multiple subspecialties. In their previous mentoring structure, only those in the sub-specialty really knew the candidate when he or she came up for tenure. This sometimes caused problems, so now they require at least one member of the mentoring committee to be outside the sub-specialty of the candidate. This had benefits for general inter-department collaboration as well.

Outside of the department?

Departments that are trying to emphasize interdisciplinary research or team teaching may require an outside-the-department committee member to make sure there is an adequately cross-disciplinary perspective in evaluating the work. In departments where the faculty members were recruited because of new approaches or methods, it may be helpful to have at least two mentors, one in the department who can shepherd the new faculty member through the culture, politics, and processes of the unit's promotional system and one (perhaps outside the discipline or even the university) who can help the new faculty member further develop the new line of inquiry.

If outside-the-department mentors participate, they must know and understand the department's process for promotion and criteria (or the program must find another way to impart that information to the mentee.) If the mentoring program is being established to benefit faculty on the tenure track, then it makes sense that the lead mentors be tenured faculty members in the department. Only they have the "inside knowledge" of what it will take to get a favorable tenure vote in the department.

Associates or just full professors?

How ranks are treated is an important consideration in deciding who mentors and whether outside-of-department mentors are needed. Small departments may not have the luxury of assigning mentoring tasks to full professors only, so associate professors take on mentoring tasks as well. Alternately they may go outside the department for mentors in some cases. The unit by-laws may be relevant here. If senior and associate ranks vote on promotion, then perhaps they should be part of the cadre of mentors. If not, then there may be other reasons for including associate professors as mentors. They may have critical methodological or sub-specialty knowledge to impart that senior faculty might not have.

Fixed-term (contract) faculty?

If the mentoring program is to benefit fixed-term faculty or lecturers, then it makes sense to engage the outstanding exemplars in those roles as key participants in any mentoring arrangement. Given the hierarchical nature of academic units, tenured faculty may be needed to support or even direct the mentoring activity, but it makes more sense for the hands-on mentoring and guidance to come from those faculty members (tenured or fixed-term) who have a more intimate knowledge of what is expected and how to perform effectively.

Required or optional?

Being a mentor can be time-consuming and not all have the skills and inclination to be good mentors. It may make sense to stipulate that not everyone has to mentor, but they can perform other departmental service in lieu of mentoring. Or mentors can come in and out of the mentor pool as other demands on their time ebb and flow. When people resume the mentor role after some years of absence, it makes sense to assure they are up to speed on current standards and processes.

Non-faculty mentors?

Staff members such as teaching experts, research methodology experts, or service experts should not be excluded from being part of an extended network of helpers and might be designated as ex officio members of certain committees. In some cases, e.g., where the goal is to build ties with industry, these mentors many not even be higher-ed employees. If a mentoring program hopes to get participation of the non-tenured faculty or other experts, it should do what it can to make those individuals feel welcome and valued in the process (given the hierarchical inclinations of academic culture) so as to get their full participation on behalf of the new faculty member.

NOTE TO THE READER

Ideally the mentoring program's formal description will include an indication of who may be included as mentors and an explanation of why this decision has been made. Therefore, if circumstances change, it will be clear why new categories of mentors are needed.

---

5. Decide on the program's format

Is the format:

a) One mentor to one mentee?

b) A mentoring committee?

c) A group mentoring model?

d) Faculty members are not assigned but are "on call"?

e) A division of labor model where a mentee has two separate mentors for different purposes?

f) Some blend of different approaches?

Once the core goals are established and it is decided who the primary beneficiaries are, these choices can drive the choice of format from among these six options. As I have noted above: faculty size, ratio of ranks, sub-disciplinary differences, and the nature of the culture and structure of the unit will figure prominently in this decision.

In the paragraphs that follow, I will discuss the advantages and disadvantages of the main mentoring models—and how, in some cases, the disadvantages might be addressed. (5)

One-to-one mentor-to-mentee model

The assigned mentor in the one-to-one mentoring model most often is the point person for the academic unit relative to guiding the new faculty members through the early stages of their promotion process. The simple one-to-one mentoring model prevails in the smaller humanities and social science departments I surveyed, but I saw great variation in how formal these relationships are, what the structure is, and who initiates. The key is that a new faculty member has a "go to" person for questions and a first line of assistance.

The mentors in this model should not be expected to provide everything for new faculty members. They should have clearly defined and delimited roles (e.g., answer questions about the tenure process and/or provide help on research or teaching). Furthermore, even if a unit adopts a one-to-one model for its formal mentoring, it should stress that current thinking emphasizes that a new faculty member also needs a broad support network. The single, formal mentor should be part of the network, not a substitute for the network.

New faculty members should be strongly encouraged to seek out additional resources in the department, on campus, and in the discipline to support their career development. Female faculty members may want to locate at least one informal confidant with whom they can share gender-related issues and the same is true with under-represented minority faculty members. Each faculty member will have a unique set of needs and no one faculty member will be able to address all of those needs. This principle applies to all the mentoring models listed in this section, but it is especially important to emphasize in the one-to-one model.

The mentor committee model

Larger departments and schools have the luxury of adopting mentoring committees when the ratio of senior to early career faculty is large. As mentioned previously, in several large medical departments, the preference is to have a mentoring committee of 3-5 people. Usually there is a chair of the committee appointed by the department head, but in some cases, the mentee is responsible for assembling the committee. This has the advantage of assuring that the mentee is likely to be comfortable with the committee, but it provides no assurance that the mentee will have all the resources he or she needs.

A compromise is to have the mentee assemble the committee in consultation with the chair, head of the division or the mentoring program leader. In some units, they are required to have one member outside the department, but then again, in other programs, sometimes outside-the-department mentors are not allowed to be members of the formal committee. What's best depends on goals and other dimensions of the situation.

Often mentoring committees have a particular rationale for multiple members. In addition to extending the resources available to the new faculty member, there may be the need to include another subspecialty representative to promote an interdisciplinary orientation, or a translational science emphasis, or someone in another department who shares the faculty member's research interest, or one who is a good teacher, etc. A mentoring committee may or may not meet as a committee, and the mentee may access resources on an individual basis.

However, I think that every mentoring committee needs a chair who is fully committed to the mentee; otherwise (if there is no chair), the situation devolves into informal and, perhaps, inconsistent mentoring.

Division of labor models

It may be desirable to have one mentor for teaching and one mentor for research for an individual or groups of mentees. In such situations, it might be that the unit chair or vice chair takes care of the coaching about tenure or promotion.

The group mentoring model

A group model is a good option when there are few senior faculty members to mentor and a relatively large number of early career faculty members who need to be mentored, as may be the case in new and growing units. In an Information and Library Science School I worked with, an associate dean holds a monthly educational program for those new to the school. The new faculty help define the agenda and the associate dean brings in the speakers. Other mentoring needs are met informally. The associate dean also helps faculty members prepare their tenure dossiers.

In the example of the area studies department discussed earlier, there were a large number of fixed-term faculty who provided required and elective language instruction. Appointing a mentor for the early career faculty in these situations gives them someone to go to for pedagogy questions, problems that arise, and for guidance on promotion guidelines and processes. This is another application of the group approach. A third group model, also introduced earlier, is the mentoring group offered by an interdisciplinary unit where mentees are drawn from a number of different departments.

Designated mentors "on call"

This is a clearly specified group of mentors a new faculty member may call on. However, they are not a committee *per se*, and multiple mentees may use the pool of mentors.

This model increases mentee choice over the one-to-one model. It is especially important in this model to monitor the experience of the mentors and mentees to assure that mentees are using mentors, and the mentors are able and willing to do what is expected of them when contacted. It is also possible in this model that some mentors are overused and some under-used.

Mixed models

Mixed models may be occasioned by special circum-stances. In one well-regarded social science department on the campus, the chair serves as mentor as far as the tenure process is concerned, but mentoring in all aspects of research and disciplinary engagement is provided through a well-established interdisciplinary research center that almost all faculty in the department affiliate with. In the area studies unit discussed previously, the tenure track faculty have a one-to-one model, and the language instructors have a group model.

QUESTIONS FOR THE READER

Is there one model that stands out in your mind as most practical for your unit?

What are the factors that lead you to believe the model you have in mind is best for your unit at this time?

What additional models might supplement this preferred model, if any?

6. Determine the specific program activities

For example, decide from the start on the frequency and duration of meetings, special events, etc., and how these are related to the program goal. Formal mentoring programs are defined by the decision of who mentors and also how the mentoring process is supposed to be carried out. Some activities are required while others are informal and optional. Those activities that are required in the mentoring initiative should be clearly related to the goals of the program.

If a main goal of the program is to keep the mentee appraised of his or her progress toward tenure, then annual feedback sessions and well-defined action plans are the required activities. If the main goal of the program is to make sure the mentee has an advisor when questions arise, then the requirements may be one or more documented meetings per semester. Additional interactions between mentee and mentor may be the norm or strongly encouraged, but not at the expense of the required activities.

Monitoring progress

In highly structured programs a report of the mentoring committee must be filed with the department chair or dean. In one college of arts and sciences, each chair is required to have an annual review with each tenure track faculty member and put a written assessment of progress toward tenure in the faculty member's file. In some departments the mentors and mentoring committee are required to provide information to the chair relative to that review. In some cases, the chair makes an independent annual assessment and inserts this into the record on which a tenure recommendation is partly based.

Teaching and research

Similarly there may be required activities related to teaching and research. Most mentoring programs for faculty that teach have a provision where at least one class must be observed and a chair or member of the mentoring committee is assigned to do this. Some go farther and appoint a mentor for teaching and a mentor for research. Where research is key to promotion, some mentors may be required to develop clear written plans and goals related to their research program and progress. The committee reviews these plans. Other mentoring programs may offer or require courses on teaching or professional writing, or offer or require involvement in the relevant national professional meetings.

Group activities

Some mentoring programs have special activities and practices that are part of the process of mentoring faculty. At one private university I know, there is no formal mentoring requirement, but the dean meets privately with the tenure track faculty in each of three divisions in three separate group gatherings to answer their questions and hear their concerns. She reports the concerns they identify to the divisional deans so they can follow up. In one department, the chair has an annual dinner meeting with the untenured faculty to hear how things are going. In another program, there is an annual celebratory dinner for new faculty. Some units assign new faculty a collective task, like organizing the monthly research seminar. This gives them an important role in the department and the authority to contact potential speakers at other universities and build their contact network.

Peer mentoring

In this model, the mentees meet together to discuss common issues or to help each other in various ways, such as in writing groups or teaching support groups. Since peer mentoring models lack a formal leader by design, they need to be well structured. Often peer mentoring is an adjunct to a more formal mentoring process, rather than the entire mentoring program. Peer mentoring programs that are sponsored by Teaching and Learning Centers, or Interdisciplinary Institutes may be more likely to succeed than those that are ad hoc and episodic. (6)

In summary, thoughtful design is needed in order to assure that a mentoring program for early career faculty will address the most pressing needs. Setting clear goals is the first step. Next, program planners should consider what mentoring services and specific activities are required to meet those goals, who receives those services and participates in these activities, and who mentors. Finally, planners must decide which program format is really most practical and efficient. When a planning group has made these core decisions, then it can begin to focus on the important operational details. These are discussed in the following section.

QUESTIONS FOR THE READER

What required group activities might supplement or enhance your mentoring initiative?

Are these activities necessary to achieve the most important goals or desirable for other reasons? Which can be voluntary?

Making Mentoring Work: 7 Operational Decisions

The following are seven operational decisions that deans and chairs must make in deciding how to implement the mentoring program design. This section takes you through the mentoring program operation from first contacts with mentors to the stage of evaluating the effectiveness of the mentor-mentee relation-ship. You will be able to identify what decisions are needed and what options exist at each stage. These include operational decisions about:

- Program timing and duration.

- How participants are informed of the program.

- Who initiates the mentoring relationship.

- How formal the processes are supposed to be and what is to be documented.

- How relationships will be monitored.

- How mentoring will be recognized, rewarded, and supported.

- What the confidentiality rules are.

Program timing and duration: When mentoring starts and when it ends

Not all mentoring programs for early career faculty have the same timing and duration. Some programs start with the hiring decision and the mentor is expected to be in contact with the faculty member before he or she comes to campus. In other programs, the mentees are told they have six months to decide who they want for a mentor.

Despite these diverse practices, unless there are special circumstances that argue for a late onset of mentoring activity, it seems to make intuitive sense for some aspects of the mentoring program (e.g., clarification of expectations for tenure and promotion) to begin as early as feasible. So, if there is a time of exploration before settling on who is a mentor or serves on a mentoring committee, then it seems that this activity (of exploratory discussions) should be for limited period. During this time the mentee needs a clear "go to person" as well, i.e., provisional mentor, chair, or mentoring program head. In most units I observed, mentoring ceases after the tenure decision or appointment to associate, but in an increasing number of units, faculty members have an option for post-tenure mentoring on the way to full professor.

How mentors are informed

It is important to clarify how mentees are informed about the program:

- Is the mentoring program emphasized in recruitment of new faculty?

- Is it stated as an expectation during the hiring process?

- Or, is it an optional benefit that is discussed after the new faculty member arrives on campus?

If the mentoring program is partly instituted to show that the unit or IHE is a good place to work and that the IHE has a progressive attitude towards faculty development, then the mentoring program should figure prominently in the recruitment of new faculty. A statement on the website might say something like: "At department X, we help new faculty members launch their careers and establish themselves in the discipline through effective mentoring and faculty development opportunities."

If participation is required or expected in the unit, this should be part of the written agreement that the new faculty member signs. If it is truly voluntary and optional, then talking about it might wait until the faculty member comes to campus. As the reader is by now no doubt aware, I favor stating, as early as is reasonable, a clear expectation that faculty will participate in the mentoring program.

It is often true that there are implicit promises of mentoring when a faculty member comes to campus to "work with professor" X or Y. The chair of the unit or the head of recruitment committee should be alert to this and try to clarify how serious this commitment is from the likely mentor in order to prevent future problems. One approach is to have a pre-employment discussion between the mentor and the prospective mentee.

It would not be a surprise if candidates for faculty positions ask about your mentoring arrangements during their visits to your campus. They may query both older and younger faculty to get their views, so it makes sense to assure that all faculty members understand exactly what the mentoring arrangements are for their departments so they can give out correct information.

How mentees are paired with mentors

Decide who initiates the mentoring relationship. Are mentors assigned by the chair or program leader, or is it up to the mentee to seek out and obtain a mentor? Who can terminate a mentoring relationship?

I have stressed this function from the outset. If the main goal of the mentoring program is to support the new faculty member's research progress, then (in a well-defined program) usually the chair will make an assignment after consultation with the faculty members and after seeing whose interests match with that of the new faculty members. If the focus is process (i.e., knowing standards, understanding how to build the tenure dossier) then the chair can choose any faculty member who is eligible to serve, who can be depended upon to deliver this information, and who will be sufficiently attentive to the new faculty member. (7)

Departments that want to emphasize the responsibility and agency of the young faculty member ask the new person to identify a mentor within a set time period. As previously mentioned, it would best if the chair or mentoring program head will be available to assist the new faculty member by brokering the mentoring relationship or at least being available to advise. This choice of leaving it up to the mentee can be risky if the new faculty member is shy about asking or resistant to mentoring. The new faculty member may not get connected. In any case, as I have consistently emphasized, some unit leader needs to be accountable for seeing that the mentoring connections take place so that the intended processes, as much as possible, produce the desired results. Even if your department assigns a mentor, you should still emphasize to the new faculty member that he or she needs to seek out and develop a broad informal network of additional mentoring contacts. (In the workbook in Appendix B, I provide a worksheet for mentees on this topic.)

No matter how relationships are initiated, there are risks. The relationship chemistry may not always prove to be that good, not all mentors have the temperament and skills to be effective, and circumstances may change. Mentoring relationships may change because the mentor goes on leave, the mentee's interests change, the mentor may take on a big project that uses all available time, etc. The change of a mentoring relationship does not necessarily imply a failure on someone's part. So, some units create "no fault divorce" provisions to make sure those relationships that are not working can be terminated easily. I have already mentioned that it is "a fail-safe" in many programs for the chair or head of the mentoring program to check in with both parties in the first year to make sure the relationships are going well according to program goals and intervene if they are not.

How formal are mentoring arrangements?

Decide how formal mentoring arrangements are supposed to be in your unit, including written guidelines, defined program roles, and written records.

In a small department that is committed to helping its new faculty members succeed, there may be no need for a lot of formal process and documentation. In small departments, the chair is often in charge of organizing and monitoring the mentoring regime (e.g., linking a new faculty member to one or more mentors). In close-knit departments, the faculty as a group feels a mentoring responsibility toward the new member. In some departments, the whole senior faculty has regular discussions about the progress of the juniors and what they might need in terms of guidance. However, if the mentoring commitment is real but the program is less structured, then the department needs to be able to demonstrate a good track-record in supporting its early career faculty through the tenure and promotion process if asked to justify their approach by senior administration. In low paperwork programs, it will at least be necessary for the chair or other mentoring program leader to document that each mentoring relationship was periodically reviewed and changes were made as needed.

In units where faculty have somewhat distant relationships or where there are major ongoing conflicts, new faculty members will need more help to navigate the environment. A more formal arrangement may be a necessary step. I often heard about departments that made the shift from more informal to more formal programs as they increased in size or their space expanded and they no longer interacted on a daily basis. If a unit has a more informal mentoring arrangement, then it usually falls on the chair to make sure the new faculty member is getting the help he or she needs. This can be a problem, though, because in a small department, the chair is often overloaded with duties and he or she has little help. Adding a mentoring program may be the reason for the chair to appoint a deputy to handle the mentoring program and other duties or take on some routine chair duties that releases the time of the chair to address mentoring.

In large units, some clear structure and formal process is generally needed because new faculty members can "get lost." There can be a mentoring program chair or associate chair whose job it is to make sure the process and activities are carried out effectively and efficiently. In a really large unit, this program chair may be in touch with a dozen mentors or mentoring committees. The school or department may require mentoring committees to keep records of meetings, require the mentee to submit plans, and provide records to the chair of the program. Centralized record keeping and routine communications (e.g., mentoring committee meetings) may be assigned to a paid staff member.

In my interviews and surveys, I learned about at least one department that was so worried about litigation in cases of conflict over tenure and promotion decisions that they instituted a "no paper rule," whereby advising is all informal. The concern seemed to be that a document will turn up whereby the department made a promise of promotion that was not honored, or that somehow documents discrimination or an unacceptable personnel practice. This caution seemed excessive to me, but university counsel should probably be consulted to assess how probable or serious such an occurrence would be. One might also be concerned that the lack of documentation could be a risk if someone alleges they have been treated unfairly. Without adequate documentation, it might be hard to show that the unit performed all the required administrative procedures and was compliant with applicable rules.

Requirement—or incentives? And how are mentors and mentees recognized?

Required participation

In some programs, participation in the mentoring program is a requirement for new hires. In others, it is all but required. In most cases, chairs and deans report that early career faculty are only too happy to be part of the program. There may be special circumstances, however. If a new faculty member has been an assistant professor at another university for a number of years and seems to have mastered the basics of teaching and research, he or she may need a modification of mentoring arrangements in place. In rare cases, a faculty member may resist participating in the mentoring structure. This becomes one of the many challenging personnel issues that a chair must handle with sensitivity to the needs and wants of the individual but with also due deference to the needs of precedent, written procedure, and overall equity.

Educating mentees about the mentoring process

How to be a good mentee and to get the most out of a mentoring relationship is not always obvious and the quality of the relationship between the two people is important. Effective practices that can help those being mentored include:

- Holding panel discussions (campus-wide) of early career faculty who have been successful and/or overcome difficulties with their mentors. These discussions would be open to early career faculty who want to learn about how to navigate the mentoring relationship.

- Having a person that mentees can talk to either in the unit or on campus when they are having problems with their mentor.

- Providing readings that give tips and appropriate general guidance to mentors and mentees alike. (Please see the many examples provided in Appendix B.)

- Creating a written mentoring agreement between mentor and mentee. (See Appendix B.)

Supporting mentors

Mentoring is an unfamiliar role for many and while it has many satisfactions it can have its challenges. Therefore, it also makes sense for departments and schools to give practical support for mentors in various ways such as:

- Holding panel discussions of faculty who have won mentoring awards in which they share their approaches with new mentors.

- Having an experienced person that mentors can talk to either in the unit or on campus when they are having problems with a mentee.

- Creating opportunities for mentors to get together informally and confidentially to talk about their experience as a mentor.

- Creating a formal workshop where mentors practice their skills of listening, guiding, giving feedback, and connecting mentees with resources.

Recognizing mentors

Most mentoring is uncompensated, except for cases when a mentoring stipend is provided by an endowment or where the unit has provided a special award for mentoring service. So, once mentoring programs are established, then a follow-up step is to raise funds for rewards and recognition. (8) Some units pick a faculty mentor of the year and provide other forms of recognition, such as an annual dinner for mentors. Most mentoring programs reported in my surveys of UNC-CH units were low- or no-budget operations, though a few units provided funds for mentors to take mentees to lunch. Ideally, faculty will take pride on their own in their mentoring roles and come to consider it an integral and important part of their positions. However, chairs, deans, and provosts should find ways, as a matter of course, to recognize and celebrate the contributions that mentors make to the unit and to the campus.

While mentoring is mostly uncompensated, it does not have to be considered low value. Unit leaders, in developing or improving their mentoring efforts, need to give attention to how they show they esteem this function and make that known to others. By valuing mentoring, they also implicitly value the careers of their early career faculty and the importance of faculty development overall. By valuing mentoring, academic leaders also strengthen the bonds of collegiality. If the department or school makes clear that it is proud of its mentoring and values the job of the mentor, that makes it easier for faculty members to get involved with the role.

Ground rules about confidentiality

One type of mentoring program tends to position the mentor as a helper only. The designated mentor is specifically excluded from the evaluation of the new faculty member so that the mentoring relationship is private and confidential. Everything is done to make the mentor a safe haven for the faculty member and this aspect of the program is emphasized to all parties.

In other programs, the mentor is seen as a helper but also a liaison to the department and a source of information about how the faculty member is progressing. In this model, mentors have mixed roles as both helpers and evaluators. It would be important to go over these rules in advance with each mentor and mentee and also to include them in program descriptions.

This is a challenge that every program has to deal with: How to make the mentoring relationship safe enough to uncover real problems in time to help the young faculty member? How to proceed when the faculty member may feel that by uncovering problems he or she may hurt his or reputation in the department?

Whatever the agreements about confidentiality or the roles of mentors in evaluation, probably the key factors in program success are whether, firstly, the department and the mentors convey a genuine desire to help young faculty members and, secondly, whether young faculty members trust the department to have their best interests at heart. Hopefully, this trust can be built if the department is transparent about its philosophy, and if it uses the information gained in the mentoring relationship to promote the best interest of the faculty members being mentored.

EXHIBIT 1.4: SAMPLE MENTOR-MENTEE CONFIDENTIALITY GUIDELINES (SOME OR ALL MAY APPLY)

What we discuss will not be talked about with others and will be kept strictly confidential.

If we feel we may have breached confidentiality inadvertently, we will discuss what happened.

We may decide to share some conversations with others, e.g., to get their help on a particular problem identified.

What we discuss here may be shared with the chair or others for the purpose of feedback and evaluation.

What we discuss is required to be shared with the chair or others for the purpose of feedback and evaluation.

The mentor will/will not be asked to give his evaluation of the progress of the mentee.

If a problem arises in the mentoring relationship that we cannot resolve, we may choose to discuss that confidentially with the chair.

In some universities, there are designated officers (e.g., ombuds) where faculty members can get help on a strictly confidential basis (9). This provides a safety valve for concerns that the young faculty member feels uncomfortable sharing with those who may vote on his or her tenure or promotion.

When I did workshops for early career faculty on mentoring, I would occasionally be consulted afterwards, in private, by an early career faculty member who was struggling with a problem she did not feel she could talk about in her department. In these cases, I was able to provide coaching or refer to an appropriate resource on campus. It is the responsibility of the campus overall to provide outlets for early career faculty who are having problems that they do not feel comfortable sharing inside their department.

Having said this, the focus of those outside resources should always be, if possible, to help the faculty member work within the department or school to work out a solution to the problem.

Monitoring and assessment

You also need to decide early how will you assess whether mentoring relationships are working—and how the mentoring program as a whole is working.

Monitoring mentor-mentee relationships

It is a critical departmental task to monitor mentoring relationships periodically to see if they are going as planned and, if not, to intervene by talking to the participants to solve a problem—or substitute a new mentor. As mentioned previously, there are multiple reasons to intervene. For example:

- The original mentor becomes too busy with his or her own projects.

- The mentor gets sick or goes on leave.

- There is a poor quality relationship.

- Another faculty member joins the faculty who is a more appropriate mentor.

- A new faculty member joins who needs the mentor more.

The important thing is having someone who is paying attention to the quality of mentoring relationships that have been established. An unhelpful (e.g., hypercritical, poorly informed, or more often, non-performing) mentor may be worse than having no mentor at all.

The "how is it going?" inquiry is an important one. It should not come as a surprise to either the mentors or mentees when they are confidentially queried either in person, over the phone, or electronically. This is one reason a chair of mentoring is appointed in a medium size or larger department where there are several mentoring relationships going on simultaneously. This is a serious responsibility, and you will recall that in the first section of this chapter, I offered some sample check-in emails.

Monitoring the mentoring program

It is also critical to assess whether the program is working overall. This might involve assessment of:

- How the mentors and mentees are experiencing the relationship.

- What benefits are observable.

- What needs are being met.

- What needs remain unmet.

- How many times mentors or mentees meet.

- How long the meetings are.

- What is covered in the meetings.

In very small programs, this task can be handled by discussion at a faculty meeting.

In larger units, a formal survey and report may be required. (See Appendix B for examples of evaluation forms.)

In either case, it makes sense for there to be some regular faculty discussion of the mentoring program, perhaps annually, to check in on how it is proceeding and how it might be improved. Such regular internal review is, in my opinion, as critical as establishing the mentoring program in the first place.

9 Factors That Influence the Program Design

There are nine factors that faculty members should consider when deciding among the program design options laid out earlier in this chapter.

Three of these considerations are related to the department's competitive position within the university or the discipline. These include:

- Mandates or guidance from senior administration.

- What other institutions are doing.

- Standards and practices in the discipline.

The other six considerations are unique to the unit. These include:

- A history of recent problems to be solved.

- Departmental culture.

- Departmental strategic goals.

- Frequency of new hires.

- Faculty capabilities and interests.

- Needs for documentation and training.

But before launching into an analysis of these nine factors and how they will shape your mentoring program, there is one thing every academic leader must do:

Get the faculty involved.

No mentoring effort can succeed without the support and involvement of the faculty. In fact, the mentoring program of the unit will be only as good as faculty make it. While chairs, directors, and deans should make the case for mentoring, they should also enlist faculty leaders to support the adoption of a strong mentoring plan that fits the needs and capabilities of the department, institute, or school.

Ideally, it would be best to assign the task of program design to a faculty committee made up of people the dean or chair trusts to do a good job. Someone in whom the dean or chair has great confidence should head this committee. Typically, a committee recommendation would be thoroughly discussed and/or voted on by the faculty and then implemented by the chair or dean. Some departments and schools have by-laws for decision-making and the choice to start a mentoring program would need to respect those by-laws. (In Appendix B, you will find a sample charter for a faculty mentoring planning committee.)

The rest of this section briefly discusses each of the nine considerations. Any committee assigned to recommend the design of a mentoring program would benefit from reviewing the following pages.

Check mandates or guidance

Planners should consider whether the establishment of a mentoring program is voluntary or required by senior leaders (e.g., if there are mandates or guidance from provost, dean, and chair, or promotion and tenure committee, or other campus-wide faculty committee).

If required, are there any criteria for the program design that have been stated or implied by the campus or system authorities? If so, what is the best way for the department, school, or institute to incorporate these required aspects into a program that also genuinely reflects its needs and local conditions?

Check what other institutions are doing

It is not hard to find many good and detailed discussions of mentoring programs. In fact, descriptions of Developed Mentoring Programs are readily available for download from the Internet.

A simple approach is to identify half-dozen peers or aspirational peer institutions and to see if they have their mentoring programs described on the Internet. Direct inquiries can follow. A Google search of "faculty mentoring programs at universities" reveals the details of programs of such disparate institutions as the University of Arkansas, Boston University, Columbia University, Northern Illinois University, Northern University, Stanford University, University of California at San Francisco, and the University of Nebraska. In addition to programs faculty mentoring tool kits can also be accessed. (10)

Check what other departments in the discipline are doing

For some units having a strong mentoring program is a comparative advantage in hiring. If this is the case, the department, center, or school's program should be at least as robust as its competitors. This suggests that as a prelude to designing their mentoring program the faculty should invest in reconnaissance about what competitor departments in peer universities and colleges are doing to mentor their faculty.

Consider any recent history of problems

Was there a recent problem that the unit wants to prevent from recurring? As mentioned above, awareness of an unfortunate incident (e.g., a failed tenure case; a minority faculty member drops out; a lawsuit is filed) can spur desire for an upgraded mentoring effort. If so, how will the proposed plan address the issue that caused the problem, and, in addition, what benefits should the new plan bring beyond that particular type of situation?

It is important not to overreact to the recent past (e.g., the problem may have had more to do with the people than the structure) but also to consider what could have prevented the problem and determine the practicality of adding that feature as part of a mentoring program.

Consider departmental culture

Planners might ask: Is this a department where things have traditionally been handled very informally? If so, then what is the least structured program that will produce the desired results? If the unit is very hierarchical and process oriented, what would a mentoring program look like that fits into the way the unit does things? Are there relevant aspects of the departmental culture that might need to be addressed as a prelude to implementing a mentoring program? For example, is there an "old school" belief, among some or many, that a "sink or swim" approach is the best for the department or young scholars? If so, those attitudes might need to be addressed by discussion and help people update their perspectives in light of current academic thinking and recommended practices. If these attitudes and values are not directly addressed, the program may just go through the motions but its intent will be subverted.

Are faculty members comfortable giving feedback about whether academic work meets departmental standards? If not, there may be a need for discussion and coaching. If there is reason to suspect implicit bias in hiring and promotion against women and people of color, this may require real soul-searching and strong, continuing leadership in the service of equity. Is discussion and dialogue a way to change the culture? Are there campus resources or outside experts that can help lead such a discussion in a way that is truly helpful? In one department I consulted with, the faculty committee developed a more structured mentoring program but also asked that the university's central unit charged with diversity come in and do some training for the faculty. They suspected that not everyone was on board with the latest thinking about how inclusive searches should be conducted.

Consider departmental goals and plans

Should the mentoring program be conceived as a part of the unit's strategy for success in competing for resources and raising its relative standing? If so, the mentoring program should be designed to create synergy with that strategy.

For example:

- One professional school framed the mentoring program to support its goal of being a leading school in evaluation research and designed hiring criteria and faculty development activities to reflect this goal.

- A pharmacy school that aimed to lead in cross-disciplinary health research structured mentoring teams to include representatives from other schools and from the pharmaceutical industry.

- A research institute designed its mentoring programs to help new investigators become independent scholars and grant-getters.

If the mentoring program is designed to explicitly help the unit achieve its goals, then, arguably, there will be more motivation to participate in and support the mentoring effort.

Consider the number and frequency of new faculty hires

The ratio of potential mentors to mentees is a key factor to consider when choosing a format for your mentoring program:

- If the department is growing slowly, a one-on-one model may be feasible.

- If there is a large ratio of senior faculty to juniors, a committee model is an option.

- However, a department that is growing rapidly or has a high ratio of younger to older faculty might want to consider a cohort mentoring program rather than a one-on-one or committee model. In the cohort or group model, the new faculty meet as a group to discuss common issues with a mentoring coordinator who links them to other resources.

Consider faculty skills and interests

In a small department, there may be only a few people who are capable of being good mentors and who want to be mentors. In larger departments, there may be more willing participants, but also a few people who are "star mentors." How can roles be structured so these individuals are not overloaded? In some units, faculty members have unique skills to contribute, e.g., they are good coaches for research proposals, or excellent role models as teachers, or good conflict resolvers. Planners might consider how the program might be designed to take advantage of these talents. If faculty members do not want to serve as mentors, can there be an option for "alternative service" so as to take some of the load off those who do serve?

Consider needs for documentation, training, and information

Each department or school must fashion a program that is sustainable and responds to the needs of the unit and conforms to the policies of the institution. Once the design is developed, the program should be documented as a written policy. A well-documented program is clear about the expectations for tenure and promotion, how the mentoring program works, the role and expectations for mentors, and the role and expectations of mentees.

Beyond that, the needs for written plans, mentoring contracts, and formal evaluations should fit the department's style and resources.

Concluding Thoughts

This section is the end of the beginning. Once the components of the program have been carefully considered, the academic leader needs to combine them into a coherent program.

In the exhibits that follow, I provide five descriptions of actual mentoring programs that show how these various choices add up to a program that is tailored toward the needs of a specific unit or campus. Each program is quite different and responds to a different scenario. I recommend reviewing these five examples closely with your colleagues.

EXHIBIT 1.5: A SOCIAL SCIENCE DEPARTMENT MENTORSHIP PROGRAM AT A RESEARCH UNIVERSITY

Objective: The objective of the department mentorship program is to provide feedback to assistant and associate professors in the department from a committee of their senior colleagues in order to help them achieve their career goals. The program does not involve evaluating the faculty member and is solely for the purpose of giving advice solicited by mentees.

Primary Mentor: Assistant professors will be paired with a mentor (associate or full professor) who can appreciate the significance of their research. Associate professors will be paired with a full professor. It is suggested that the faculty mentor and mentee meet once per semester in any mutually agreed upon format. In addition, the faculty member should be available to answer questions on an ad hoc basis.

Mentorship Committee: The mentorship committee for assistant professors consists of at least one full professor and two other committee members who are associate professors or above. The committee for associate professors consists of at least two full professors. One of the members of each committee will be the primary mentor. It is suggested that the faculty mentorship committee and mentee meet once per year and also provide ad hoc advice at the mentee's request throughout the year.

EXHIBIT 1.6: HUMANITIES DEPARTMENT AT A PUBLIC RESEARCH UNIVERSITY

The department hereby establishes the following departmental mentoring program:

> The chair of the department shall meet, as early as possible, with every newly hired untenured professor for the purposes of establishing a tenure cluster.

Typically such a cluster shall comprise three faculty members as follows:

> The primary mentor may be either requested by the newly appointed professor or appointed by the chair from those faculty whose work is most closely affiliated with the work of the new member;

> A second member shall be appointed by the chair from other faculty in the department;

> A third shall be appointed by the chair from outside the department upon consulting with both the new faculty member and relevant members of the department.

Once formed, the mentoring cluster shall meet as a group as soon as possible to establish their expectations and procedures. Once these are agreed upon, the cluster shall inform the chair of the department of their agreement in writing.

The mentee and the primary mentor agree to meet at least once a semester.

The mentee and mentoring cluster agree to meet at least once a year.

EXHIBIT 1.6 CONTINUED: HUMANITIES DEPT.
AT A PUBLIC RESEARCH UNIVERSITY

Additional meetings with the cluster can occur if either the mentee or the primary mentor initiates it. The mentee can also request to meet individually with any member of the cluster.

The mentee and all mentors agree that exchanges within the mentoring relationship are strictly confidential (unless all agree otherwise).

The mentee and mentors agree that the mentoring relationship does not signify advancement toward tenure and promotion.

A mentee-mentor relationship is for one academic year, although it is strongly recommended that untenured faculty continue to participate in the formal mentoring process. If they do, the chair and the mentee shall each year consider whether the membership of the cluster should be changed to reflect the evolving interests and work of the mentee.

Although newly hired tenured professors are not required to participate in the mentoring process, it is strongly recommended that they do negotiate a formal mentoring agreement with a single faculty member.

The topics mentees and mentors discuss are not prescribed. Rather, they should reflect the individual problems, concerns, and interests of the mentee. (The requirements and standards for tenure and promotion are not topics of discussion for the mentee and mentor; the mentee should discuss these topics only with the chair of the department.)

EXHIBIT 1.7: MENTORING PLAN FOR *ABC* SCIENTIFIC RESEARCH CENTER, WITH JOINT APPOINTMENTS

Goals: ...Effective mentoring is particularly important to the success of new tenure–stream ABC faculty members as there can be unique challenges to meeting the expectations ... when faculty members are jointly appointed at ABC and a campus department, where their tenure resides...

Who participates: All tenure stream assistant professors and untenured associate professors with appointments at ABC will be expected to establish a mentoring committee consistent with the ABC Faculty Mentoring Plan (below) and the goals and requirements of the College and campus department where they are jointly appointed.

Mentoring will continue for tenured associate professors as requested or required by their campus department. A mentoring plan will be established for all fixed-term faculty and academic specialists with ABC appointments. Faculty members can decide not to participate in mentoring. If so, they must submit a letter to the ABC director and their department chair indicating this decision.

Specifics of the ABC Mentoring Plan:

- Mentoring is ... the responsibility of all senior faculty ... appointed at ABC. [Mentors] will be recognized for these efforts as part of their annual review and evaluation.

- Tenure and promotion of ABC-appointed faculty is a joint decision and responsibility of the tenure-home academic departments and ABC. Thus understanding the culture of all of the academic departments who have faculty appointed at ABC is important to the success of the mentoring program.

EXHIBIT 1.7 CONTINUED: MENTORING PLAN FOR
ABC SCIENTIFIC RESEARCH CENTER

- Differences in the expectations and roles of the mentoring committee between campus departments and those outlined below will be resolved by the ABC director and department chair when the mentoring committee is established.

- The mentoring committee will be established jointly by the mentee, the chair of the tenure-home department and the ABC director, and will consist of at least one ABC regular faculty member and at least one faculty member from the mentee's tenure home department. The mentoring committee will be selected to provide expertise and guidance to the mentee in meeting the expectations for research, teaching, service and extension…

- The mentoring committee will meet with the mentee at least once per year, and a summary of this meeting and any other mentoring activities during the year (e.g., classroom visits, manuscript and grant proposal reviews) will be reported in writing to the mentee, the ABC director, and tenure-home department chair by February 1. This report will not be an evaluation of the mentee, but should report on issues of concern that the committee and mentee agree are barriers to the mentee's success that need to be shared with the ABC director and department chair. The summary report of the mentoring committee will be discussed with the faculty member at their annual evaluation with the ABC director and department chair.

EXHIBIT 1.7 CONTINUED: MENTORING PLAN FOR *ABC* SCIENTIFIC RESEARCH CENTER

- All discussions between the mentee and mentors are strictly confidential unless the mentee explicitly states otherwise.

- Mentees may change mentors at their discretion. Decisions to change the mentoring committee should be made in consultation with the ABC director and department chair.

- The ABC mentoring plan will be reviewed every three years and revised as appropriate.

EXHIBIT 1.8: NEW FACULTY MENTORING PROGRAM AT A COMMUNITY COLLEGE

[Edited for brevity.]

...The following is an overview of the mentoring program provided for new full- time faculty hired at TCC starting with the 2012-13 academic year.

…Each mentoring team should establish at least four goals that the two will commit to accomplish for the academic year and which can be measured at the end of the academic year, e.g., grant seeking, promotion plan, develop online teaching. Obviously, these are simply a few suggestions. There are many others that may be pursued through a written plan for the academic year. Both the mentee and mentor should strive to keep the goals attainable and measureable while recognizing that there is a limited amount of time to accomplish the goals.

Exhibit 1.8 Continued: New Faculty Mentoring Program at a Community College

At the end of the academic year, the mentor and mentee will complete an evaluation form that will be submitted to the Office of Academic Services to help evaluate the effectiveness of the mentoring program and make appropriate changes as needed. These forms will be kept confidential in nature and will not be shared with the supervising academic dean/director of either the mentee or mentor unless the mentor or mentee requests in writing that it be shared with her/his dean/director. However, the supervising dean/director will be notified that one of her/his faculty members is being mentored or is serving as a mentor, and this may be used as part of the faculty member's self evaluation to document service to the institution.

Roles and Responsibilities

Both mentors and mentees are responsible for establishing a relationship built on trust and confidence and interacting with each other in a collegial manner. Both are to remember that the intent of the mentoring program is to provide information and services to the new faculty member that will enhance student learning and thus promote the mission of the Community College.

Mentors are responsible for the following:

1. Making initial contact with the mentee within one month of the beginning of fall classes to develop mutually agreed upon goals and staying in touch with the mentee throughout the academic year (best method of communication to be determined jointly by mentor and mentee). Providing appropriate guidance to the mentee's questions, needs, or concerns, and developing measureable goals for the mentee.

2. Maintaining the confidentiality of all shared information.

3. Committing the necessary time to the relationship and being available at the mutually agreed upon times.

4. Sharing knowledge and experience with the mentee in a way that benefits the mentee in her/his career at the College.

5. Completing an evaluation form at the end of the academic year about the mentorship program and submitting it to the Office of Academic Services.

Mentees are responsible for the following:

1. Committing the necessary time to the relationship and being available at the mutually agreed upon times.

2. Exchanging ideas and experiences with the mentor in a collegial manner and developing measureable goals for the academic year.

3. Taking advantage of the experiences and opportunities provided by the mentor. Maintaining the confidentiality of all shared information.

4. Keeping the mentor informed about any problems, concerns, or progress made during the academic year.

5. Completing an evaluation form about the mentorship program and submitting it to the Office of Academic Services.

EXHIBIT 1.8 CONTINUED: NEW FACULTY MENTORING PROGRAM AT A COMMUNITY COLLEGE

Mentor Selection Process

The academic deans/directors submit names of faculty to serve as mentors to the office of the vice president for student learning... Faculty members are encouraged to let their dean/director know if they are interested in becoming a mentor. Each nominee will complete an application to serve as a mentor for a new faculty member...being a mentor is simply one way that a faculty member may choose to serve the college. The vice president will assign the mentor to the new faculty member and will provide training to the mentors. All mentors must have a multi year contract and excellent service and teaching evaluations and be approved by their division directors.

EXHIBIT 1.9: FACULTY MENTORING PROGRAM IN A LARGE MEDICAL SCHOOL DEPARTMENT

[Edited for brevity. From 2012.]

Goals: The Faculty Mentoring and Development Program will help provide faculty with support, direction and intentional academic guidance through collaboration with experienced faculty mentors who will facilitate appropriate academic progress. Further, the program will: provide support for the faculty member in the demanding academic health center environment, lead to the creation of a career development plan, ensure that academic activities meet established performance goals, facilitate networking and collaboration inside and outside the department and the university, help identify opportunities, and provide written feedback for the faculty member being mentored, the division chief and the department chair.

Participants: MD and/or PhD faculty who are on the main campus and at the rank of assistant professor or associate professor are expected to participate. The faculty member's division chief, with input from the department chair, will ensure that the individual is participating in the program.

Structure: The faculty will have both a primary mentor and a faculty mentoring committee to help meet the goals of the program. The faculty member and the division chief will propose committee members by submitting to the mentoring program coordinator 3-5 names of individuals from both our department and other appropriate departments. Faculty will begin assembling their committees as they begin their appointment in the department, under the approval of the department chair. The composition of committees may change over time, reflecting change and evolution in scholarly interests…

Ideally, at least one individual from outside of the department will be included on each committee. Among identified committee candidates, one person (typically the primary mentor) will serve as chair of the committee. The department chair and/or the mentoring program coordinator will ask each of the committee candidates if they are willing to serve on the committee…

Activities: The faculty member will meet with the entire mentoring committee a minimum of twice a year initially and then once annually (more often as needed).

...The primary mentor and will be responsible for meeting regularly with the faculty member. The frequency of these meetings will vary according to the faculty member's needs and mission focus.

Reporting: The faculty member being mentored will provide the mentoring group with both short-term and long-term goals on an annual basis. The committee will be expected to provide appropriate feedback (see attached form) (after each meeting) to the division chief and the mentoring program coordinator. These reports will serve as part of the documentation of faculty performance during annual faculty reviews and for promotion and tenure applications.

Learning: The faculty member will develop a formal development plan that will include specifics about goals and further training. The faculty member and primary mentor will meet regularly and will focus on progress toward the goals of the plan and consideration as to how the plan should be modified, per changes in the faculty member's focus. Under the mentor's guidance, the faculty member will develop core academic skills, including but not limited to: oral communications and presentations, scholarly writing and critiques, grant, program, and/or contract development, academic and other professional networking and collaboration, leadership and professionalism.

Notes

1. See evidence base for elements of effective mentoring structures in: Fountain, Joselynn, and Kathryn E. Newcomer. "Developing and Sustaining Effective Faculty Mentoring Programs," *Journal of Public Affairs Education*, vol. 22, no. 4, 2016, pp. 483–506

   www.naspaa.org/JPAEMessenger/Article/vol22-4/05_Fountain%20Newcomer%2020160916.pdf

   Also see Bland, Carol J., et al. *Faculty Success Through Mentoring, A Guide for Mentors, Mentees and Leaders*, ACE Series on Higher Education, Roman and Littlefield Publishers, 2009. pp. 35-44.

2. A good description factors that go into mentor selection can be found in Phillips, Susan L., and Susan T. Dennison. *Faculty Mentoring, A Practical Manual for Mentees, Mentors, Administrators and Faculty Developers*, Stylus, 2015, p. 43-44

3. See Phillips and Dennison cited above, pp. 28-9.

4. Straus, Sharon E., et al. "Characteristics of Successful and Failed Mentoring Relationships: A Qualitative Study Across Two Academic Health Centers," *Academic Medicine*, vol. 88, no. 1, January 2013, pp. 83-89.

   www.ncbi.nlm.nih.gov/pmc/articles/PMC3665769/

5. For a complementary discussion of mentoring models and mentoring program structure, see Bland, Carol J., et al. *Faculty Success Through*

Mentoring, A Guide for Mentors, Mentees and Leaders, ACE Series on Higher Education, Roman and Littlefield Publishers, 2009, pp. 21-34.

6. For a report on Emory University's Peer Faculty Mentoring Program, download the Academic Exchange, Spring 2015, see pp. 1-6. This is a publication of the Emory University Center of Excellence and Faculty Development. It may be accessed at:

    http://www.emory.edu/ACAD_EXCHANGE/2015pdfs/print.pdf

7. Bland, et. al. (2009), have a good discussion of the "Making the Match" in Chapter 6. p. 67-70. They also recommend there be "a negotiation phase" culminating in a mentoring agreement. This formalizes the commitment on an individual level and may or may not generate a lot of document-ation, see p. 79. The Faculty Mentoring Program at the UNC Eshelman School of Pharmacy provides a particularly good example of a well-defined mentoring program and relationship. See Harold Kohn, "A Mentoring Program to Help Junior Faculty Members Achieve Scholarship Success" in *The American Journal of Pharmacy Education*, 2014, March 12, 78 (2). 29 or access the program's description at:

    https://pharmacy.unc.edu/faculty/faculty-mentoring-program/

8. The Bill and Susan Campbell Program mentioned in the previous footnote is one of the few examples of compensated mentoring, and it is supported by an endowment. Another UNC-CH example of recognizing and supporting the mentoring function is the Women's Leadership

Council Mentoring Award, established by alumni to recognize outstanding mentors of students and faculty on the campus. The program provides a $5,000 annual award for three individuals: one who has mentored faculty, one who has mentored graduate students, and one who has mentored undergraduates. A fuller description of the program may be accessed at:

http://giveto.unc.edu/supporters/get-involved/womens-leadership-council/areas-of-support/faculty-mentoring-award/

I also provide additional examples in Chapter 5.

9. Campus ombuds programs provide highly confidential advisory services to faculty on campus and they are often able to quietly head off major problems. (See http://ombuds.uci.edu/general-information/).

To be effective, such resources would need to be effectively publicized to new faculty. Sometimes staff of a Center for Teaching and Learning or similar organization on campus can be a safe space for new faculty to talk about concerns in their units. However, the staff needs to have a set protocol for fielding complaints and concerns, which by their nature can be politically sensitive and involve critique of specific mentors.

10. See UCSF's Faculty Mentoring toolkit: https://academicaffairs.ucsf.edu/ccfl/media/UCSFFacultyMentoringProgramToolkit.pdf and the University of Maryland's Junior Faculty Mentoring Guide: https://pdc-svpaap1.umd.edu/faculty/documents/MentoringGuide.pdf

CHAPTER 2
WHAT MENTORING SERVICES ARE NEEDED TO SUPPORT EARLY CAREER FACULTY ON YOUR CAMPUS?

Chapter 1 focused on *structure* and *process*. In Chapter 2, I focus on the *substance*, i.e., what services your mentoring program is going to deliver to faculty members and the institution. Of course, in practice, structure, process and substance are intertwined, but it makes sense to highlight each area separately so as to clarify the choices you may have in designing your mentoring program. So in this chapter, I will discuss the five areas that campus, school, and unit level faculty mentoring and development programs should address:

1. Providing guidance about the promotion and tenure process.

2. Supporting the development of teaching skills.

3. Supporting research and publication.

4. Encouraging professional development.

5. Addressing the particular concerns of women and faculty members of color.

I will provide examples, cases, and guidelines for each of these functions.

There are other positive things that can also be done, such as:

- Welcoming and on-boarding faculty.

- Providing them with help in building leadership and organizational skills.

- Assisting (where appropriate) in public engagement and developing clinical competence.

However, based on my research and experience, the first five I mentioned above are the key mentoring services that most early career faculty and even mid-career faculty want and need. Specific services that might be included in these four areas of mentoring service are summarized in Exhibit 2.1 below.

EXHIBIT 2.1: TYPICAL MENTORING SERVICES THAT MIGHT BE PROVIDED AS PART OF EARLY CAREER FACULTY DEVELOPMENT PROGRAMS

1. Helping early career faculty members understand standards for tenure and promotion and take effective action to meet those standards, such as:

- Required and documented conversations where the standards and expectations are clarified and expressed by mentors with mentees.

EXHIBIT 2.1 CONTINUED: TYPICAL MENTORING SERVICES FOR EARLY CAREER FACULTY

- Periodic discussions with mentors and others about the candidate's progress toward advancement, including written feedback on progress.

- Development of explicit goals and plans to address expected milestones and correct identified gaps.

- Training activities directly related to promotion processes such as: dossier preparation workshops and simulations; supervision in preparing tenure file and dossier, including providing examples of required recommendation letters, as well as guidance on what documentation to provide about teaching or research effectiveness.

2. **Assisting the development of teaching effectiveness, such as:**

- Departmental/disciplinary workshops on teaching (required or recommended).

- Options for classroom observation, feedback, and coaching in first years.

- Teaching methods courses and consultations (e.g., technology in the classroom, active learning approaches, etc.), either provided by the unit or by a campus teaching and learning center.

- Reduced course load the first year.

- Assistance in interpreting and acting on student evaluations.

- Connect to teaching mentor or mentors.

EXHIBIT 2.1 CONTINUED: TYPICAL MENTORING SERVICES FOR EARLY CAREER FACULTY

- Connect to center on teaching and learning.

- Support group for new teachers.

3. Providing research support, such as:

- Required or recommended workshops on writing and publication.

- Targeted grants for research methods development.

- Peer writing groups.

- Access to research support units (Centers, Institutes, Training Programs).

- Access to travel and research funds.

- Connect to research mentor or mentors.

- Assistance in writing grants and developing research opportunities.

4. Supporting professional development. For example:

- Brown bag lunch/research or teaching seminars to which new faculty are invited/expected to attend.

- Junior-help-junior activities (e.g., new faculty support group).

- Activities to help faculty engage with the community, profession, or relevant industry or government agencies.

- Financial support, released time, and encouragement to attend professional meetings.

- Guidance about how to appropriately get involved in the most relevant professional organizations.

- Identification of service tasks that are helpful or required for promotion.

- Protection from service tasks or teaching or research engagements that are not helpful for promotion at this time.

Helping Early Career Faculty Understand and Prepare for Tenure and Promotion

The goal here is to assist early career faculty members as they seek to understand standards for tenure and promotion and take effective action to meet those standards.

The keys to doing this are:

- Establishing clear standards.

- Providing good process guidance.

- Providing sensitive coaching, counseling, and advocacy.

- Providing opportunities for skill development and faculty accomplishment.

- Providing clear feedback that identifies where improvement is needed.

Establishing clear standards and requirements at the unit level

Ten years' experience with the largest national study of tenure track faculty shows that faculty on the tenure track want, most of all, clarity of expectations of what it takes to get tenure, and a collegial departmental climate. Studies of young professors on the tenure track all cite the hunger for clear standards of promotion and tenure. This information is also sought by contract faculty who have an opportunity to advance in rank. The landmark COACHE study (1) identified key items that universities should address as part of their mentoring effort to clarify tenure and promotion practices:

- Discuss expectations in the selection process and again on arrival.

- Set weights and priorities for different expectations (e.g., teaching vs. research).

- Be explicit about other less measureable standards (e.g. collegiality).

- Provide written information, orientation sessions, and Q&A sessions.

- Provide sample dossiers, education sessions, and open communication channels.

Productivity standards vary greatly by discipline and by institution. To receive tenure, a biology professor at a research intensive university may be expected to develop as many as 40 short research reports showing progress in a given field of inquiry; a history professor may be expected to produce several peer reviewed articles and a book; a creative writing professor may be expected to create a series of short stories, or a book of poems, and so on. A research professor in a school of Medicine or Public Health will likely live or die by the ability to attract funding or to be funded on other grants, or by developing valuable methodological skills that are in high demand and can be hired on multiple grants. A faculty member in the professional track in a journalism program may be expected to write strong pieces about the development of the field but not necessarily produce the kind of research valued by the academic side of the school.

So that means standards must be individualized and tailored to the department and sub-unit of the discipline. The new faculty member has to have a good understanding of how much is expected, the quality criteria, the favored forms and methods. He or she must develop a workable plan to produce the desired result.

Faculty who are primarily teachers rather than researchers should also understand expectations in some detail: e.g., how many courses, what role student evaluations play, what are the expectations for student counseling and campus engagement, what the service norms for the unit are, what the measures are, and so on.

A variety of descriptions of promotion and tenure processes are readily available on the Internet (2). The

English Department of the University of Loyola at Chicago has posted a particularly detailed account of its procedures. I provide an edited version of it in Exhibit 2.2 below to illustrate both the intricacy of promotion procedures and the detail to which they need to be explicated.

EXHIBIT 2.2: GUIDELINES FOR PROMOTION AND TENURE - ENGLISH DEPARTMENT, LOYOLA UNIVERSITY, CHICAGO

[Source: https://www.luc.edu/english/tenure.shtml

Edited for brevity.]

I. Introduction

Candidates for promotion and tenure in the Department of English are assessed according to the procedures set forth in these guidelines for promotion and tenure, which are supplementary to the by laws of the department. ... The responsibility to make recommendations concerning promotion and tenure is shared among the appropriate voting members of the faculty, the appropriate elected council of the department who constitute an advisory body, and the chairperson. These guidelines are subject to the provisions of the faculty handbook, ...

II. Areas of Assessment

Candidates for promotion and tenure...are expected to have engaged in teaching, scholarship, and service to the department, to the university in its appropriate units and to the profession.

Teaching duties in the Dept of English consist of regular meetings with groups of students as

Exhibit 2.2 Continued: Sample Guidelines for Promotion and Tenure

as listed in the schedule of courses and in courses listed as special studies and directed readings...

Teaching includes...maintaining regular office hours and otherwise making oneself available for individual consultation on matters pertaining to one's courses; advising students more generally on curricular matters; proposing and creating new courses; participating in peer teaching evaluation groups; supervising independent studies, graduate theses and dissertations; serving on thesis and dissertation committees; and serving on examination boards of the department.

Four sorts of **scholarship** are relevant: (1) published or publishable scholarly work in composition, language, and literature in such modes as literary-critical, cultural, historical, and textual studies (in print or digital media); (2) published or publishable creative writing—e.g., poetry, fiction, drama, and nonfictional prose; (3) published reviews of work in the two categories listed above; (4) presentation of papers, or participation in panels, at recognized professional meetings, or, by invitation, at other institutions.

Service includes membership on departmental, college, and university committees; advising student groups or moderating student activities...administrative service in department, college, and university; offices held in professional organizations; journals edited; such professional service as reading manuscripts for journals or publishers and evaluating candidates for promotion and tenure within the department or at other universities; membership on

EXHIBIT 2.2 CONTINUED: SAMPLE GUIDELINES
FOR PROMOTION AND TENURE

college and university evaluation teams; and community service and other activities consistent with the mission of the department and its programs.

III. Means of Assessment

Teaching is assessed in several ways: (1) the chairperson or a delegate visits the classes of each untenured member at least once a year until the member is considered for tenure (and) prepares a written report after each visit and discusses its contents in a conference with the teacher. The report is placed in the member's file in the department. (2) (student evaluations are read by the chairperson, who inserts a summary of them into the teacher's file…(and) then passed to the faculty member; untenured faculty must keep their forms until tenure has been granted. (3) Other pertinent information may include results of surveys of graduates; service on dissertation and exam-ination committees; development of new courses and teaching materials;… Candidates for promotion and tenure are encouraged to submit a portfolio of materials related to their teaching….

Scholarship: At the time of consideration for tenure or promotion, the candidate shall submit published and unpublished work for consid-eration by the members who are eligible to vote… Candidates may also submit evidence of their recognition as scholars or writers in their fields, such as reviews of their work, awards, citations by other scholars, election to member-ship on boards of professional organizations, appointments as editor of scholarly or literary journals, and invitations as keynote (or similar) speakers.

EXHIBIT 2.2 CONTINUED: SAMPLE GUIDELINES
FOR PROMOTION AND TENURE

The chairperson shall request written evaluations of the candidate's scholarship. These shall total four, one written by a senior member of the department and three written by external evaluators.

The chairperson shall ask the candidate to submit at least five names of qualified external reviewers in his or her field of expertise. Candidates may also submit up to two names of persons who should not be invited to serve as reviewers. The chairperson shall select at least one external reviewer from among those suggested by the candidate and at least one on the basis of consultation with the Department Council and members of the department in the candidate's field. None of the outside reviewers should have any vested interest in the candidate's career;...

Service: Ordinarily a candidate's services to the department, the university and the profession are matters of public record. It may be necessary for the chairperson to ask those acquainted with the candidate's service (e.g., chairs and members of committees) to estimate the quality of it.

IV. Criteria for Tenure and Promotion

...It is necessary to emphasize...that no specific quantity of published material can guarantee a favorable or trigger an unfavorable recommendation for tenure or promotion. The department seeks evidence that a candidate has produced scholarly, critical, or creative work that has merited positive recognition in the profession through acceptance and/or publication... Nevertheless, in most cases four or five

EXHIBIT 2.2 CONTINUED: SAMPLE GUIDELINES FOR PROMOTION AND TENURE

articles or a book would be required. Professional and scholarly work in digital or other media may also be presented. If the faculty member is at work on a long-term project (e.g., a monograph, edition, or bibliography), he or she may submit the incomplete or unpublished manuscript for consideration. In all cases, the department values the quality of scholarly work (as judged by the departmental and external evaluators) above the quantity of such work.

Overall Criteria for Tenure: [The Department] places emphasis on a member's teaching and on his or her scholarship; service and the willingness to serve and perform administrative tasks are important but cannot substitute for success in teaching and scholarship. Candidates for tenure, like other members of the department, are expected to maintain appropriate professional relations with other members of the university community.

Criteria for Teaching and Service to Students: The department recognizes that styles of teaching vary according to the personal attributes of each individual teacher. We seek evidence of the faculty member's dedication to teaching and effectiveness in achieving the objectives of each course.

Criteria for Scholarship: ...as soundness of argumentation, originality, quality of presentation, and importance of the published material to the candidate's field; reputation of the journals and/or presses publishing it; reception by the profession, as evidenced by published reviews or citations of the candidate's work; and promise of future productivity.

EXHIBIT 2.2 CONTINUED: SAMPLE GUIDELINES
FOR PROMOTION AND TENURE

Tenure is normally granted only to faculty members whose performance gives evidence of scholarship and productivity which, if sustained, would merit eventual promotion to the rank of professor...

Criteria for Service: Service to the profession, as officer in national or regional organizations, as editor of a professional journal, as manuscript reader, or the like, is considered important evidence of professional standing. Service to the department and to the university is critical to faculty governance. Everyone is expected to contribute in meaningful ways.

V. Process

[Each candidate who is qualified by years of service] is asked by the chairperson to submit a letter describing the candidate's scholarship, teaching and service; CV; and any other supporting material... The letter, CV, and supporting materials, including the chairperson's statement quoting student opinions of the candidate's teaching, as well as four evaluations of the candidate's scholarship or creative work by three external and one internal evaluator particularly qualified in the candidate's area, are distributed to all the eligible voting members of the department... The chairperson calls a meeting of all eligible voting members... the purpose of which is to discuss the candidate's teaching, scholarship or creative work, service, and any other matters relevant to the application. No voting takes place at this meeting. Proceedings of this meeting are strictly confidential. The chairperson calls for a written vote of the eligible voting members to be received soon after the meeting.

> ## Exhibit 2.2 Continued: Sample Guidelines for Promotion and Tenure
>
> ...All letters, which are to be signed, are treated with strict confidentiality by the Department Council. The Department Council now reviews the written poll of the eligible voting members, the evaluations of scholarship, and whatever other evidence can be gathered. No member of the council of a rank equal with, or lower than, that of the candidate will take part in the discussion of, or voting on, that case. On the basis of all this information, the council makes a recommendation to the chairperson... The chairperson attaches to the recommendation of the Department Council his or her own recommendation, the result of the poll of the faculty, and the evaluation of scholarship. The results are submitted to the Dean of the College of Arts and Sciences and the Dean of the Graduate School...

Providing good process guidance

Providing clear standards, while crucial, is not enough. Junior members also need good guidance on how to meet those standards and navigate the associated processes. Political and social factors are important in the fraught world of tenure and promotion. For researchers these include: which journals to submit to, which remarks of a journal editor or reviewer to pay attention to and which to ignore, and who to ask for a pre-proposal review on a grant application. These are all questions that require a sophisticated understanding of the unit, the campus nuances of the tenure process, and the disciplinary politics.

A knowledgeable mentor is often required to help over-come hurdles at all these levels.

Young teachers need to know how to interpret student evaluations so as to understand how to improve their classes, who to reach out to get help to become a better lecturer or discussion leader, how to handle student complaints, predictable problems, how to help students who are struggling, how to promote civility in the classroom, what the university standards are for grading, designing a syllabus, giving exams, independent study, and so on.

Also, standards for promotion are constantly shifting (mostly increasing) and the application of the standards may vary at unit and school and university levels as members of appointment, tenure, and promotion committees come and go. So, astute mentoring is needed as a complement even to clear written standards in most cases.

Another reason careful mentoring is needed has to do with timing associated with tenure and promotion processes. Young faculty members may not understand the import-ance of obtaining letters of recommendation from disciplinary leaders in other universities or know who to seek these from. This in turn relates to why, therefore, that they need to be visible in the national professional association. They may not realize they have to put their student evaluations in the tenure file or understand other technical requirements of the review process. They may not know that completion of a manuscript is not enough, but acceptance for publication is required, or that the date of publication must be before the completion of the third year review. Or they may not understand that unpublished material that has been externally reviewed can be submitted and when this helps their case and so on.

Units may resort to creative methods to assure that each new faculty member can "dot the I's and cross the T's" in understanding how to prepare the tenure dossier, or meet promotion criteria and plan ahead to get this done in time to meet hard deadlines. One psychology department I profiled went further and provided tenure track candidates with redacted files of real tenure applications and had them go through a mock review of these cases. This opened their eyes to the process they would undergo and gave them the detailed understanding of the process they would need to be prepared. This is also one of "effective practices" mentioned in the COACHE study cited above.

Providing sensitive coaching, counseling, and advocacy

Coaching is needed to help faculty members address special issues related to diversity. What if a young faculty member suspects racial or ethnic bias? Whom can s/he turn to? What if a female faculty member needs to strategize about whether she should ask for an extension of the tenure period while caring for an infant, etc? In the case cited earlier, where the department lost a promising African-American faculty member because, ironically, she was working too hard, it is clear that no one had established a trusting relationship with this faculty member to help adjust expectations to a reasonable level.

Units and campuses need to provide a rich network of resources for faculty to use so as to be able to discuss the things that may be "un-discussable" with their mentors. At the same time mentors need to do what they can to assure that the mentoring relationship is a safe space in which to broach delicate issues.

The lesson here is that even having formal mentoring in place does not assure the faculty member will get all the guidance they feel they need to have and the department wants them to have. It is also critical that the relationship feel safe enough so that the faculty member trusts that she or he can explore deep concerns and questions with the mentor without fear of being negatively evaluated.

Diversity issues are not the only reasons that sensitivity is needed in helping a new faculty member. Problems with relationships, health problems, even drugs and alcohol may appear. Mentors may not want to get involved at this level, but they should be able to recognize issues and refer to appropriate resources on the campus or in the community. At the very least the mentors themselves need access to a knowledgeable professional, if they suspect there are problems of this sort.

The culture of the unit (e.g., the degree to which new faculty are expected to be reticent or outspoken, hard-driving or laid-back, preferred methods and theories, factions and personality conflicts) may also be a source of concern. New faculty members may experience problems and do not fully understand the source of those problems. As a faculty developer at UNC-CH, I offered a "lunch and learn" program for new faculty on how to assess the fit between their academic preferences and the dominant culture of their unit. The session was on how to discover the areas of congruence and incongruence and how to deal with the results of that inquiry, so as to enhance rather than derail their careers, and how to deal with the unfortunate situation of discovered "bad fit." (See Appendix B for a unit culture assessment form.)

National culture factors may be significant. In one discussion with a professional school faculty, it was asserted that early career faculty needed to aggressively make their case for tenure and promotion to assure the greatest success with internal promotion committees. Faculty members on the school committees were anxious that all of their recommendations would be acceptable at the higher level, so they wanted very strong self-promotional statements. It was pointed out that new faculty members from several Asian countries were socialized to be more modest in presenting themselves. Mentors needed to help these faculty members adapt to a different cultural standard if they wanted to maximize their chances of success.

Sometimes coaching must be combined with advocacy. A classic problem for young faculty members in the research university can be carving out time for writing or other activities required for tenure and promotion. Chairs who need bodies to fulfill service tasks or senior faculty who need help on their projects may try to recruit the early career faculty member. If he or she has a problem saying "no," the early career faculty member may wind up spending too much time mentoring students rather than doing his or her own work. It is with situations like these where experienced mentors can save the day. The mentor can strongly advise the young faculty member to block out time for promotion-related tasks, and as mentor, he or she can run interference for the young faculty member who has been asked to take on a task that distracts him or her from what they should be doing to get promoted or achieve tenure.

In one private research university I worked with recently, a science department chair required his approval before any untenured faculty member could accept a project offered to him or by another faculty member. This gave the early career faculty members "cover" if they felt that accepting the job would distract from their main priorities In a teaching focused institution, a mentor can be alert when an early career faculty member is assigned too many new preparations in the first year and intervene. Good mentors at both teaching and research-focused institutions look out for their mentees.

In Exhibit 2.3, I provide an excerpt from a University of Michigan manual that lists the variety of career advice that early career faculty may need from mentors. (3)

EXHIBIT 2.3: PROVIDING CAREER ADVICE TO EARLY CAREER FACULTY (UNIVERSITY OF MICHIGAN)

[The ADVANCE Program at the University of Michigan published a set of guidelines for giving career advice. The following is excerpted from page 3 of their manual and is slightly edited as to format and brevity. The full text may be accessed at:

https://advance.umich.edu/resources/]

What is the goal of providing career advice?

The ultimate goal of giving career advice to early career faculty is to enhance their chances of career success in earning tenure (for instructional faculty) or advancement and promotion (i.e., for research or clinical track faculty) through achievements in scholarship, success in obtaining external funding, teaching, and/or service. Thus, senior faculty can offer information and assistance not only by providing advice about one's area of scholarship, but by: providing information about promotion and tenure processes, demystifying departmental, research center, college, and university culture, providing constructive and supportive feedback on specific work or on career progress, providing encouragement and support helping to foster important connections and visibility, and looking out for early career faculty interests.

Junior and senior faculty alike should consider these topics for their discussions:

"The inside story" on departmental culture, how to navigate department and institution, grant sources, strategies for funding, publishing outlets and processes, teaching, research, key conferences to attend, service roles inside and outside the university including work on committees...

[Faculty members should seek] feedback from a supervisor, such as a department chair, including:

- Review of research, publishing and grant activity, service on campus and nationally, teaching activity and mentoring students, clinical assignments. and review of documents like CVs annual reports and required professional statements.

- Critical feedback in the crucial years prior to tenure reviews or promotions, with delineation of the exact criteria by which that faculty member will be evaluated at the annual or third year review.

- Personal advice on sensitive issues that individuals do not feel comfortable discussing in groups, such as: relationships to cultivate, how to recruit students or post-doctoral fellows to your research group, advice about the career ladder and alternative tracks, how to plan a career trajectory, external visibility, tenure and promotion processes, family issues, national sources of support, publishing outlets and processes...

Providing clear and constructive feedback

Telling faculty members where they stand in relationship to the standards for tenure and promotion is a useful practice. The more that the feedback can specify in some detail areas of needed improvement, the more helpful it is to the faculty member. The more that the feedback is combined with specific assistance, when needed, the more likely it is to contribute to the faculty member's success.

In some units it is the responsibility of the chair to meet with each tenure track faculty member and to state in clear terms where they are on track to meet departmental standards and where they are falling short. Since there are potential legal liabilities for chairs saying, in effect, "If you do this you will get tenure" (in case the faculty member is not awarded tenure), this is usually couched in terms like:

- "What you have accomplished here strengthens your case."

- "Not having X, Y, Z in place is a problem in addressing this or that standard."

- "Your case would be strengthened if you accomplished X, Y, or Z by this time frame," etc.

These comments should be recorded in a letter to the faculty member and put in the faculty member's tenure file.

The chair may gather information from faculty member mentors, or may conduct his or her own assessment based on the CV or required annual report. In some departments, each early career faculty member's progress is discussed on an annual basis by the senior faculty. That feedback is then provided to the early career faculty member by the assigned mentor. This feedback becomes the basis for the early career faculty member's goals for the next year. In some units the mentoring committee provides this feedback, and in highly structured programs, they file a report with the chair.

Sometimes such an evaluation may indicate improvement is needed in one or both critical areas: teaching and research. The next sections of this chapter deal with effective practices for mentoring young faculty members in those critical areas.

Providing feedback can be challenging because in general, people may not be skilled at providing constructive criticism or recognizing accomplishment or progress. They may avoid important topics, be hypercritical, or lack specificity, timing, or sensitivity. At some point in each mentoring program, the mentors and mentees should discuss what kind of feedback is truly helpful both in general and in the context of the individual relationship. Keys to good feedback include: good timing, constructive tone, clear focus, specific guidance, and dialogue to assure the feedback is understood and accepted. (4)

The general principles of feedback are useful for mentors to learn and practice. In addition a more broadly developmental form of feedback can provide actionable information about where mentees stand in their progress toward tenure.

The following generic format would be a useful tool for any mentor-mentee team to complete and discuss. Exhibit 2.4 provides a format for that kind of feedback. When the cells of the table are completed and fully discussed by the mentor-mentee pair, the mentees know what they should do next to stay on the path to promotion and tenure.

EXHIBIT 2.4: PROVIDING PROMOTION-RELEVANT FEEDBACK FOR MENTEES				
Criteria for promotion and tenure	Scholarly productivity	Teaching excellence	Service excellence	Other
Accomplishments /projects this academic year				
Relevance of these accomplishments to the most important standards				
What indicators of high quality are there? How are these likely to be regarded in the department?				
Next steps toward progress in this area?				

Once possible next steps have been discussed, mentors and mentees could then identify which of the projects would contribute most to the mentees' promotion case. This could lead to an action plan for the next year based on the priority needs and goals. If the mentee has a problem with the priorities indicated by the mentors, then that may be an indication there is not a good fit between the preferences of the mentee and the expectations of the unit. If the mentee embraces the suggestions then that may indicate that the mentee is quite willing. If problems arise in execution of the plan, that may indicate lack of skill and knowledge. Hopefully, then, any problems can be corrected through professional development activities that are part of the ongoing mentoring plan.

Supporting the Development of Teaching Skills for Early Career Faculty

It has long been known that the most prestigious doctoral programs emphasize research over teaching, and in many disciplines a new faculty member arrives on campus without much teaching experience. However, it is often expected that the new faculty member jump right in, prepare several new courses, teach, and get good evaluations.

In addition to lack of preparation for teaching, there can be other obstacles that arise. For example, in the case of a faculty member from another country, there can be deep differences in the cultural expectations (e.g., the relationship between teacher and student in some European countries is more formal and distant than is the norm in American classrooms). There can be differences in what is considered good teaching from unit to unit. In one unit, there is a bias in moving toward active learning, and in another, the faculty member is expected to be a spellbinding lecturer. (5)

Young professors may have attended a 4-year residential college and then a PhD granting university. What if they land a job teaching in an urban setting that caters to adult working students, or if he or she is white and middle class and their students are predominately people of color from working class backgrounds? What is the role that mentoring should play in these types of situations? New teachers may appear apologetic, indecisive, and timid in the classroom or they may compensate for lack of experience by being arrogant, distant and dictatorial, or they may err in trying to be too friendly with students and blur boundaries. (6)

How teaching competence is valued in relationship to other duties will vary by the level of the institution. Typically community colleges and four-year institutions place a much greater emphasis on this than research-intensive universities. However, as competition for students increases and standards of accountability rise, assuring good teaching is becoming more important at all types of institutions: large and small, public and private.

My surveys of campus units revealed a number of creative responses to this challenge some of which related to mentoring. Other units deployed other faculty development modalities: education, technical assistance, and peer support. These other supports were "folded-in" or "wrapped-around" the mentoring program. Here are some examples:

- One physics department regularly sends new faculty members to a national program for new college teachers offered by the main professional society.

- In another unit, the chair regularly sits in on a new faculty member's courses once or twice a year and provides advice and guidance.

- In some departments, faculty members have a mentor for research and a mentor for teaching who serve as the "go to" persons for new faculty with questions and concerns about those functions.

- Many universities limit teaching responsibilities and the number of new preparations a faculty member must do in the first year or first several years until they establish their confidence in the classroom, and/or launch their research program.

- In many universities and colleges, there is a campus teaching and learning center and new faculty are urged to consult the experts there who can provide guidance on core teaching activities: lecturing, syllabus, discussion, grading, technology in the classroom, and active learning.

Almost all universities and colleges require some kind of student evaluation, and those are often used in promotion and tenure decisions. Ideally, there would be someone who could help early career faculty members make sense of those evaluations and correct problems or make improvements after the first semester or certainly after the first year, well before a contract renewal decision or a tenure vote. This review of student evaluations seems like an obvious topic to discuss with mentors or the chairs as part of a mentoring activity.

The main point of the section, though, is to suggest strongly that no mentoring program is fully effective unless it explicitly addresses how the unit or the institution plans to help young faculty meet the institution's expectations for effective teaching. Many colleges and universities have recognized this and have specialized units to help young faculty members do a good job in the classroom. The role of faculty developer has become a routine job category in higher education and there are now hundreds faculty development units that include assistance in teaching and learning on college campuses in the U.S. The main association (Professional and Organizational Development Network for Higher Education) for these specialists has more than 1,300 members. The Society for Teaching and Learning is another national and regional source of support for instructors interested innovative pedagogy. (7)

Mentors working with faculty members who are interested in improving their teaching should alert their mentees to these and other similar networks. Mentoring programs should make such information available to all mentors so they can pass it along.

Supporting the Development of Research and Writing Skills for Early Career Faculty

Supporting the development of writing research skills and publication is one of the main roles of formal mentoring programs, particularly in the research-intensive university and in those units and in the many institutions attempting to raise their research profiles. In the research-intensive university, the focus on scholarly work is a "do or die" proposition, much more so than teaching. So in these institutions effective research mentoring is an essential part of a strong mentoring program. For some schools and departments, having a good research mentoring effort is key to their strategic plan, as in Exhibit 2.5.

EXHIBIT 2.5: RESEARCH MENTORING IN A GRADUATE PROFESSIONAL SCHOOL

Based on an interview with the Associate Dean for Research in 2012.

The school...has a structured program of mentoring. Each faculty member has two mentors that are appointed by the Associate Dean for Research. The Associate Dean for Research also sits in on most meetings. Each mentoring committee meets with the new faculty member and lays out a plan for accomplishment. The plan is monitored and updated on a yearly basis.

The main focus is on helping the faculty member establish a research program, show appropriate levels of productivity, develop a capacity to write and win research proposals, and to build a research network.

The plan lays out the nature of the research that will be pursued, the recommended journals for publishing, and the potential funding sources. The new faculty member receives help from the committee and others in carrying out this plan.

By the time faculty members come up for tenure, they are already very productive scholars and quite capable of developing their own funded research. Early in the process, if the committee spots a deficit in training, the School provides the funds to get the faculty member the training they need, such as a seminar in which they learn a particular research and statistical technique.

EXHIBIT 2.5 CONTINUED: RESEARCH MENTORING
IN A GRADUATE PROFESSIONAL SCHOOL

We in the school believe this structured mentoring program has helped us develop a strong cadre of associate professors who are capable and committed to doing the impactful research that the future of the school is premised on. In this sense, our mentoring approach is integral for our vision of the school.

Not all programs for helping faculty develop research programs are as focused and integrated as the above program. However, effective mentoring programs in the area of research and writing provide at least some of the following services to faculty. This list is consistent with the general guidelines for new faculty mentoring mentioned earlier in the chapter but specialized for the research function including:

- Clarity about the levels of productivity required for tenure and promotion.

- Assistance and support relative to research projects and specific papers.

- Small amounts of funding that enable faculty members to undertake projects.

- Training in methods and approaches where needed.

- Linking faculty members to opportunities and projects.

Clarity about research expectations and feedback on progress toward goal achievement

Effective programs provide clear statements about numbers and types of publications that are expected of tenure track and fixed-term faculty including the preferred journals or outlets and a timetable of production that is tied to the promotion and tenure calendar. They also provide regular feedback on the progress that is being made.

One health science department at a research university says that a tenure candidate should expect to publish about 20 articles in a short list of particular peer-reviewed journals during their candidacy or about three or four a year. Each year the senior faculty members meet to review the work of each of the early career faculty member and a mentor is assigned to communicate the results of that review and create a work plan. The plan is filed with the department chair and reviewed annually in a one-on-one discussion between the faculty member and the chair.

As standards for promotion change, there may be a need for increased mentoring and faculty support. There are trends toward requiring teaching faculty to do research on pedagogy in order to rise to higher ranks, or requiring extension service faculty to write about improvements in methods of extension, or requiring clinical faculty to produce cases studies and other clinically based research and professional writing. In these situations, it may be necessary to provide support for new and current faculty to rise to the new standards of productivity.

Some support activities in this situation might include the following:

- Provide individuals a template and model for how to do this kind of writing.

- Identify role models who can mentor.

- Provide a short course on how to integrate this kind of research into a busy professional teaching, clinical, or extension practice.

- Help each person pick one subject and work it through to completion and publication.

- Coach people on how to set aside the time for this activity.

- Create a writing support group for first time writers in this situation.

- Recognize and reward those who are successful.

Provide review and comment on early drafts of papers

Effective mentoring programs assign senior faculty to be available to review drafts of papers by early career faculty and to advise early career faculty on how to respond editor's comments on early drafts. In one law school, the dean for faculty development helps young faculty members to have his or her work peer-reviewed by eminent scholars outside the department at least a year in advance of any departmental review. After the senior scholars have reviewed the early career faculty member's work, a phone conference is held between the established scholars and the early career faculty member. One political science department has a monthly informal gathering in which a research paper is presented and critiqued. The paper may be from a junior or senior faculty member.

Provide research and travel funds to support the work of early career faculty

Early career faculty members are in particular need of support to launch their research programs. These funds can be provided by a department, school, interdisciplinary center or the university or college itself, or they can facilitate faculty members locating and applying for outside resources.

The History department at one private university provides each new faculty member with a $3,000 travel fund. At UNC-CH, the Institute for the Arts and Humanities has a grants program that provides significant support for early career faculty. Early career faculty may compete for one of eight grants that sponsor semester-long research leaves. The program is funded by a multi-million dollar endowment raised by the Institute's staff and the University.

Some schools do not have the benefit of internal resources to support faculty members, but they link their faculty to outside resources such as Wilson, Guggenheim, NIH, NSF, and other sources of funding. Arizona State Engineering Research Service lists federal (NSF, NASA, DOE, DARPA, etc.) and non-federal sources (AAAS, Microsoft, Cancer Society, Alzheimer's foundation, etc.)

that early career faculty can apply for on its website. UC-San Diego's Office of Corporate and Foundation Relations Opportunities for Young Investigators lists not only grant sources but specific RFPs and deadlines.

Support specialized research and writing skills training

Promising early career faculty are sometimes hired while lacking specialized training in certain methods that are favored by the department. In a strong mentoring program, these faculty members would be sponsored to get that training so they could join with more senior faculty on research efforts. A School of Social Work recently established itself as a leader in evaluation research. Accordingly, new faculty are sponsored to attend certain advanced courses in statistics and methodology so they can contribute to this strategic thrust.

Sometimes departments will offer that training in-house if they have a faculty member who is interested in teaching writing and is skilled in that area. In my survey of UNC campus academic units and their mentoring programs, I discovered that in the Classics Department, a faculty member known for her ability to write and teach offered a free summer course for new faculty on how to write for the leading Classics journals. George Mason University Provides "write ins" several times a semester where faculty participants meet for a half a day, check in, and quietly write together. They also provide opportunities for two-day faculty retreats. DePaul University and The Office of the Provost at Purdue University offers extensive writing group support. (8)

EXHIBIT 2.6: THE PURDUE UNIVERSITY
WRITING GROUPS

This is excerpted from:

https://www.purdue.edu/provost/faculty/faculty
Initiatives/faculty-writing-groups.html

The Faculty Writing Groups include faculty of all ranks and from many units, who meet weekly in small groups so that members can read, edit and critique each other's writing projects. Participants report that working in a group improves their writing quality and productivity, and connects them with colleagues across disciplines. Tenure-track, clinical, and research faculty working on papers, monographs, book chapters, grant proposals and other academic writing projects are welcome. The Provost's Office handles the logistics each semester – assembling groups, assigning times to meet based on participants' weekly schedules, and booking rooms. If you'd like to join a Purdue Faculty Writing Group, please email…

Link new faculty members to research and writing opportunities

I once had a conversation with an associate provost who was in charge of faculty development campus-wide. I asked him what the greatest predictor of young faculty success as a researcher was in getting grants in the complex system of National Institute of Health Programs that provided funding for many on campus. He said that in his experience it had to do with whether the young faculty member found membership and a role within a currently successful research group. When this happened, the young faculty member gained the confidence and experience to go on to become an independent researcher, write proposals, and win awards and then return the favor to those coming behind him or her.

In one panel of very experienced faculty members talking about mentoring, a woman who had become a senior researcher in her journalism department talked about how important it was for her when a senior faculty member invited her to do a joint paper combining her strengths (empirical researcher) and his (theoretician).

It's critical to engage the new faculty member in research programs and networks. Mentors should be familiar with those opportunities in their disciplines.

For example, the Southeastern Association of Law Schools (SEALS) holds an annual call for papers. This event provides an opportunity for young faculty members to develop their writing and publication skills.

Providing Effective Professional Development Services for Early Career Faculty

The SEALS program illustrated in Exhibit 2.7 actually does double duty as a developmental activity. It both helps the new faculty member have an opportunity to write in a way that could lead to publication, and it also introduces the young scholar to the regional professional community.

EXHIBIT 2.7: WRITING OPPORTUNITY FOR EARLY CAREER FACULTY

Excerpted from SEALS Call For Pages:

https://sealslawschools.org/boards-and-committees/call-for-papers/

The mission of the SEALS Call for Papers Committee is to solicit, identify, and honor outstanding scholarship being prepared by faculty at our member schools. Each fall, the committee solicits new papers that have not yet been published. Each committee member reads each of these papers, judging the contribution that each makes as well as the quality of the writing. At the annual meeting, the committee hosts a luncheon at which authors of the top papers are recognized and invited to make brief presentations.

The literature suggests that attending to academic socialization and helping early career faculty form professional networks are key to academic success and advancement. (9) Exhibit 2.8 condenses the advice offered by Bland, et. al. in their *Faculty Success through Mentoring: Guide for Mentors, Mentees, and Leaders* (2009).

> ## EXHIBIT 2.8: HOW MENTORS SHOULD WORK TO SUPPORT THE PROFESSIONAL GROWTH OF EARLY CAREER FACULTY
>
> **Mentors should help new faculty:**
>
> - Develop their own career vision.
>
> - Understand the structure and dynamics of their unit and campus.
>
> - Assess the fit between campus goals and expectations and their own preferences and goals.
>
> - Understand the daily activities that lead to success; understand the products that lead to promotion and rewards (e.g., relevant journals); and understand the expected teaching load and measures of quality.
>
> - Maintain frequent contact with researchers in allied areas on their campus and in other institutions.
>
> - Seek opportunities to collaborate and participate in relevant professional groups on campus, in the community, nationally, and globally.
>
> - Build contacts with funding sources and project and program offices.

In a seminar of young humanities professors, we discussed what their greatest needs were for faculty development. First among these were getting appropriate guidance about which funding opportunities (for travel, released time, research assistants) were realistic for them and which they should invest time in applying for. Mentors need to inform themselves about the realistic opportunities that exist for early career faculty so as to help them pursue the most promising opportunities, saving them precious time.

Sometimes opportunity development takes the form of helping a young faculty member navigate the professional association that is most important in the profession, e.g., how involved to get, where to set limits, what groups and committees are going to be most helpful, and where and how to be visible and establish relationships. It is through the national and regional professional organizations that the young faculty members make contact with those all-important outside evaluators who will prove key to the tenure process later on.

Providing Effective Mentoring and Faculty Development Services for Women and Under-Represented Minority Faculty Members

The problems, causes, and solutions related to the issues facing women and under-represented minority faculty members in the academy are much broader than mentoring and faculty development per se. Yet, as I pointed out in the introduction and overview of the book, the mentoring movement in the academy is inextricably bound up with the increasing diversity in American higher education.

While mentoring and faculty development services are an essential part of the solution to the problems I discuss in this chapter, they are not the whole solution, nor will be they be effective unless they are part of a broader institutional approach to diversity and inclusion. Accordingly, my general discussion of diversity issues in this and later chapters takes a wider-lens viewpoint than some of the other parts of the book.

Designing programs and policies that address the special concerns of women in the academy

Statement of the problem

The general situation of the academy with respect to equity for women faculty. The pioneer of feminist organizational theory in the academy, Joan Acker (10), identified 5 ways in which organizations seem to be gender neutral but in fact perpetuate male domination and push women down and out:

1. Through gender-based divisions in work, physical locations, power, labor market structures, family, and state.

2. Through symbols and images that reinforce gender divisions.

3. In interactions between men and women and among men and women, where patterns of submission and dominance reinforce gender divisions.

4. Those processes that enhance individual gender identities in men and women that may promote inequality.

5. Finally, organizations, while seemingly gender neutral, have a "gendered substructure" of policies and procedures.

In 2017 the American Council on Higher Education produced a report that suggested that Acker's ideas were more than theoretical. The report concludes in part:

> The data show that women are not ascending to leadership roles, given that they hold a greater share of the entry-level, service, and teaching-only positions than their male counterparts. This is true for all women when looking across degree- granting postsecondary institutions; the trend is exacerbated for women of color. ... Overall, during the 2015–16 academic year, male faculty members made an average of $89,190, and female faculty members made an average of $73,782. No matter the academic rank, men make more than women and are more likely to hold a tenure track position. (11)

A major cause of this situation is conscious and unconscious bias in promotion decisions. (12) It is also generally accepted that women in the academy are more reticent about entering into salary negotiations and may ask for less than men when they do negotiate. This has significant systemic consequences. In a peer mentoring session for department chairs I facilitated, one of the female chairs related how, as an early career faculty member, she was proud of herself for negotiating a good contract with a private university. After she became chair and had access to everyone's salaries she found she was the lowest paid faculty member.

Another cause of slower promotion has recently been documented: women perform more service work than men do. Students expect women faculty to do more and they suffer for this in promotion and reviews, reflecting a low value put on these activities. Put simply: the academy has a problem with effectively valuing the work that women are expected to do. (13)

STEM Disciplines. The 2010 AAUW Report *Why So Few Women in STEM?* explores the long-standing social and cultural causes of the lack of female faculty in STEM disciplines. They show that pervasive stereotypes, e.g. "that women are not good at math" translates into lower performance on tests and reduction of interest in STEM-related fields among girls and young women. They show also that where there are accurately measured differences in performance (e.g., spatial skills), these differences are not inherent but can be erased by simple training. Unconscious biases persist through the college period affecting choice of major. Despite increases in the number of women majoring in STEM fields (especially biology), there is still a big discrepancy in women representation in chemistry, physics, information technology, math, and the engineer-ing disciplines.

COACHE study data from 56 universities cited by the AAUW indicates women are more unhappy than male faculty on all ten measures of departmental climate used by COACHE. A major factor is a sense of isolation since many units have only token representation. Women may feel unwelcome and may fail to be included in informal networks where valuable information (like salary ranges) is exchanged and where different kinds of professional opportunities are discussed. (14) A recent study of retention and promotion within STEM disciplines at four large land grant universities suggested that men and women were not advancing differently though differences did show up at one institution and between various disciplines. More telling though, was that the researcher said numbers were so small that they could have not strong confidence in their conclusions. (15)

Academic Medicine. This report in *Stanford Medicine* in 2017 sums up the situation. (16)

> The gender disparity in academic medicine can no longer be attributed to the so-called pipeline problem: Women make up roughly half of U.S. medical students and more than half of those receiving PhDs in the biomedical sciences. But they make up 22 percent of the tenured faculty at U.S. medical schools, according to 2013 data from the Association of American Medical Colleges. Their proportion declines as they rise in academic rank: Women are 44 percent of assistant professors—the early career faculty position that represents the first step toward tenure—but only 34 percent of associate professors and 21 percent of full professors (are women). The only rank at which women outnumber men is that of instructor, (which is) a separate, non-tenure-track faculty line. And while women are increasingly likely to serve in medical schools' leadership, their numbers in key positions are still small. Nationwide, they make up just 15 percent of department chairs and 16 percent of medical school deans.

Recent studies (2015, 2017) show that women in academic medicine have not progressed as rapidly as their male peers and that 40% of the schools of medicine have no programs to counteract this trend despite the fact that women now constitute the majority of MDs graduating from medical schools. (17)

Practices that institutions have adopted to improve the status of women faculty

Some academic institutions are making efforts to address these conditions. Many of these initiatives are potential services for an institution's programs of mentoring and faculty development. A partial listing is included in Exhibit 2.9. (18)

EXHIBIT 2.9: BROAD AREAS OF PRACTICE THAT PROMOTE EQUITY, INCLUSIVE CLIMATES, AND THE RETENTION OF WOMEN ACADEMICS

Assessment

- Regularly assessing the status and particular needs of various groups of women faculty, by rank, by status (i.e., tenure vs. non-tenure track, part-time, full-time), and by unit.

- Careful measurement and reporting of progress toward goal achievement.

Awareness

- Implicit bias training for all faculty.

- Information on the history of gender in the university.

- Discussions of gender bias and diversity issues.

Policy

- Creating robust policy statements about increasing the numbers of women at all levels of the faculty and in leadership.

Recruitment

- Setting aggressive recruitment goals related to gender equity.

- Training search committees to counter built-in bias in hiring practices.

- Gender-blind screening of CVs.

- Expanded phone interviews and campus interviews.

- Requirement of gender-diverse candidate pools at final stages.

Mentoring and social support

- Offering mentorship programs, including participation in formal unit-based programs and institution-based programs.

- Women's mentoring groups.

- Access to coaches and counselors in addition to the mentoring process.

Opportunities

- Offering programs that provide leadership training and advancement: e.g., emerging leadership programs that include women especially.

Professional development

- Life/balance training

- Career planning

- Time management training

- Network development programs

- Assertiveness and negotiation training

Family-related issues

- Offering policies that recognize child-care responsibilities: family leave, stopping the tenure clock, onsite child care, support for child care, research support for women with young children.

- Training and coaching on life-balance issues.

- Provide Dual Career Support.

Leadership

- Diversity and inclusion training for leaders.

- Expanding the number of women in positions of authority.

- Creating a faculty development leadership role that has the responsibility to address the particular needs of women.

EXHIBIT 2.9 CONTINUED: LIST OF EQUITY, INCLUSION, AND RETENTION PRACTICES

Salary and promotional equity

- Institutional reviews of outcomes and practices.

- Surveys of faculty concerns.

- Training for leaders on pay and salary equity.

The role of mentoring in supporting women faculty

Because women tend to be in the minority in many departments in the academy, and because the academy was built with men, not women, in mind, they tend to experience more stress. As a consequence women faculty often appreciate counter-balancing social support. Effective mentoring is a supportive relationship and also a way to build faculty capacity.

Professors Girdler and Colford's 2017 study of mentoring of medical school women faculty at UNC-CH employed focus groups of mentors. The mentors reported that mentees had particular needs for support in negotiating, relationship building, having an advocate, saying "no to service," establishing work-life balance, and being able to express themselves emotionally in the mentoring relationship. (19)

In recognition of the special role that mentoring can play in the support of women faculty, some campuses have developed mentoring programs specifically for women in addition to their formal, departmental mentoring structure. For example, the Mayo Clinic has offered a one-year program of peer mentoring for women that led to increased academic productivity. (20)

The use of mentoring groups for women is not limited to medicine, however. The University of Wisconsin at Madison is one example of this type of program that extends to the entire campus—as described in Exhibit 2.10.

EXHIBIT 2.10: UNIVERSITY OF WISCONSIN-MADISON MENTORING PROGRAM FOR WOMEN

Edited for brevity and relevance.

(This program is supported by the Office of the Provost and housed within the Office of the Secretary of the Faculty and is coordinated by the Faculty Services Coordinator—Apply to the Office of the Provost.)

- Each assistant professor is matched with a tenured woman who shares similar interests, but who is outside her department and, therefore, removed from her promotion and tenure process. ... It offers additional information and resources that build upon the work of departmental mentoring relationships.

- Each year, mentoring pairs are asked to evaluate their relationship and are invited to suggest event topics, and to offer advice to the advisory committee and fellow program participants.

> **EXHIBIT 2.10 CONTINUED: UW-MADISON MENTORING PROGRAM FOR WOMEN**
>
> - In addition, the program is home to a number of peer mentoring groups. These informal networks are intended to foster collegiality, promote learning, spark new ideas for research, and help women find their way throughout the university. The program also offers a series of panels and seminars and holds an annual luncheon.

To summarize, equity and the creation of a positive work environment for women faculty is a pervasive and long-term issue in the academy. Mentoring and faculty development have an important role to play as part of a broader diversity and inclusion effort. In the next section, I will focus on creating inclusive environments for other under-represented faculty groups.

Designing programs and policies that address the special concerns of under-represented minorities defined by color, ethnicity, nationality, LGBTQ+ status, or differences in ability (e.g., hearing, sight, mobility, etc.)

Statement of the problem

There is a broad consensus that diversification of the faculty is an imperative for IHEs if the US is to become the pluralistic society to which it aspires, the recent surge of white nationalist sentiment notwithstanding.

Yet less than 20% of University faculty members are non-white. If you separate that into proportions of faculty members of Asian (9%) African (5%), and Hispanic-descent (4%), then the percentage of faculty members within any racial/ethnic category is likely to be in single digits, and Native American and Pacific Islander groups less than 1%. As a consequence, it is not surprising that a key issue for inclusion of under-represented senior faculty is a sense of isolation.

In their chapter on retaining diverse faculty, Damon Williams and Katrina Wade-Golden cite a 2010 study that refers to a "culture that sometimes breeds a sense of isolation and exclusion, creates confusion about how to meet job responsibilities and advance professionally, and imposes unreasonable work burdens on faculty from (racial and ethic minorities)." (21)

Writing in *Inside Higher Ed* in March 2017, Berea College Historian Dwayne A. Mack writes about the experience of the under-represented minority faculty member (URMF). While speaking primarily of the experience of people of color, he may also be voicing the feelings of other people who are not the typical faculty member, e.g. women in a predominantly male science unit, a disabled faculty member, a faculty member from outside the US, etc.

> Academe is a challenging environment for faculty of color. Depending on the situation, predominantly white campuses treat faculty of color as though they are invisible, and then, when it is convenient, they become hypervisible. On your journey to tenure, you will find that your contributions are often devalued, margin-alized, ignored and, in some cases, appropriated by

white faculty. For those failing to adjust to these campus customs, it is often difficult to maintain an effective work-life balance. If you accomplish this balancing act, you will achieve professional success, along with a healthy mind, body and soul.

Mack's description is backed up by broad based empirical studies that find concerning evidence of stress disorders among UMRF, especially women of color. (22)

Williams and Wade-Golden, cited above, conclude that "any faculty diversification effort that does not address mentorship, improving the institutional culture, or attending to dual career needs may end up fueling a 'revolving door' with respect to new minority hires." This was also the conclusion of an earlier study by AACU. (23) Ethical considerations aside, considering the effort and expense required to recruit URMF, it is self-defeating not to make a strong effort to create a campus climate that is friendly and inclusive.

Some institutions of higher education have not ignored the problems that under-represented faculty members face. To their credit, they have been at the forefront of enunciating principles, policies and programs to strengthen faculty diversity. However, few are truly satisfied with the progress to date as faculty diversity lags student diversity and student diversity lags population diversity.

Options for improvement

Studies that surveyed multiple campuses show that there are three broad lines of action that are helpful in overcoming the barriers to creating a truly welcoming culture for under-represented minority faculty and women. They can be seen as a series of "nested" strategies, starting with URMFs themselves and expanding outward to embrace system change. These three lines of action are:

1. Improve direct support through mentoring and peer networks.

2. Work with senior faculty to build greater understanding and empathy for URMFs and to understand their own pre-conceptions and biases.

3. Engage in systemic changes that affect rewards, policies, student diversity, faculty diversity, and curriculum.

A 2016 University of Southern California at Davis Faculty Senate committee studied 16 campus diversity and inclusion initiatives at major universities. (24). They reported that "The strongest existing support for faculty diversity initiatives is reflected in mentoring programs, including programs from UC Berkley, Dartmouth, University of Notre Dame, and Columbia." (You can see more detail on these 16 programs in Appendix A.)

They also singled out Cornell's program for special mention:

> Cornell offers a small group mentoring program, which features 3-9 women and/or faculty from under-represented racial and ethnic groups who share an interest in a broad topic, a discipline or broader disciplinary group (e.g., "engineering") or a career stage (assistant or associate professor). The group serves to assist with each individual's career and community needs.

The second approach is directed toward educating those senior faculty members who represent the majority about the aspects of the academic culture that are challenging to faculty of color or women who are severely under-represented in some disciplines.

In a 2012 report on the experience of six geographically dispersed research universities, the University Leadership Council of the Educational Advisory Board found that effective programs for helping senior faculty overcome "generational bias" have the following characteristics: they are faculty led, they bring senior faculty and early career faculty into dialogue, they work together on collaborative projects, they involve mentoring, and they share data about unconscious bias so as to create a non-blaming environment for senior faculty to re-examine their thoughts and feelings. (25)

The third approach to faculty diversity sees it as a subset of system change: i.e., overall curriculum, policy, admissions, and rewards changes. In an AACU-sponsored study (26) of five institutions of higher education, including both community colleges and universities, the authors concluded that a supportive campus climate is essential and faculty diversity is furthered by:

- Supportive policies, structures, and reward systems.

- Student diversity, and when there is support for curriculum and research topics that address issues of diversity.

- Staff training and campus preparation.

The authors also suggested that while pursuing diversity in recruitment is important, providing mentoring and support for promotion and tenure is *more* important, because it does no good to recruit a diverse faculty if conditions do not favor retention of those recruited.

The idea that faculty diversification depends on whole system change is supported in a recent series of articles critical of the pipeline concept of diversity. These authors suggest that while we need to do a better job of deciding which graduates to admit to advanced degree programs, we also need to do more to recognize and reward minority faculty members' desires to address under-served commun-ities, and attend to unconscious biases. We should make our campuses reflect more the populations of the region and the nation, and undertake bold and audacious initiatives like Brown University's goal of doubling under-represented minority faculty in ten years.

A lot of work needs to be done at the system level, but in closing, I should acknowledge the importance the role of the dean or chair in supporting under-represented minorities and women in the STEM areas. The most important leader for all faculty members is the department chair or divisional head with whom they work most closely. The relationship the faculty member has with the chair is key to morale especially when the faculty member feels vulnerable in some way.

So, if chairs and deans articulate their support for diversity and equal opportunity, and back that up with activities that make the unit's recruitment, selection, and development programs more inclusive, this will make a difference. Similarly, if they demonstrate concern for all faculty members by fostering meaningful and supportive career conversations and then work to help faculty members gain the resources they need to achieve their goals, then the issues of faculty development are a long way to being addressed.

To summarize, isolation and stress can be a significant problem for women (especially in STEM disciplines), faculty of color, and other under-represented groups. Combined with environments that are not welcoming and supportive of diversity, this can lead to low morale, reduced productivity, and turnover.

Institutions of higher education can work to improve the climate for diversity by supporting peer mentoring and support groups, by conducting systematic efforts to educate all faculty about negative process such as micro-aggressions and unconscious bias, and by systematically examining and addressing all aspects of campus life: admissions, curriculum, climate, and faculty and staff development from a diversity and inclusion lens. The chairs and deans play a crucial role in supporting URMF in their units through showing awareness, personal interest, and a commitment to equal opportunity and diversity.

Conclusion: How to Get Started

How do you identify which of the various mentoring and faculty development services for early career faculty is needed right now for your campus?

I will spend more time on the question of program implementation in Chapter 5. However, it may be useful to conclude Chapter 2 by commenting on the first part of the implementation process: assessing needs, and setting goals and priorities.

Of course, the answer will vary depending on where you sit in the organization. As a provost, you are looking at the needs of the campus as a whole. As a dean, you are assessing the needs of your school or college. And as department chair, you are looking at your own faculty group. If you head an interdisciplinary center or center for teaching and learning, you would want to see where the gaps in research or teaching support are, respectively, and address those.

Your approach to the question of which services should be a priority for development will also vary based on whether you are starting your mentoring program from scratch or whether it has been ongoing for a while. Finally, the approach will vary based on whether you are extending existing services to new groups (e.g., extending mentoring already provided for tenure track faculty to fixed-term faculty) or creating new services (e.g., developing a writing support group).

The factors in deciding what to do next include asking the following questions:

1. Where are the "felt needs"—i.e., what services do people lack and want?

2. Which of these are most connected to important institutional goals or concerns?

3. Which of these needs can be implemented at your level?

4. Which can be implemented with current resources?

To answer these questions, it may be important to conduct several different inquiries:

- Survey or interview the current group being mentored, the mentors, and those recently mentored about their experiences and the gaps they see.

- Talk to those involved in tenure and promotion processes, and those who assess the quality of research and teaching at the institution, about their views of strengths and weaknesses.

- Assess the comprehensiveness of current programs compared to near and aspirational peers; are there any gaps? What would it take to be the leader?

- Assess the current program in place and resources that are available.

What might result from these inquiries is a set of overlapping perspectives, sort of a Venn Diagram where felt needs, competitive concerns, and current resources align, i.e., proverbial "low hanging fruit"—a change that could be relatively easily implemented and do immediate and significant good. There may be important gaps in programming, but the resources are not yet there. In that case, the implementation is deferred but the search for resources begins.

Here are examples of what this process may look like in practice:

- A new associate provost decided that in his first year he could not easily change policies, but he could institute a series of training workshops that educated department chairs about best practices in promotion and tenure.

- A new dean of the College of Arts and Sciences saw that her departments did not have mentoring programs in place, and so she convened meetings with early career faculty to get their concerns and questions and then held meetings with her chairs to discuss what to do about them.

- A health sciences dean sought and gained funds for an endowment to support faculty mentors, thus distinguishing the school from peers.

- A natural sciences department saw a recommended promotion turned down by the central appointments, promotion, and tenure committee of their college, so the chair used the setback to institute a general review of their mentoring program and make changes.

- The head of an area studies department saw that tenured early career faculty had a good mentoring system. However, fixed-term, limited contract faculty, the language teachers who provided half the instruction in the department, lacked a similar support system. She moved to create a mentoring position for her fixed-term faculty.

- In a psychology department, the chair saw that early career faculty were not doing a good job in preparing their tenure applications, so he had a workshop in which they looked at successful and unsuccessful tenure applications with names redacted.

- The head of a center for faculty excellence surveyed the strong support existing for young researchers in the natural sciences and social sciences and decided to partner with the humanities center to create writing groups focusing on new faculty in the humanities and qualitative social sciences.

- A humanities chair noted that one faculty member had a gift for mentoring so he built a mentoring program around this person's talents.

- The head of a history department received a grant from a donor to improve their mentoring efforts internally. He used the funds to send a faculty team to study the mentoring program of three of their aspirational peers.

- In a health sciences department, the chair thought it was a problem that standards for promotion were not clear, so she had a committee review and publish new standards. Then she instituted a new process to make sure new faculty got feedback each year about where they stood in relationship to those standards.

Throughout this book, I will emphasize a persistent but incremental approach: assess the needs and resources, take the next step, then the step after that, and keep going until at least the major needs are effectively addressed. As the proverb says, "It's not just a destination, it is also a journey."

Notes

1. See Trower, Cathy Ann, *Success on the Tenure Track: Five Keys to Faculty Job Satisfaction.* John Hopkins University Press, 2012. pp. 61-62.

2. A number of universities have published promotion standards. Here is a sampling:

   a. https://compsci.appstate.edu/faculty-staff/promotion-and-tenure

   b. https://www.northwestern.edu/provost/policies/faculty-promotion-and-tenure/tenure-and-promotion-standards-and-procedures.html

c. https://www.uh.edu/class/spanish/faculty/p-and-t-guidelines/

d. https://medschool.ucsd.edu/som/surgery/faculty/Pages/Faculty-Promotion-Standards.aspx

3. For a description of the NSF ADVANCE Program go to: https://www.nsf.gov/funding/pgm_summ.jsp?pims_id=5383

4. Some mentoring programs offer general guidelines for providing good feedback to faculty, e.g.:

a. http://www.ohsu.edu/xd/education/schools/school-of-medicine/faculty/mentoring/mentoring-best-practices/communication/giving-and-receiving-feedback.cfm

b. https://pdc-svpaap1.umd.edu/faculty/documents/MentoringGuide.pdf

5. For an account of how the movement for improved teaching is developing, see: https://www.nytimes.com/2016/06/23/education/teaching-professors-to-become-better-teachers.html?mcubz=3&_r=0.

6. This is the case Rob Jenkins makes in "Tips for new Teachers." *The Chronicle of Higher Education.* August 17, 2009.

https://www.chronicle.com/article/Tips-for-New-Teachers-at/48003

7. For the POD website, go to: https://podnetwork.org; for SOTL, go to: https://www.stlhe.ca/sotl/what-is-sotl/

8. You can see the relevant programs at UNC, ASU, and UCSD here:

    a. https://iah.unc.edu/faculty-resources/apply-for-a-fellowship/iah-faculty-fellowships/

    b. https://research.engineering.asu.edu/early-career-grant-funding-opportunities/

    c. http://foundationrelations.ucsd.edu/funding-opportunities/index.html

9. See Bland, Carol J., et al. *Faculty Success Through Mentoring, A Guide for Mentors, Mentees and Leaders*, ACE Series on Higher Education, Roman and Littlefield Publishers, 2009, pp. 55-64.

10. You can read a quick summary of Acker's main concepts here: https://thesocliterati.wordpress.com/2012/07/09/hierarchies-jobs-bodies-a-theory-of-gendered-organizations/

11. Johnson, Heather L. "Pipelines, Pathways, and Institutional Leadership: An Update on the Status of Women in Higher Education," Washington, DC: American Council on Education, 2017. www.acenet.edu/news-room/Documents/Higher-Ed-Spotlight-Pipelines-Pathways-and-Institutional-Leadership-Status-of-Women.pdf

12. For example, note this definition of implicit/ unintentional bias offered on Texas A&M University's ADVANCE website:

https://advance.tamu.edu/implicitunintentional-bias/

The authors cite numerous studies of bias against women in employment processes. In one, Katherine Weisharr suggested that gendered bias accounted for a significant proportion of the discrepancy between outcomes for men and women in the academy. See: Katherine Weissharr, "Publish and Perish? An Assessment of Gender Gaps in Promotion to Tenure in Academia," *Social Forces*, Volume 96, Issue 2, 1 December 2017, Pages 529–560. Also, see Victor Ray's argument that student evaluations of teaching also reflect gender stereotypes: "Is Gender Bias an Intended Feature of Teaching Evaluations?" *Inside Higher Ed*. Feb. 9, 2018.

https://www.insidehighered.com/advice/2018/0 2/09/teaching-evaluations-are-often-used-confirm-worst-stereotypes-about-women-faculty

13. See Colleen Flaherty, "Relying on Women, Not Rewarding Them," *Inside Higher Ed,* April 12, 2017 and Colleen Flaherty, "'Dancing Backward in High Heels'," *Inside Higher Ed,* January 10, 2018.

14. See Catherine Hill, Christine Corbett, and Andrese St. Rose, "Why so Few Women in Science, Technology, Engineering and Mathematics?" AAUW, 2010.

15. See Gumpertz, M, et al. "Retention and Promotion of Women and Underrepresented

Minority Faculty in Science and Engineering at Four Large Land Grant Institutions" *PLOS One*, 2017.
www.journals.plos.org/plosone/article?id=10.137 1/journal.pone.0187285

16. See Kathy Zonana, "Pursuing Parity." *Stanford Medicine*. Spring 2017.

https://stanmed.stanford.edu/2017spring/wome n-faculty-use-data-to-seek-parity-in-academic-medicine.html#

17. See Carr, Phyllis L., et al. "Inadequate Progress for Women in Academic Medicine: Findings from the National Faculty Study." *Journal of Womens Health (Larchmt)*, Mar 1, 2015, vol. 24, no. 3, 2015, pp. 190–199. Also see Carr, Phyllis L., et al. "Recruitment, Promotion and Retention of Women in Academic Medicine: How Institutions Are Addressing Gender Disparities," *Journal of Women's Health Issues*, vol. 27, no. 3, Jacob's Institute for Women's Health, 2017, pp. 374-381.

18. The list offered in Exhibit 2.9 draws on the following sources:

   a. The Faculty Retention Toolkit for the College of Engineering and the College of Arts & Sciences at the University of Washington. Available through the ADVANCE Center for Institutional Change at the University of Washington.

   b. "Effective Policies and Programs for the Retention, and Advancement of Women in Academia." *Worklife Law*. UC Hastings College of Law, 2012.

c. Carr, Phyllis L., et al. "Recruitment, Promotion and Retention of Women in Academic Medicine: How Institutions Are Addressing Gender Disparities," *Journal of Women's Health Issues*, vol. 27, no. 3, Jacob's Institute for Women's Health, 2017, pp. 374-381.

19. See Girdler, Susan, and Christin Colford, "Mentoring Junior Faculty in the UNC School of Medicine." Presentation to the UNC-CH School of Medicine Association of Educators, November 2017.

20. See Varkey, Prathibha, et al. "The positive impact of a facilitated peer mentoring program on academic skills of women faculty," *BMC Medical Education,* vol. 12, 2012, p. 14, www.ncbi.nlm.nih.gov/pmc/articles/PMC3325854/

21. See Chapter 7, "Best Practices for Improving Faculty Diversity Recruitment and Retention," in the book, *The Chief Diversity Officer [CDO]: Strategy, Structure, and Change Management*, by Damon A. Williams and Katrina C. Wade-Golden. Stylus Publishing, 2013.

22. See Mack, Dwayne A. "Sick and Tired of Being Sick and Tired," *Inside Higher Ed*, 2016, www.insidehighered.com/advice/2016/03/25/how-faculty-color-can-achieve-good-work-life-balance-academe-essay

See also the summary of a national study of occupational stress at URMF published by Ruth Enid Zimbrana of the University of Maryland Consortium on Gender, Race, and Inequality:

http://crge.umd.edu/wp-content/uploads/2018/01/Zambrana_PP_Summary_POST.pdf

23. See "The Revolving Door for Under-Represented Minorities in Higher Education, An Analysis from the Campus Diversity Initiative." A Research Brief From the James Irvine Foundation Campus Diversity Project. AACU, 2006.

24. See "Faculty Diversity Training and Programs and Best Practices: Draft Report of the University of Southern California Climate Committee of the Faculty Senate." Nov. 10, 2016:

https://academicsenate.usc.edu/files/2015/08/Climate-Committee-Faculty-Diversity-Best-Practices-11-10-16.pdf

25. See "Addressing Generational Change with Senior Faculty Members, Custom Research Brief," University Leadership Council, Educational Advisory Board, April 23, 2012.

https://www.umass.edu/provost/sites/default/files/uploads/Addressing%20Generational%20Change%20with%20Senior%20Faculty%20Members.pdf

26. See Taylor, Orlando, et al. "Diversifying the Faculty," *Peer Review*, vol. 12, no. 3, AACU, 2010.

See also "Reconsidering the Pipeline Problem/Increasing Faculty Diversity." *Higher Ed Today*:

https://www.higheredtoday.org/2016/02/10/reconsidering-the-pipeline-problem-increasing-faculty-diversity/

And Bryan Monesson-Olson, "Pathways, Potholes, and the Persistence of Women in Science: Reconsidering the Pipeline." UMASS blog, March 28, 2017.

https://blogs.umass.edu/bolson/2017/03/28/pathways-potholes-and-the-persistence-of-women-in-science-reconsidering-the-pipeline/

And Mark Toner, "Diversifying Diversity." The Presidency. American Council on Education. January 11, 2016.

http://www.acenet.edu/the-presidency/columns-and-features/Pages/Diversifying-Diversity.aspx

CHAPTER 3
DESIGNING AND IMPLEMENTING MID-CAREER MENTORING AND FACULTY DEVELOPMENT PROGRAMS

NOTE TO THE READER

If you fully understand the challenges and dilemmas faced by newly tenured faculty members, I recommend skipping ahead to the section "Creative Responses to the Mid-Career Faculty Crisis at the Unit Level" on page 169. This will allow you to jump right to immediate recommendations for action.

On the other hand, if you want to learn about the causes and consequences of the "mid-career crisis" in higher education, read on.

Too often the department or school thinks their faculty development responsibility is done after the early career faculty member is tenured or promoted. It should not end there. There are great benefits for the institution, the individual, students, and society at large if faculty members are engaged and growing professionally throughout their careers. There is a great loss of productivity and a waste of talent if faculty development stops abruptly at the point of tenure and promotion. (1)

In this chapter, I discuss the needs and concerns of associate professors and recently promoted fixed-term faculty members. I also show how academic leaders can move toward a full-career cycle of faculty development activities by addressing those concerns. Throughout the chapter, I describe promising approaches to implement mid-career faculty development. In Chapter 4, I will discuss how the process may continue for senior faculty.

Sometimes Promotion Can Be a Career Crisis

Academic leaders may think all the work that they have put in to make mentoring services available for early career faculty would be enough to assure a career-long trajectory of faculty development and to ease the transitions to higher ranks. So, it could be a rude shock to realize that the transition to associate professor has been a challenging and exhausting ordeal for many early career faculty members. It is now well documented that by the time they reach the associate status, they have the least job satisfaction of any rank on the tenure track. (2)

Faculty members who have successfully completed the tenure process may be feeling relieved and happy at their achievement, but at the same time depleted and perhaps resentful of the sacrifices required to reach that point.

Non-tenure-track faculty may achieve promotion, but may have no clue about what the next step in their career is or how to get there—and not being on the tenure track, they may feel relatively disadvantaged.

Senior faculty, i.e., full professors (perhaps because they belong to an earlier generation of scholars with different attitudes and life situations) may not understand (or have forgotten) the inner toll the tenure or promotion process has taken. They may expect their newly elevated juniors to be energized and on to the next project. While some faculty members easily find their next challenge, others are more typically at a "pause" in terms of ambitious new initiatives. In fact, the challenge of "the next big thing" for some may add anxiety to the list of adverse reactions to getting tenure or being promoted.

The newly tenured/promoted professor may now be expected to address the backlog of needs for attention from children and spouses that built up while the tenure clock was ticking. If marriage, childbearing, or relationship building has been put on hold, those needs may now take center stage in the newly promoted faculty member's life.

For its part, the unit usually places additional demands on the newly promoted faculty member. The rationale for this is reasonable: they were protected from service work in the department while on the tenure track or at junior grade and now must "pull their weight." Departments also withdraw supports *de facto* in that most departmental mentoring programs end when tenure/promotion is achieved. The new associate professor may interpret the message from senior colleagues as: "Now you are on your own," and "By the way, for the next leg of the journey, here are some additional burdens you must bear." Whatever "rough justice" in workload adjustment this may reflect, the emotional costs have not been taken into account.

A new associate professor, faced with such a disparity between the inner feelings, outer demands, and the conventional thinking may experience a sense of disappointment—even betrayal—followed by social disconnection and loneliness. They need mentoring and support too, particularly now. Too often, though, this need is not recognized even (or especially) by themselves. A final irony is that they may also be called upon to mentor younger colleagues but given no training or recognition for the time spent.

Despite all this, some associate professors do just fine and progress toward full professor status without incident. They may have very supportive family situations, unusually supportive departments, or they may be particularly well adapted to the demands of the mid-career passage, but this is not the typical case.

Instead, faculty members who are elevated to tenure or who receive a promotion may be struggling with one or more of the following conditions. The faculty member might:

- Feel fatigue (e.g., from the pressure of publishing the book that assured his or her promotion).

- Become overwhelmed (e.g., from new administrative demands or demands at home that were deferred during the period of tenure and promotion seeking). Some of these new tasks (e.g., chairing the graduate program of the unit) may be difficult to perform, be consequential, and have a steep learning curve.

- Experience various adult life stage development changes. (3)

- Find that they are done with the scholarly interests they pursued so avidly during their graduate student and early faculty careers and are at a loss (perhaps temporary, but perhaps not) to develop a new focus for scholarly work.

One common response of associate professors and other mid-career faculty members to this crisis is to become absorbed by service work. Associate professors, male and female, take on and solve problems that bring them accolades within the institution and in the broader society. They may run important programs for students, become associate deans, and take on faculty committees. However, if they do not meet the demanding and somewhat narrow criteria set for advancement by their colleagues, they remain associate professors. They do not receive salary increases or advance to full professor-status in a timely way.

In the case of under-represented minority faculty members, they also have the burden of being asked to sit on many committees and advise minority students in the name of advancing diversity. This is a compelling obligation for some but also detracts from their research productivity and their ability to advance in the research university. (4)

Gender is also a factor. There is reason to suggest that female faculty members in the research university are more likely to be derailed by service work and other non-research assignments once they reach the associate professor status. Studies show that female faculty do not negotiate as aggressively as their male counterparts for resources and support that would help them advance. Of particular concern currently are the situations of female associate professors in science who progress to full professors at lower rates, and under-represented minorities who may have additional reasons to feel alienated and lonely, particularly at the vulnerable post-tenure period. These gender-correlated behavioral differences may exacerbate a sense of inequality. This is such a common problem that the National Science Foundation has created a whole series of programs known as ADVANCE to address problems of women assistant and associate professors in male-dominated science fields. (5)

As a consequence, many associate professors experience at least a pause in their progress, and for as many as half of new associate professors, this pause becomes extended, such that the professor may be said to be "plateaued," then "stuck." Sometimes this leads to "burnout." In the end, a very few professors in each department, in his or her later years, wind up with the reputation as "deadwood" essentially non-performing, but tenured. This, of course, is a bad outcome for the professor in question, the department, and the university or college. (6)

Additional Consequences of the Mid-Career Crisis

When faculty members fail to advance to the rank of full professor, this can leave the faculty members unsatisfied and feeling they have under-achieved, and the senior faculty cohort may feel both guilty (about how they may have failed that person) and resentful that their colleague has not gone "all in" as they had hoped and expected. It is a problem—across all disciplines and units—when a significant number of mid-career faculty members do not progress to the final rank. There is also a risk the feelings that are particularly acute post-tenure would consolidate into a deeper sense of alienation from colleagues over time.

Kerry Anne Rockquemore writes evocatively about these emotions in several essays on the emotional spectrum of the mid-career and the problems of "stuckness." (7) Faculty members may feel "stuck" but are emotionally numb and cannot move. She says they need to figure out what they feel and why, but most of all commit to a program of moving forward. However, if environmental support is not forthcoming, there may not be enough positive energy in the situation to help faculty overcome the inertia. As I have just reported, the newly promoted faculty member encounters many barriers and obstacles, both internally and externally.

Since those promoted to full professor are usually paid significantly more than those at the associate level, failure of a significant group of associate to move to full professor accentuates general wage disparities and associated jealousies. If minority and women faculty members are promoted more slowly than white men, this adds to race and gender-based salary disparities as well.

Mid-career issues can also lead to turnover. Research on faculty turnover suggests there usually needs to be a "push factor" (i.e., a reason for dissatisfaction in the current job) as well as a pull factor (i.e., an attractive new opportunity) to cause a faculty member to leave one school and go to another. (8) The situation of the newly promoted faculty member provides many occasions for "the push factor" to emerge, and so new associate professors who are in the doldrums of transition may be particularly vulnerable to offers from other institutions. It provides institutions no benefit to have good mentoring and tenure and promotion processes at the assistant level if their best new professors are then hired away at this vulnerable moment. Unwanted turnover is a huge cost to universities and recruiting replacements is a time-consuming and often unpredictable process.

For all these reasons, leaders of institutes, departments, and schools have more than enough justification to put programs in place to retain, develop, and enhance as their faculty transitions through the crisis of the mid-career. Often these programs are not costly but they require sustained attention and sometimes a shift in attitudes.

EXHIBIT 3.1: HOW ONE UNIVERSITY TOOK DECISIVE ACTION TO ADDRESS MID-CAREER ISSUES

This story is based on N. Douglas Lees and Jane Williams' article, "Progressing Toward Creating a Campus Culture of Faculty Mentoring." The Department Chair. January 15, 2018. Wiley Online Library. See:

https://onlinelibrary.wiley.com/doi/full/10.1002/dch.30179

At Indiana University-Purdue Indianapolis (IUPI) which comprises 17 schools and 30,000 students, the campus underwent a major upgrade of mentoring services since 2012, starting with pairing early career faculty with mentors. Within several years a demand for more dimensions of mentoring became apparent. The Office of the Provost responded. After a yearlong planning process that involved a fact-finding task force and a campus-wide training effort in mentoring issues, a strategy for extending mentoring services was established. The Provost empowered the original task force as a campus-wide mentoring planning committee and provided it with funds to offer $10,000 challenge grants to the schools who developed the best mentoring proposals. Seven received grants to implement programs in the first round and four of those have focused on mid-career mentoring.

EXHIBIT 3.1 CONTINUED: HOW ONE UNIVERSITY TOOK DECISIVE ACTION TO ADDRESS MID-CAREER ISSUES

In the School of Science, the Dean and the faculty, after undertaking a survey of faculty needs set the following goals for their mid-career faculty program:

1. Increase the number of faculty members with an active plan for promotion.

2. Increase the amount of feedback given to faculty.

3. Increase faculty perceptions of the school's commitment to their development.

4. Establish mentor-mentee pairs.

5. Generate developmental plans at the end of the year.

To start the first iteration of the program, interested early career faculty were asked to submit applications as mentees and interested senior faculty were asked to submit applications as mentors. The mentoring committee operating the program for the School of Science decided to pair faculty from different departments within the school. They required three mentoring sessions. Each session brought the pairs together as a group for presentations and structured activities to guide the pairs in later interaction. Each mentee created a career development plan through the process. The plans were then shared by each mentee with the department chair. Sixteen associate professors participated in the first round of the program. They represented about 1/3 of associate professors in the school. The program was evaluated after the first year and significant benefits were identified for the school and participating faculty. Recommendations for future rounds included the need for even more interaction between mentors and mentees, clearer structure for evolving the plans, and adding a same department mentor to the cross department teams.

IUPI's experience (see Exhibit 3.1) suggests that it is possible to make progress at the campus, school, and department level within a few years if there is sufficient commitment and leadership is aligned around the goal of mentoring and faculty development. In addition to focusing on the mid-career in four schools, other funded proposals in that case included programs of assistance to under-represented minority faculty members, a program to support women faculty, and a program to support non-tenure-track faculty.

Creative Responses to the Mid-Career Faculty Crisis at the Unit Level

In addition to the campus-wide approach described above, there is an emerging a body of practices that leaders at the unit level can implement to help faculty careers keep on track, prevent stalling, and forestall raiding by other institutions of higher education. In this section, I identify a number of strategies and related actions (with actual examples from universities and colleges) that you can deploy at your institutions to assist mid-career faculty:

1. Assign greater priority to mid-career faculty needs.

2. Help mark the transition to mid-career.

3. Make the pathway to the next promotion more transparent.

4. Provide opportunities for reflection and goal setting in early mid-career.

5. Foster faculty career conversations during mid-career.

6. Secure financial support for mid-career development.

7. Extend mentoring support after tenure and promotion.

8. Work supportively with long-time associate professors.

9. Explore modifications to tenure and promotion policies to support mid-career faculty transition.

10. Recognize the challenges facing mid-career women in the STEM disciplines.

11. Support under-represented minorities in overcoming obstacles to advancement.

In the pages that follow, I will give examples of how to implement each of these practices.

1. Assign greater priority to mid-career faculty needs

In fact, this is the major point of this chapter! If, as I have argued, supporting faculty in the mid-career is an excellent investment for an academic unit, it stands to reason that unit leaders (i.e., deans, chairs, center directors, etc.) should make this a priority for their own time or delegate this responsibility to another senior faculty leader in the unit and charge them with responsibility to take practical steps relevant to the situation at hand.

The Ohio State University Office of Academic Affairs has published a comprehensive guide to how academic leaders and full professors may support promotion to full professor. (9) A few of their many suggestions include:

- Set positive expectations

- Serve as mentors

- Provide examples of successful dossiers

- Review each associate professor annually

- Provide clear definitions of specific service, teaching and research expectations

- Make mentoring a valued activity in the unit

However, beyond any specific set of recommendations, the brochure underlines my key recommendation that full professors and academic unit leaders step up and take responsibility for addressing the needs of faculty at mid-career.

To accomplish this, chairs and deans can deploy a variety of engagement approaches. They can assess needs through interviews, surveys, or focus groups. They can schedule discussions with faculty leadership; they can engage the support of key leaders; and they can appoint committees to make recommendations for change, set goals, institute policy changes, assign mentoring tasks, and raise funds. In these and other ways, they can call attention to the need to act. The rest of this list outlines the specific activities that many units may consider as they go about trying to improve the mid-career experience.

2. Help mark the transition to mid-career—by ceremony, celebration, education, and peer support

Organizational psychologists now make much of recognizing organizational transitions which have three stages: letting go of the past, managing a period of anxiety and confusion in adjusting to a new situation, and finally exploring alternatives to create a new structure. (10)

Use ceremony to provide acknowledgement

Ritual, ceremony, and celebration are traditional and important ways of marking a passage. While a ritual or ceremony can make important contributions to the cohesion of the social group, it can also confer psychological benefits on those being initiated into a new stage. Too often the transition to mid-career is "a ho-hum affair" and bureaucratic process may conspire to make elements of the transition a de-motivator. One leader of a transition group for newly tenured faculty told me that it took months for the university's recommendation of tenure to be approved by the system board of Governors and by then it was an afterthought and anti-climax. In the interim, nothing had been done to mark the transition at a time that it would have been meaningful for the faculty member. For some when they finally did receive the letter telling them their tenure had been finally approved, it almost seemed like an insult, rather than recognition.

Failure to acknowledge the transition in a significant way can support the tendency toward denial of change. Recognizing the transition with a small ceremony, in newsletters, and by other means can help with the emotional struggles and fatigue associated with tenure and promotion. One former chair of the faculty at a large public university suggested to me that a newly tenured faculty member be presented with a cap and gown. At the very least units and campuses should find some small but genuine ways to recognize faculty members who advanced in rank during mid-career.

Educate newly tenured faculty and associate professors about their situation

In interdisciplinary seminars and workshops held outside the department, newly tenured and promoted faculty can read some of the literature on the mid-career transition and discuss their current career thoughts and feelings. Even a single lunch and learn on "The Transition to Mid-Career for Recently Promoted Professors" could be an important benefit for some faculty members who are feeling "shell-shocked" by the big change in their lives. They would realize "they are not alone" in this, and it's not due to a failing on their part. This in itself would be a big plus.

Use a peer mentoring/education program to help faculty through the initial shock of promotion and its aftermath

At UNC-CH, where I worked, the Institute for the Arts and Humanities initiated a program of dinner meetings open to newly tenured faculty in the College of Arts and Sciences. The program provides all three of the elements I have been talking about in this section: ceremony, education, and peer support. A well-regarded senior professor and former chair with excellent group skills was convinced to convene and facilitate the group. With his leadership each cohort of faculty are able to discuss their situations in a confidential setting outside of their home departments, commiserate, celebrate, brainstorm together, and take stock of their situation. This is how the program is described:

> Throughout academe and across disciplines, newly tenured and promoted professors face unique professional and personal challenges. This program is designed to support them as they enter this transitional period. The Associate Professor Program is co-sponsored by the Institute and the College of Arts and Sciences. All College faculty are invited to participate in the program in the first year following their promotion to associate professor. The program typically consists of four dinners and two lunchtime events. [The] Dinners ... will provide time and space for participants to forge connections beyond their departments and to discuss professional and academic issues of common interest. Lunch events will focus on topics such as: sustaining work-life balance at mid-career, managing increased expectations and opportunities for university service, developing leadership and negotiating skills, preparing for promotion to full professor, and positioning oneself in the academy as an established scholar. (11)

3. Make the pathway to the next promotion more transparent

Too many new associate professors or fixed-term faculty who have been promoted have no idea about the path to full professor or the next stage. Part of the problem is that the standards are vague and changing and the process is much less structured than that for achieving tenure (or the first promotion for the fixed-term faculty member). Departments and schools can address this by publishing standards and expectations at this stage and having discussions with mid-career faculty about how this might translate in their situations. Publicizing the accomplishments of faculty who have been recently promoted to full professor or the equivalent rank for the fixed-term faculty member will help make expectations more concrete.

EXHIBIT 3.2: DUKE UNIVERSITY MEDICAL CENTER PROMOTION TO FULL PROFESSOR

Edited for brevity.

Source:
https://medschool.duke.edu/about-us/faculty-resources/faculty-appointments-promotion-tenure/clinical-science-apt/faculty/track2

The title of **Professor with Tenure** is reserved for faculty members who have attained extraordinary national and international eminence, especially as demonstrated by significant scholarship, publications, participation in NIH study sections and equivalent review groups, offices in professional societies, and/or prizes and awards. …

Clinical Work – The faculty member must have a national or international reputation for excellence. Referrals should come from across a multi-state region. Further evidence of reputation can be demonstrated by inclusion in national and international guideline-setting panels, or by participation in national boards and leadership groups within the faculty member's field. Other markers of clinical excellence (outcome measures, patient satisfaction indices, etc.) will be considered. National awards will be considered.

Teaching – Faculty in this rank are expected to participate in teaching exercises across a wide arena. Activities may include invited lectures at national and international meetings, seminars, teaching rounds, and workshops. Participation is expected in medical student, house staff, and/or graduate student curricula.

EXHIBIT 3.2 CONTINUED: DUKE UNIVERSITY MEDICAL CENTER PROMOTION TO FULL PROFESSOR

Research – Establishment of a national reputation as a researcher, especially as demonstrated by significant scholarship, publications, participation in NIH study sections and equivalent review groups, and/or offices in professional societies.

- Faculty granted the rank of Professor with tenure will have established a record of sustained funding through peer-reviewed grants.

- Clinical researchers should be in leadership positions within the field. They should have participated in multiple major clinical trials as a team leader ... On at least 10 publications, the researcher should be: 1) first author; 2) senior author; 3) study chair; 4) study co-chair; or 5) lead study designer. In addition, at this rank clinical investigators must have leadership positions in clinical trials groups or organizations (e.g. steering committees, executive committees, organization chairperson, etc.).

Publication – Usually a minimum of 50 co-authored, peer-reviewed publications will be necessary to be considered for this rank, with at least 20 as first or senior author. Publications should be based on outstanding, original, and innovative research findings and/or important clinical applications of basic science. For appointment or promotion to this rank, the 10 most important will be reviewed for evidence of original and significant scholarship by the candidate...

4. Provide opportunities for reflection and goal setting in early mid-career

Offer mid-career self-assessment and planning workshops

Kiernan Mathews, head of the COACHE study at the Harvard School of Education recommends that institutions implement a career re-visioning program. He gives several examples:

> At the University of Missouri - Kansas City, one dean conducted a series of visioning exercises, with annual updates, in which faculty discussed their passionate interests, determined what excited them about being a faculty member, and built their reflections into revitalized career plans. The dean exhorts faculty that if they do what they most enjoy doing—and do it well— he will advocate for their promotion. If that fails, he promises his recognition in other ways. In any event, the exercise ensures that faculty are doing the work they love. Versions of career redevelopment activities can be found also at James Madison University and the University at Albany. (12)

This type of program is something that might be sponsored by a center for faculty development and include professors from a variety of disciplines. For nine years as part of a semester-long leadership seminar on faculty leadership development, I led a series of weekend seminars for mid-career professors. Some were associate professors; some were full professors. The seminar went from 1:00 p.m. on a Friday to 1:00 p.m. on a Saturday and was held at an off-campus (but nearby) conference center and included an after-dinner session. In the first session (usually early in the semester), faculty simply told their personal story about how they arrived at their present career situation including the crucial decisions they made along the way. In the second session (usually after the end of exams but before graduation) the same group of 8-10 participants went through a mapping exercise using Ernest Boyer's varieties of scholarship framework to describe their work over the last ten years (i.e., scholarship of discovery, teaching, integration, application.) Then they used the same format to describe what they hoped the map would look like ten years from now. They considered what might happen in their personal lives and professional careers that could affect their ability to concentrate on those goals and then developed a multi-year plan that they discussed with their peers in the group and got feedback. When the seminar ended, participants were invited to form self-directed support groups to help them work on their plan. Some of these self-help groups have continued for a decade or more. Exhibit 3.3 suggests how universities are beginning to realize the need for more faculty development programming at the mid-level.

EXHIBIT 3.3: EXAMPLES OF PROMISING PRACTICES

The following are excerpts from The Report on Promising Practices In Mid-Career Faculty Development, which was prepared by the staff of the Wallace Center for Faculty Career Services at Rochester Institute of Technology.

See:

https://www.rit.edu/academicaffairs/facultydevelopment/sites/rit.edu.academicaffairs.facultydevelopment/files/images/FCDS_Mid-CareerRpt.pdf

EXHIBIT 3.3 CONTINUED: EXAMPLES
OF PROMISING PRACTICES

Michigan State University

What they did: Instituted faculty orientation to mid-career and started workshops to help associate professors develop leadership and managerial skills since so much of the job is about directing and serving on committees. In addition to workshops specific to leadership and academic life, MSU offers an annual program, *From Associate Professor to Professor: Productive Decision-making at Mid-Career*, for associate professors in the tenure system.

Who owns the effort: Office of the Provost, Faculty, & Organizational Development.

The Ohio State University

What they did: Implemented annual workshops that focus on providing tools and information relevant to a successful progression from associate to full professor, including a *Mid-Career Faculty Symposium*. Also: a *Mid-Career Faculty Release Time Program* (MFRP), designed to provide support to tenured associate professors who would benefit from concentrated time to advance their research or creative work.

Who owns the effort: Academic Affairs, Office of the Provost, Faculty Development.

University of Nebraska-Lincoln

What they did: The *Academic Leadership Program* is designed to develop the leadership and managerial skills of faculty who have demonstrated exceptional ability and promise.

Who owns the effort: Academic Affairs, Faculty Development.

5. Foster supportive career conversations

Leaders must disrupt isolating patterns of non-communication

Too often these conversations never occur because of old habits of thinking about academic freedom and autonomy. The idea of absolute freedom to teach and to conduct research has great resonance within the academy. Unfortunately, this strongly-held value, combined often with a reluctance to engage in potentially uncomfortable personal discussions about expectations, leads to misunderstandings.

Chairs or deans may think they are respecting faculty members' autonomy by leaving them alone. Yet, faculty members may feel that they are invisible or neglected if no one in authority takes the trouble to inquire seriously about their work and goals. The reverse may also be true, i.e., the well-intentioned chair or dean may find the faculty member feels his or her space is infringed upon or he or she is being condescended to if the chair broaches this topic. Hopefully, leaders can begin to change these norms by setting expectations that they should and will have career discussions with newly tenured faculty and other mid-career faculty members on at least an annual or semi-annual basis.

Create more options for how faculty may contribute at mid-career

Faculty members at mid-career may need to take a break from what they have been doing and explore other scholarly pursuits. Chairs can use the "Creativity Contract" suggested by Ernest Boyer, in a chapter of his classic Carnegie Foundation Study, *Professoriate Reconsidered.* Boyer suggested chairs "contract" with each faculty member around an area of productivity (e.g., one Boyer's four varieties of scholarship) that most corresponded to their current sense of internal motivation. One science department chair I know is experimenting with a form of this approach. He identified five areas the department needed to develop in order to demonstrate its growth toward excellence (i.e., teaching innovation, funded research, advising graduate students, etc). He then asked each of his faculty members to commit to excel in just one of those areas and to be OK "in the others, as a way of tapping the motivated talent of each person. He reasoned this approach would yield an enhanced group product, based on the combined initiatives of individuals, each optimizing a single area of scholarly endeavor. Such an approach can allow newly tenured professors to renew their motivation by focusing on some new area of endeavor they have neglected in the push for tenure, but at the same time feel that they are helping the department achieve its goals.

Leaders need to discuss faculty member career goals

Using the 'creativity contract' and other methods, chairs of departments and associate deans in schools can meet periodically one-to-one with midcareer faculty to discuss career goals. If the faculty member has participated in any of the mid-career programs discussed in the previous section, this conversation is a natural follow up to that experience. If not, senior leaders may need to set a context and describe a process over time by which goals can be set and revised. UNC Charlotte's ADVANCE program has produced a mid-career self-assessment form to help faculty think through their choices. (See Appendix B, Section 3.3.)

As I have reported, units can go farther and have an annual review of each associate professor's progress by the senior faculty along with a process of providing the faculty member honest and constructive feedback.

Chairs or other senior leaders who hold career conversations with mid-career faculty can use this opportunity to state the unit's hopes and needs as well. Ideally, the career plan of each mid-career professor will be some integration of the individual's needs and goals with the needs and goals of the academic unit. The likelihood of that occurring is usually increased if there is a good exchange of information and expectations between the faculty member and the representative of the unit, usually a chair, division head, or associate dean.

6. Secure more substantive support for mid-career development

Once leaders are more familiar with the goals of their faculty, they are in a position to be more helpful. In my work with chairs and other senior leaders (e.g., associate deans, division directors), I have often heard them comment on how positive it is for morale when they are able to offer opportunities to faculty. In order to be successful at this two things are required: 1) they must know their faculty members and their interests; and 2) they must pay attention to the opportunities that might benefit their faculty that they become aware of in the course of their leadership duties.

Opportunities provided could include funding for a professional conference, an opportunity to get into a new research area, or a summer seminar on teaching. Putting an opportunity in front of a mid-career faculty member may be the thing that helps them re-start and get moving in an area that will sustain their interest and produce results over the next several years.

It is one thing to simply forward this information to the faculty; it is more powerful to forward with a note that shows concern and knowledge of how the opportunity relates to a faculty member's goals or to put a notice in front of faculty member personally with a suggestion that it might fit their interests.

The career development conversation between the chair and the new associate professor or just promoted fixed-term faculty member will be easier if it's not just about new expectations but also about possible support. When the unit or institution has something to offer, the conversation can be about what the institution can do to support new goals. Listed below are some common offerings:

Provide a sabbatical semester for newly tenured faculty

Do this in the first three years after tenure, and provide travel funding as a way of helping mid-career faculty find a new focus for their writing or teaching. Many universities have adopted similar policies, recognizing that the newly promoted faculty member may need some time out from increased burdens post promotion to develop a new or refined focus for teaching and research.

Support the acquisition of general professional development and leadership skills

Human Resource units in IHEs often offer professional development skills for staff such as stress and time management, communication, change management, conflict, negotiation, supervision, leadership, meeting management, budgeting, and the like. Yet seldom are short courses like these adapted for the needs or schedules of faculty. Mid-career faculty may now be considering taking on leadership jobs. Finding ways to support their interest by sponsoring participation in core professional skills training that is adapted to their needs would be another supportive activity for faculty at the mid-career, but chairs may have to seek out offerings on campus or elsewhere that will make sense to the faculty involved.

Raise money for mid-career development

Once mid-career development is recognized as a major problem and opportunity, chairs and deans can begin to ask donors for contributions to promote mid-career faculty development: released time for research, travel funds, sponsorship to conferences, and needed equipment. If faculty see the department investing in them, they are more likely to be motivated to reenergize their careers post-tenure. At UNC-CH donors were asked to commit to a "Chairs Say Yes Program," i.e., a flexible use of funds that chairs could use in small amounts (a few hundreds or thousands) to support faculty projects. Versions of this program were implemented at the department level, in a humanities institute, and throughout the College of Arts and Sciences. (13)

EXHIBIT 3.4: SHORT COURSES FOR FACULTY PROFESSIONAL DEVELOPMENT

UNC-CH Center for Faculty Excellence 2014: Five Core Skills for Faculty Leader Series, Lunch and Learn, Room 308, Wilson Library.

Friday, Sep. 5: Leading Groups and Meetings.

Effective faculty leadership almost always involves group work. This session will focus on the key points in organizing successful meetings including: agenda building and management, facilitating discussion, and handling difficult group members.

Friday, Oct. 10: Setting Goals for Individuals, Groups, and Organizations.

Goal setting is critical to success in completing most faculty leadership tasks. This session will focus on setting goals that are motivating, realistic, strategic, and measurable.

Friday, Nov. 7: Supervising One-on-One in the Academic Setting.

The dimensions of supervision vary with the context: directing students, guiding postdocs, working with colleagues, or managing employees; but there are general principles and practices that all leaders should know.

Friday, Nov. 21: Managing Challenging Interactions.

Sometimes faculty leaders need to address a problem with an individual and a "crucial conversation" is needed to put things right. At these times, it's good to have a step-by-step approach to follow.

Friday, Dec. 12: Negotiation Skills for Academic Leaders.

An expert on negotiating within the university setting teaches win-win approaches to achieving results and strengthening relationships. Participants will come away with specific methods they can use to bridge differences and a template for how to approach negotiations.

Friday, Feb. 6: Leading Change, Adapting to Change.

When it comes to organizational change, as the song goes, "Sometimes you're the windshield; sometimes you're the bug!" It is important for leaders to know how to be a proactive agent of change and also how to help others adjust to change.

Friday, Mar. 6: Resolving Conflicts.

Differences are inevitable in university life, and we all have our own distinctive style of approaching conflict. This seminar is a chance to review your typical approach to conflict and consider how you might improve your results in conflict situations.

Friday, Apr. 10: Resilient Leadership Under Stress.

Explore the stresses inherent in the leadership role, review what is contributing to your own current stress level, and add to your repertoire of stress management approaches.

7. Extend mentoring support after tenure and promotion

Some departments and schools are now offering mid-career faculty members a mentor who can help them build a next-step career plan and/or continue the mentoring committees formed at the junior rank into the next stage. Ohio State University Prof. Robert Fox, writing for the American Speech and Language Association, lays out a strong program of what mentoring programs should cover at the associate level: establishing clear professional goals (with a view toward meeting departmental standards for promotion), setting a timetable and specific roadmap for a new research program, assistance in identifying funding sources, peer reviews of teaching, and defining the necessary service commitment required for promotion. (14)

For schools and departments extending mentoring services to mid-career faculty members, a key decision will be whether participation will be voluntary or required. If voluntary, units will need to make sure that those choosing to be mentored are not seen as "needing extra help" or those who choose not to join the program are not seen as "rogue actors."

Departments could provide a menu of post-promotion mentoring services including:

- Annual conversation with the chair or mentoring program leader about goals and progress.

- Ability to apply for leave, travel funds, and research support.

- Access to a teaching advisor or teaching support group.

- Having a mentor or mentoring committee to assist with the progress toward the next rank.

8. Work supportively with long-time associate professors or those at equivalent rank

Another critical mid-career mentoring program design decision is how to deal with faculty who have been in rank for ten years or more. If a program is established only for newly tenured faculty then those faculty may feel the department has "written them off." On the other hand, some of these faculty members may have made peace with their permanent associate status and might find going into a mentoring program a kind of admission of failure or having their career placed in "receivership status." Faculty development does not have to be directed toward promotion only. An enlightened department chair will help the "permanent associates" set new challenges for themselves, and engage them in the department in ways that use their strengths and maximize their contributions. Career plans that identify these significant goals are just as important as career plans that lead to promotion.

It will also be important to differentiate any negative post-tenure review improvement plans from new mentoring arrangements lest the mentoring program is seen as remediation instead of advancement. Probably, the best approach would be to make post-tenure mentoring services optional for those in rank for, say, ten years or more. However, I would emphasize this does not mean that associates who have been in rank a long time and do not want to progress to full should be ignored by the chair or senior colleagues.

Each faculty member deserves to have a good discussion about their careers going forward on a regular basis, to set goals, and to receive assistance in meeting those goals.

Assuming a faculty member is a strong contributor, despite not progressing in rank, there is no need to push going up for full professor. He or she may be doing just fine as a teacher, scholar, and citizen of the department by any reasonable judgment.

On the other hand, if the chair and colleagues feel the individual is not making a strong enough contribution, the conversation should be about meeting expectations and upping one's game. The trick here is to find the sweet spot between what the department needs done and the faculty member is willing to do, and good at doing. Finding this spot requires patient and honest dialogue and some creative thinking.

If a person has ceased to do original research, he or she may contribute to the literature through integrative research or writing about pedagogy. He or she may contribute through service to the department or the campus or the discipline, or through innovative teaching. He or she may be an excellent advisor to graduate students, or a mentor to undergraduates. The important criteria are (a) that the unit and the individual get to the place where they both feel comfortable about the level of effort, and (b) that, objectively speaking, the individual's contribution demonstrably advances the unit's goals.

9. Explore modifications to tenure and promotion policies to support mid-career faculty transition

In some institutions (particularly research intensive institutions) the lack of advancement opportunities outside the tenure track, combined with rigid requirements for granting tenure disadvantage the following classes of mid-career faculty:

- Faculty members who want to focus on teaching, university service, public service, or entrepreneurship after tenure (e.g., associate professors who take on leadership of the university's writing program, or honors program, or who lead a major public service initiative).

- Faculty members who take on major family responsibilities (e.g., child-rearing, ailing parents).

- Faculty members who are in emerging disciplines that use innovative methodologies for which national standards of excellence are not yet clear (e.g., digital humanities) or who focus on new topics within traditional disciplines (e.g., study of rap and hip hop within music departments, emerging social media tools within journalism, or use of robotics within surgical departments).

The means of addressing these separate issues vary but they include some of the following approaches:

- Provide an alternative promotion track for faculty who make a strong contribution to the institution but who may not meet the traditional criteria of the research-intensive university. The president of Ohio State University floated this idea in 2010. (15)

- Give serious attention to how gender and family responsibilities affect advancement in the mid-career and develop additional mechanisms to help promising academics continue to advance while raising their families (e.g., increase child care services, provide extended time expected to reach full professor, additional research leaves, etc). (16)

  Exhibit 3.5 showcases the University of Colorado's program for stopping the "tenure clock."

- Provide an alternative track to promotion and tenure that goes from assistant to full that is more focused on teaching, clinical, application (i.e., translational research, entrepreneurship, or public service.) Set up means to shift between tracks. The medical centers at Duke and Yale have begun to try out this idea. (17)

- Provide an alternative promotion system for the fixed-term faculty members including: clear ranks and salary increases with increasing accomplish-ment and multi-year contracts, as well as access to sabbaticals and other professional development opportunity. This is something the University of Denver is now experimenting with. (18)

> **Exhibit 3.5: Stopping the Tenure Clock**
>
> *Excerpt from the University of Colorado-Boulder's policy. See:*
>
> *https://www.colorado.edu/facultyaffairs/adjustments-tenure-clock*
>
> Parental leave is also grounds for stopping the tenure clock. As of July 2007, upon notification to Faculty Affairs, a tenured or tenure-track faculty member who will be the primary caregiver for a child within 12 months of birth or adoption of the child will have their tenure clock stopped automatically for one year (if not yet tenured). The faculty member will also receive up to a maximum of one semester at full pay without using accrued sick leave.
>
> In compliance with University policy, normally an eligible faculty member may receive a maximum of two parental leaves during their employment with CU.

10. Recognize the challenges facing mid-career women in the STEM disciplines

In the previous chapter, I discussed the challenges that women face in the academy—and early in this chapter, I defined the "crisis" of the recently tenured professor and by extension, the recently promoted professor. It seems logical to assume that the intersection of the stress of mid-career with the experiences related to gender inequities create special challenges for women and present additional barriers for their further advancement in the academy.

We also know that women do not advance as quickly from associate to full professor in academic medicine as their colleagues and are under-represented in leadership roles. (19)

Problems in the STEM fields in the advancement of mid-career women have also been well documented. (20) The previously discussed failure to value women's work and contribution adequately also come into play here.

One female biologist explained to me that the most likely path to full professor was to produce a large number of small research papers that represented incremental progress. She, on the other hand, produced relatively few papers but they had an outsized impact on the field. She also was a widely-acclaimed major champion of trans-formative innovations in the curriculum campus-wide. She finally got the promotion but only after strong intervention by the chair who saw the injustice of the situation. Another female faculty member in that department had a strong track record of research, sat on NSF panels, and because she was an African American provided extensive support to minority students in the department—but she had not received the promotion to full professor.

In STEM departments, women throughout their careers continue to face issues related to lack of availability of child care, the danger of being in labs late at night, insensitive or sexist interactions with colleagues, and lack of responsiveness in terms of HR organizations relative to policies—all of which may tend to be very problematic for morale for women in STEM in mid-career. I started this chapter by showing how faculty morale may reach a nadir in mid-career. In the STEM disciplines, too often these misogynistic factors may be the last straw for mid-career women faculty.

Raising awareness may be one solution component. In one STEM department at a major research university, female faculty leaders began to meet with the early career women faculty, the post docs, and the graduate students to talk about how women experienced the department. Once they had built trust among themselves and clarified their perspectives, they invited supportive male faculty to hear their views, including the chair. With the chair's support they then had a series of discussions throughout the department. My understanding is that these activities transformed the department in many positive ways and made it a more comfortable environment for women at all levels.

Ultimately, the most important intervention academic leaders can make to support women in the STEM fields is to work persistently to create a strong positive organizational climate where both men and women feel valued for their particular contributions and where any gender-related concerns are addressed sensitively and equitably. The #MeToo movement in the US suggests that many types of organizations have a long way to go in making the workplace truly welcoming for women. Academic leaders, both men and women, can help their organizations by vowing to be leaders rather than laggards in this movement.

11. Support under-represented minorities in overcoming obstacles to advancement

For years, the ranks of under-represented minority faculty (e.g., African Americans, Hispanic faculty, and Pacific Islanders) have been stuck at levels that are disproportionately low compared to the enrollment of students in their institutions, let alone their growing proportion of the population. The long-term solution to this problem will depend on creating a truly diverse pipeline of students in graduate school and in the early stages of the faculty career, but the record shows that as minority faculty rise through the ranks, their ranks become thinner. So, this is an issue for the mid-career as well.

Professors Joya Misra and Jennifer Lundquest have recently summarized research on the particular challenges facing under-represented faculty of color. They cite evidence for the toll that institutional bias, systemic racism and micro-aggressions take on these faculty members as well as the disproportionate impact of racialized politics on their lives at work. This is in addition to the well-documented extra demands minority faculty members may face when they are frequently asked to serve on committees and other service work to ensure URMF are represented. (21)

They identify some promising practices:

- Find ways to recognize the special contributions these faculty members make to the IHE's diversity goals through their service work on committees and mentoring students.

- Create clear guidelines to combat implicit bias and double-standards by tenure and promotion committees that disadvantage minority groups.

- Help create support groups for URM faculty in addition to other mentoring opportunities.

In addition to these practices, many of the general strategies discussed in this chapter can also be brought to bear to help under-represented minority faculty members and women faculty. Most institutions have a strong need to retain minority and women faculty. It pays to make sure that minority and women faculty members who have more stress (and perhaps have more options to leave than other mid-career faculty members) also have good access to robust mentoring and faculty development programs.

Finally, under-represented minority faculty members and women faculty members may particularly benefit from some the more general policies I have discussed in the previous sections of this chapter:

- Mark the transition to mid-career—He or she may be the first in the unit or one of the few in the university, but (depending on the faculty member's perspective) he or she may want this to be emphasized or downplayed.

- Goal setting—Make sure the URM or female faculty member has an opportunity for dialogue about what is next for him or her. As Kerry Anne Roquemore wrote: "She/he may have many career paths possible. These include: change agent, public intellectual, administration, disciplinary star, master teacher, and investing energy elsewhere. Some of these paths lead expeditiously to full professor while others can take a faculty member astray from the activities that are rewarded with promotion." (22) The choice of activities should be the faculty member's but it should be made with knowledge of the potential consequences for promotion.

- Make the pathway to the next promotion more transparent—Whatever the goals, the unit should help the faculty member understand how they fit with the unit's promotion system.

- Foster faculty career conversations—If the institution has a support/educational program for mid-career faculty, make sure the minority faculty member knows about it; he or she may find it particularly beneficial.

- Provide substantive support for faculty development—Direct the faculty member to sources of funding, make them aware of potential research leaves or other development opportunities, and help them identify any programs particularly targeted to under-represented minority faculty.

- Provide encouragement for professional development—E.g., a recent American Association of Medical College seminar (23) on early career faculty minority advancement had the following goals in addition to supporting promotion-related planning.

   a. Assess professional development goals and identify strategies and tools for promotion and tenure.

b. Develop key professional competencies in academic leadership.

c. Enhance leadership skills in the areas of communication, team building, change management, and work/life balance.

d. Expand your network of colleagues and sponsors.

- Extend mentoring: It may be important for an URM faculty member to have several mentors, including some in the department who can help him or her navigate the politics of the next stage and some outside the department and even the university where he or she can share concerns (that may relate to his or her minority status in the department) and get help in a confidential setting.

- Modify tenure and promotion policies. Sometimes under-represented minorities also bring special skill and knowledge or have interest in studying groups that have not previously been the traditional focus of attention, or have experience in media and art forms that have not been part of the mainstream. These faculty members will benefit from whatever flexibility has been built into the tenure and promotion system.

The program showcased in Exhibit 3.6 is focused primarily on early career faculty, but such a program could be modified and repurposed to address the interests of under-represented mid-career faculty who have an interest in becoming academic leaders.

EXHIBIT 3.6: SAMPLE PROGRAM SUPPORTING UNDER-REPRESENTED MINORITY AND WOMEN FACULTY

This program description is excerpted from:
http://news.unchealthcare.org/som-vital-signs/2017/oct-5/acclaim-program-welcomes-new-cohort

The Academic Career Leadership Academy in Medicine (ACCLAIM) is a UNC School of Medicine one-year program, started in 2012, that provides leadership and career development opportunities to faculty members (ACCLAIM Scholars), with an emphasis on those under-represented in medicine.

The curriculum for ACCLAIM is based, in part, on the model established by the Public Health Leadership Program (PHLP) in the UNC Gillings School of Global Public Health. ACCLAIM's weekly sessions include guest speakers from across the university and span four areas of leadership: personal, team, organization, and population. The program begins with a three-day leadership workshop/retreat that helps scholars to understand the leadership styles and approaches of others as well as themselves.

In addition to the weekly sessions and workshop, one of the central requirements of ACCLAIM is that participants propose an idea that they will work on individually to advance research, strengthen teaching, and improve the health care system.

Projects developed by the scholars are designed to span boundaries and connect disciplines at the hospital and medical school; they should also improve efficiency or effectiveness.

Scholars are chosen each year based on past leadership experience and their potential for greater leadership development.

Notes

1. See Bland, Carol J. and William H. Berquist. "Conclusions and Themes to Guide Approaches to the Vitality of Senior Faculty," *The Vitality of Senior Faculty Members: Snow on the Roof--Fire in the Furnace.* George Washington University Press, 1997.

    In 2000, Jossey-Bass published an edition of the same work under that title as well. Bland and Berquist suggest that most senior faculty remain vital and productive. When there are problems with late career faculty (i.e., those that are derailed and who become "deadwood"), they argue that these can be traced to a lack of effective faculty development activities in the mid-career. A more recent study of Faculty Vitality in Academic Health Centers also docu-mented that the lowest levels of faculty vitality were found among mid-career faculty and that this group was at greatest risk of burnout and attrition. See Pololi, Linda, et al. "Faculty Vitality—Surviving the Challenges Facing Academic Health Centers: A National Survey of Medical Faculty," *Academic Medicine,* vol. 90, issue 7, July 2015, pp. 930-936.

    https://journals.lww.com/academicmedicine/Fulltext/2015/07000/Faculty_Vitality_Surviving_the_Challenges_Facing.23.aspx

2. For a research based discussion of challenges faced by mid-career faculty, see Baldwin, Roger G., et al., "Mapping the Terrain of Mid-Career Faculty at A Research University, Implications for Faculty and Academic Leaders," *Change,* September-October 2008, pp. 46-55.

For discussion of a recent study of mid-career faculty at three liberal arts institutions, see Flaherty, Colleen. "Midcareer Professors Need Love, Too," *Inside Higher Ed*, January 26, 2017.

https://www.insidehighered.com/news/2017/01/26/research-midcareer-professors-makes-case-support-after-tenure

The most general survey of mid-career faculty comes from the Director of Harvard's COACHE Project. See Mathews, K. R. "Perspectives on Midcareer Faculty and Advice for Supporting Them," *The Collaborative on Academic Careers in Higher Education*, Harvard School of Education, 2014.

https://scholar.harvard.edu/kmathews/publications/perspectives-midcareer-faculty-and-advice-supporting-them

Also see Jaschik, Scott. "Different Paths to Full Professor," *Inside Higher Ed*, June 4, 2010.

https://www.insidehighered.com/news/2012/06/04/associate-professors-less-satisfied-those-other-ranks-survey-finds

Similarly, Wilson, Robin. "Why Are Associate Professors Some of the Unhappiest People in Academe?" *The Chronicle of Higher Education*, 2012.

The argument and evidence presented by Bland et al. (2009) strongly support the general argument and specific points made here and throughout Chapter 3. See their Chapter 8, "Mentoring Mid-Career and Senior Faculty," p. 129-141.

3. The notion of adult developmental stages and developmental crisis has been recognized in the psychological literature at least early as the work of Erik Erikson and was more fully developed by Daniel Levinson. Later, this idea entered the popular culture through Gail Sheahy and was incorporated into career development theory by Edgar Schein. A more recent empirical study of life crises which summarizes this literature was published in the *Journal of Adult Development* in 2013, by O. C Robinson. See:

   https://www.therapiebreve.be/documents/robinson-ea-2013.pdf

   Though Robinson's paper focuses on the early adult stage, it has clear implications for all levels of adult crisis.

4. As co-leader of the IAH's Academic Leadership Program for nine years, a program that focused on mid-career faculty, I can say that I saw this problem in numerous situations. Some of the most respected and highly contributing faculty on campus—who, more often than not, were female—were not being promoted to full. In some

cases, these faculty served as deans or administrators of programs serving hundreds of students, but they had not "published the third book," or they had only ten articles rather than twenty. Meanwhile, their (often male) peers who focused their time with strict attention to departmental requirements for advancement were promoted to full professor after a relatively short time at the associate rank. A good description of this situation may be found in Rockquemore, Kerry Ann. "Rebrand Yourself," *Inside Higher Ed*, July 16, 2012.

https://www.insidehighered.com/advice/2012/0
7/16/essay-how-midcareer-faculty-members-can-
rebrand-themselves

Also see Misra, Joya, et al. "The Ivory Ceiling of Service Work," *AAUP*, Jan.-Feb. 2011: (https://www.aaup.org/article/ivory-ceiling-
service-work#.Wl3knWNvk5k).

5. An introduction to the NSF ADVANCE initiative may be accessed here:

    https://www.nsf.gov/crssprgm/advance/

    Numerous studies, toolkits, and other resources relevant to faculty development may be accessed through the ADVANCE portal:

    http://www.portal.advance.vt.edu/index.php/cat
    egories/resources/recommendations

6. In a telephone survey of UNC-CH department chairs, and deans, conducted across campus in 2011 by the author of this book (at that time, I

served as Leadership Coordinator at the Center for Faculty Excellence), about half reported they thought there was a problem with the advancement of associate professors post-tenure—and they suggested that only about one third of the associate professors progressed to full without much of a pause.

7. See "How Midcareer Academics Can Find Their Place in the Emotional Spectrum." *Inside Higher Ed.* July 2, 2012:

   https://www.insidehighered.com/advice/2012/07/02/essay-how-mid-career-academics-can-find-their-place-emotional-spectrum

8. In 2007, Institute of Government Professor and UNC-CH Associate Provost Steve Allred completed a dissertation at the University of Pennsylvania studying factors relating to retention. He found that the "Push and Pull Hypothesis" was dominant in the field of retention studies. See *Fighting the war at home: A case study of faculty retention at UNC:*

   https://repository.upenn.edu/dissertations/AAI3255876/

9. This resource can be downloaded from:

   http://oaa.osu.edu/assets/files/documents/FacultyPromoBrochure.pdf

10. William Bridges' work on transitions is most often cited in this regard. For a more in-depth summary of his main theses, go to:

https://www.mindtools.com/pages/article/bridges-transition-model.htm

11. For more information, visit:

   https://iah.unc.edu/faculty-resources/join-faculty-lifecycle-program/

12. See Mathews, K. R. "Perspectives on Midcareer Faculty and Advice for Supporting Them," *The Collaborative on Academic Careers in Higher Education*, Harvard School of Education, 2014,

   scholar.harvard.edu/kmathews/publications/perspectives-midcareer-faculty-and-advice-supporting-them

13. For more information, see:
   https://college.unc.edu/2014/12/12/deangift/

14. See Fox, Robert A. "Mentoring in Mid-Career Faculty," American Speech and Hearing Association, 2014,

   www.asha.org/Articles/Mentoring-Mid-Career-Faculty/

15. See Jaschik, Scott. "Different Paths to Full Professor," *Inside Higher Ed*, March 5, 2010.

   https://www.insidehighered.com/news/2010/03/05/osu

   The subtitle of that article reads: "Ohio State wants to rethink traditional patterns of faculty reward structure—starting by questioning whether research should be the only way to reach the highest rank." This was also reported in *Tomorrow's Professor:*

https://tomprof.stanford.edu/posting/1007

16. According to recent research, the most important factor is a family-friendly climate within the academic unit supported by institution-wide policies. Frank discussion and transparent administration are key. Institutions often have more family friendly policies than faculty are aware of, and it is up to deans and chairs to do a better job in communicating, discussing, and supporting the use of more family-friendly policies. See:

https://www.insidehighered.com/news/2012/10/09/authors-discuss-new-book-academic-motherhood

17. Medical schools seem to be leading the way in this area, including Duke and Yale. For example, see this post on Duke's website:

https://medschool.duke.edu/about-us/faculty-resources/faculty-appointments-promotion-tenure/clinical-science-apt/faculty/tracks

18. See Colleen Flaherty, "More than Adjuncts." *Inside Higher Ed.* February 17, 2015. The subtitle of this article reads, "The University of Denver moves to new titles, a career path and multiyear contracts for those off the tenure track. Could this be a model for other institutions?"

19. See Carr, Phyllis L., et al. "Inadequate Progress for Women in Academic Medicine: Findings from the National Faculty Study." *Journal of Womens Health (Larchmt)*, Mar 1, 2015, vol. 24, no. 3, 2015, pp. 374-381.

20. See Hart, Jeni. "Dissecting a Gendered Organization: Implications for Career Trajectories for Midcareer Faculty Women in STEM," *The Journal of Higher Education*, vol. 87, issue 5, 2016 pp. 605-634. This article cites the study by Liza Howe-Walsh and Sarah Turnbull: Howe-Walsh, Lisa, and Sarah Turnbull. "Barriers to women leaders in academia: tales from science and technology," *Studies in Higher Education*. vol. 41, issue 3, 2014, pp. 415-428. See also the discussion of Bland et. al (2009), pp. 108-114, discussed in Chapter 2.

21. See Misra, Joya, et al. "Diversity and the Ivory Ceiling," *Inside Higher Ed*, June 26, 2015.

    https://www.insidehighered.com/advice/2015/0
    6/26/essay-diversity-issues-and-midcareer-faculty-
    members

22. See Rockquemore, Kerry Anne. "How faculty members can chart meaningful post tenure career paths," *Inside Higher Ed*, June 25, 2012.

    https://www.insidehighered.com/advice/2012/0
    6/25/essay-how-faculty-members-can-chart-
    meaningful-post-tenure-career

23. See the Leadership Section of the AAMC course catalogue:

   https://www.aamc.org/members/leadership/catalog/452848/mid-careerminorityfacultyleadershipseminar.html

CHAPTER 4
DEVELOPING SENIOR FACULTY: GUIDANCE FOR CHAIRS, DEANS, AND OTHER ACADEMIC LEADERS

In this chapter, I address the major gap that exists in the thinking and programming for faculty beyond mid-career. This period spans two decades or more and is arguably the most productive phase of the faculty member's career. Both the institution and the faculty would benefit from a more systematic approach to meeting needs of senior faculty.

Once the needs for mentoring early career faculty became evident and programs to address that need became more common, it was inevitable that the needs of mid-career faculty would also come into focus. Accordingly, career development services, including mentoring are being extended for associate professors, and now, finally, the turn of senior faculty is beginning to come around.

I start by stating the case for senior faculty development (SFD) and then identify a set of six core principles to guide SFD initiatives. In this introductory section, I distinguish between programs that focus on individual level (e.g., personal goal setting and planning), functional level (i.e., teaching, research, service, and leadership opportunities and skills) and institutional level (e.g., campus-wide principles, policies, positions, and programs).

In the rest of the chapter, I provide examples at each of the three levels that chairs, deans, and senior leaders might consider as they improve SFD. I showcase exemplary programs for SFD but also (since formal SFD programming is at the early stages relative to programs for assistant to associate professors) I extrapolate from programs that are successful for mid-career faculty.

Towards the end of the chapter, I will once again consider the special needs of under-represented minority faculty and women in the STEM disciplines where isolation and attendant stress is a particular problem. I conclude by stressing the need to more closely link the needs of SFD programs, and faculty development in general to external fundraising.

By the time you have completed this chapter, you should have a comprehensive look at what a faculty development program might look like from the beginning of the faculty career to the point of pre-retirement planning. Accordingly, I conclude the chapter with a checklist for faculty development that recaps the main points of Chapter Four so you are left with a concise, high-level summary and a comprehensive programming model.

The Case for Senior Faculty Development

If early career faculty members are usually aged 30 to 40 and early mid-career is 40 to 50, then mid-to-late career faculty are typically aged 50 to 65 or older. In many institutions, they constitute the largest faculty cohort and dominate most departments. Many of these older faculty members may have attained the rank of full professor or the highest rankings available for the fixed-term (non-tenure) track. The authors of a national study on faculty development conclude:

> Senior faculty are a critical, but often ignored, group in faculty development. We say critical because they are the ones whom we are counting on to recruit and mentor the new faculty, and many of the features of a vital organization depend on them, such as leadership and maintenance of a cohesive culture and a positive climate. (1)

In fact, the most productive senior faculty are likely to be responsible for whatever national standing a given department has in the discipline, to produce innovations that attract major donor funding and to conduct research that attracts significant government funding. In teaching institutions, they may be the backbone of the administration, the gatekeepers of innovation, and repository of institutional memory.

Therefore, it makes sense to support faculty at the height of their productivity and influence, to retain them, and also to enable faculty who have reached the pinnacle of accomplishment to maintain engagement and motivation by taking on a new challenge. Arguably, the key to a long and successful faculty career is continual reinvention and renewal. SFD should include a focus on this goal.

In addition, when faculty members' productivity does decline because of advancing age, it makes economic sense and is a humane practice for IHEs to have effective pre-retirement programs in place to smooth and accelerate that transition. (2)

Key Considerations to Guide the Creation of SFD Programs

In their classic and authoritative monograph about SFD, Bland and Berquist (1997) offer guidance for the development of programs for senior faculty. They argue that programs should be *comprehensive*, should emphasize *shared responsibility*, and should be experienced as *caring and positive*. To these themes I would add three others: *diversity and inclusion, continuity* (across the age range before and during the senior years), and *sensitivity* to the specific needs of faculty members as they progress from the ages of say, 50 to 70. In the paragraphs that follow, I describe these six themes more fully, following and elaborating on Bland and Berquist's formulation. (3)

Comprehensive

Bland and Berquist assert that the development of senior faculty has three realms of activity: the *individual* realm (e.g., personal goal setting and clarification, morale, and motivation development); the *functional* realm (e.g., development of skills and knowledge in teaching, academic leadership, and research); and the *institutional or organizational* realm (i.e., institutional resources, policies, positions, and organizations that advance faculty development). This framework was also adapted for use by the staff of the Wallace Center at Rochester Institute of Technology to study mid-career faculty development at 39 universities. (4)

Shared responsibility

Bland and Berquist further suggest that the responsibility for successful SFD is distributed among: 1) individual faculty members taking responsibility for their own career management and renewal; 2) departmental and other leaders taking an active role in assessing and fostering vitality of individual faculty in their units; and 3) senior leaders establishing policies and programs, and finding and allocating resources that help develop faculty throughout the life cycle.

Positive tone

Some senior faculty policies (such as post-tenure review) are experienced as onerous, even punitive. (5) In contrast to this, Bland and Berquist argue that faculty must experience programs of development as caring, supportive, intellectually challenging, and helpful in order to foster retention and motivation. Faculty members need to feel that their value is acknowledged and that work is meaningful. They also need to feel part of a program, department, college, and university whose direction they respect and support.

Inclusive and diverse

Faculty members come in many varieties: older, younger, male and female, LGBTQ+ and straight, of African, Asian, European, Hispanic, Native American, Pacific Islander and mixed descent. They have diverse nationalities and differing abilities and disabilities. Faculty may be tenured or tenure track or long-time fixed-term, full-time or part-time. They all make significant contributions. These different identities and statuses must be acknowledged, as they may present distinctive challenges and require special supports at the senior level (as well as other levels).

Continues from mid-career

Ideally, support for faculty development is seamless and continuous from the early to late stages of the career. Problems experienced in the late stage of a faculty career may be partly the result of the fact that early stage supports are missing.

Sensitive to career stage

It is common sense that the "50ish" professor may not have the same goals or career development needs as the "70ish" professor. At the younger anchor of the age continuum the senior faculty member may be in the process of bringing to completion a major work, starting out on a career capstone project, or wanting to go in a completely different direction because of new interests. Faculty members at this age range may have aging parents to deal with and children to get through school, so financial and life balance issues may be in the picture for them. Still others may want to try their hand at academic leadership and seek to become chairs and deans or seek to lead centers and institutes.

At the older end of the continuum, faculty may need a different kind of help—talking about their legacy, wrapping things up, and planning for retirement. In the middle of the range faculty may be thinking of their "last hurrah" in terms of scholarly interests, the course they always wanted to teach, or how to be of service to their colleagues in new way. When I talk about "sensitivity" here, I mean being sensitive to the nuances and gradations of the career maturation and life cycle process so as to meet the faculty where they are and to provide help that is truly helpful.

In the next three sections of this chapter, I use the categories of individual, functional, and institutional programs and policies to frame a menu of options for SFD based on current practice and promising possibilities.

Specific Programs to Support Senior Faculty at the *Individual* Level

Individual-level programs in this three-part typology (i.e., individual, functional, and institutional) refer to programs that support individual faculty members in thinking through career goals, options, and strategies. They do not require a change in institutional policies and can be implemented at a unit level or through the person's own initiative. I discuss three types of programs in this section: *career conversations, workshops,* and *peer support and mentoring.* These are independent initiatives, but (if implemented in tandem) they can reinforce each other.

Career conversations

> *Chairs and deans can provide and encourage regular career conversation opportunities for senior faculty and work to overcome the barriers to discussing career goals.*

This section repeats and reinforces some of the points I made in the section on mid-career faculty. I make no apology for this, because the career conversation is the missing piece of the faculty development puzzle once the individual progresses from junior status.

In reality, career development takes place one person at a time. It seems elemental to suggest that every senior faculty member should have the opportunity to sit down with someone once a year and talk through where his or her career is going, including how the last year went, the hopes for the coming year, and long term goals. The Educational Advisory Board in its 2012 report "Improving the Productivity of the Faculty Post-Tenure" (based on input from 15 research universities) argued strongly for forward-looking, post-tenure career discussions. In fact, they say that "faculty productivity problems can often be traced to the failure of department chairs and deans to communicate expectations clearly and to conduct effective reviews." Such conversations, they say, should "…address obstacles to productivity, identify development resources, prepare for promotion, and craft professional goals." (6)

Unfortunately, it is not always that simple. In well-run organizations outside the academy, each employee is supposed to have such a conversation with the supervisor or career counselor. In most universities, faculty members do not consider themselves employees in the same way as non-faculty, and they don't consider the chair or dean as their supervisor, and they shudder to think the university is becoming more like an industry, well-run or not.

In fact, many would say they have no supervisor. That is part of the reason they became faculty members. They don't want people telling them what to do or to interfere with their right to follow their own inclination as to what areas they explore, write about, and teach. To suggest they might benefit from such a conversation may, in the wrong context, be taken as an insinuation that they lack what it takes to be an autonomous and self-directing faculty member. We may inadvertently reinforce this attitude when mentoring programs stop at the point of tenure or first promotion for the fixed-term faculty member.

So, there is a cultural barrier to supporting career conversations in the academy—particularly among mid- and late-career faculty who may feel they "graduated" from such discussion when they got tenure.

Some units propose to address this problem via mandate. The Johns Hopkins School of Medicine Task Force on Senior Faculty Support and Transition recently recommended that there be a documented annual review meeting for faculty of all ranks, including full professors, that includes questions such as: *"Where do you see your career in five years?* and *"What is your transition plan for teaching or research?"* The Carnegie Mellon School of Engineering mandates a full review and discussion every seven years. (7)

It makes sense for these conversations to occur, if not every year, at least every three years, and certainly no more than seven years.

Even where not centrally mandated, there are natural opportunities to promote a norm of career reflection. In almost every IHE faculty members must provide an annual productivity report. Often this report is used as a basis for allocation of small discretionary amounts of merit pay. However, this report could also be an occasion for faculty members to step back and ask questions like: *How satisfied am I with my work over the last two or three years? What was most meaningful and motivating, and why? What areas am I most excited about for the future? What shape might that take? What factors in life and work are helping me or getting in the way? How might I do things better or differently in the future?*

There are several options for actually holding these conversations:

1) *Chairs can offer this as a service.* This makes a lot of sense if this is a unit where there is a history of chairs holding career conversations with early career faculty and, if so, this can be framed as extension of this service to mid-career and senior faculty.

2) *Create a special SFD career development role.* In one medical unit, I worked with an associate chair who offered a career conversation with each faculty member every year. This conversation was consciously separated from the annual talk with the chair. That talk was more about productivity and salary than career goals. In one unit in a College of Arts and Sciences, a very well-respected senior member and past chair visited each of his colleagues to have these discussions on an informal basis.

3) *Make this a subject of discussion at a faculty meeting.* Talk about the value of career reflection for mid-career and senior faculty, and identify resources to help inside or outside the department. If the university or college has programs that are forums for this kind of discussion across the campus, promote those programs. Differentiate career reflection (the process of coming to some conclusions by asking questions) from career advice (the process of coming to a conclusion by seeking inform- ation); both are good in the right sequence and balance. (8)

4) *Provide an option for an outside the university career consultation.* Executive coaching has become commonplace at the top level of universities. Why not provide career coaching for senior faculty when it could make a real difference? Currently there are private companies that are set up to provide coaching for faculty members either in person or virtually. The private sector is rapidly developing resources to help people think about their career that can be adapted for use in universities. (9)

The career conversation may not always be easy to conduct, and it would not be a bad idea to get some training on how to make this conversation most effective. (10)

Career workshops and peer mentoring

Faculty development leaders can provide workshops for career self-assessment, planning and skill development, and can encourage peer mentoring.

As I have noted, those who are full professors or long-term associates, whether tenured or not, have special concerns. These include: *How am I going to maximize what is likely to be my most productive period?* (roughly age 50-58), *What am I going to do for "the last hurrah"?* (roughly age 59-66), and *How will I handle the transition to retirement?* (roughly age 67-75). One can easily imagine that a skillfully led discussion with a cohort group on these topics would be very beneficial to senior faculty.

Such discussion groups could be along the lines of a workshop or faculty learning community format. In such a workshop, faculty could share their situations, learn from one another, and hear about the tips and tools being developed to help those in their cohort. Participation in such a program would doubtless enrich the above mentioned career discussions and lead to more comprehensive and realistic rolling five-year plans. (See Appendix B, Section 4.2, for an example of a career planning template—the one we used in our mid-career and senior faculty development retreats at UNC-Chapel Hill.) Effective workshops need to be confidential, collegial, and whole-life based, as explained in the paragraphs below.

Confidentiality

Given that faculty are naturally sensitive and private about career choices, issues, and dilemmas, they require a high level of confidentiality.

Collegiality

In thinking about late career issues, it is important for faculty to have a place to go outside the departmental setting, yet in the presence of peers who can empathize with them, support them, and guide them. Hence there is an important role for centrally administered, outside-of-department SFD programs that address concerns at the individual level. The collegial group or forum combats a sense of career isolation and resultant loneliness that faculty at every level may feel, and that can become debilitating as they struggle with development issues.

Whole-Life Based

Organizational research suggests that at an individual level, career concerns are always embedded in life concerns, and career development programs that ignore the personal context will always be partial and incomplete. (11) The implication here is that effective career development support always occurs best in a safe, intimate, confidential context where individuals are supported to think through the past, the present, and to project the future with a full appreciation of how their career projects fit with personal needs, health considerations, other non-academic goals, and family commitments.

Examples of programs that currently exist that could be adapted for senior faculty include the following:

- *Career planning.* Michigan State, Ohio State, University of Illinois-Urbana, University of Nebraska Lincoln, University of North Carolina at Charlotte, and the University of Wyoming were recognized in a national survey of mid-career programs (12). Among the programs cited are: workshops that focus on productive career decision making, leadership and managerial skills, planning career progress, and how to strengthen teaching, research, and service. These programs could be adapted for senior faculty. The University of Illinois-Urbana holds an annual Mid-Career Faculty Symposium. It seems plausible, then, that UIA and other universities could also hold a symposium on the needs and concerns of senior faculty.

- *Career Support and Mentoring.* For nine years while at UNC-Chapel Hill, I co-led two one-day (several weeks apart) workshops for a mixed group of associate and full professors. The first day involved a review of their past career and how they made decisions, and the second day identified what they wanted to accomplish in their next ten years. The plans took into account their goals, their best guess about the demands of family life, and other trends and events that would affect their plans. They left the workshop with one-year and three-year goals and formed a continuing support network to encourage implementation.

- *Professional Development.* Almost all universities and colleges provide a series of professional development workshops for staff. These include useful strategies for time management, stress management, communications, conflict management, negotiations, communications, and the like. Would it be hard to adapt these types of programs to address the needs of senior faculty? Many universities already have seminars focused on planning for retirement. Could not the same units expand their offerings to include a broader range of issues of interest to senior faculty? For example:

    o Financial and personal planning in late middle age

    o Health and stress management past age 50

    o The dynamics of parenting adult children

    o Work-Life Balance for senior faculty

    o The role of the senior faculty member in the university

Specific Programs to Support Senior Faculty at the *Functional* Level

Functional-level faculty development means training and assistance in all of the areas of performance that are required or expected for faculty in their formal roles. This includes roles as researchers, teachers, service providers, and as leaders and citizens of the university. In the pages that follow, I outline some of the resources that chairs, deans, and senior leaders are developing that can become the foundation of a stronger career development system for faculty when they reach the late career stage.

Providing research assistance for senior faculty

Many universities clearly recognize the need to support senior faculty in developing and enhancing their research productivity. They provide travel funds and support research leaves for faculty who are looking to create, continue, or enhance research initiatives. Here is a sampling of programs available at such diverse universities as Buffalo, Dartmouth, Elon, Georgetown, and Oklahoma (13):

- The University of Buffalo provides a suite of funding opportunities for senior faculty, including: travel support, publication support, and research fellowships that support hiring a replacement teacher while the faculty member is on leave.

- Dartmouth provides $3,000 a year in research funding. Faculty may "save it up" for three years and get a $9,000 grant in one year.

- Elon University has a comprehensive statement about faculty development and also provides funds for faculty replacement, reimbursement, and stipends.

- Georgetown's Senior Faculty Research Fellowship Program provides one semester of leave time at full pay for tenured faculty members on the main campus at the associate or full professor levels on a competitive basis.

- The College of Arts and Sciences at the university of Oklahoma provides $7,500 for senior faculty doing research in the summer.

Universities also assist faculty with external grant funding, including proposal support services and grant administrative services. Purdue University is typical in this regard; see Exhibit 4.1 for a list of the services offered by their Office of Pre-Award Services.

Exhibit 4.1: Pre-Award Support for Faculty Proposals

Purdue University.
https://www.purdue.edu/business/sps/preaward/index.html

Pre-Award supports the University community in proposal development through value-added, high-quality service and professional partnerships with Principal Investigators in order to facilitate world-changing research.

Our proposal specialists work collaboratively with PIs and the Office of Research and Partnerships' Proposal Development team to prepare grant applications, serving as a dedicated central resource in all matters related to University and sponsor policies for proposal development and submission.

Pre-Award specialists provide the following services in the support of PIs:

- Review sponsor guidelines, identify key requirements.

- Assist with budget preparation, related documentation and proposal submission forms.

- Prepare required sponsor administrative forms.

- Ensure that all Purdue information included within the proposal is accurate and complete.

- Contact and collaborate with partner institutions to secure all necessary subcontract documentation.

- Assure all regulatory requirements and export control issues are identified.

- Review the final proposal package to ensure all administrative requirements have been met.

EXHIBIT 4.1, CONTINUED: PRE-AWARD SUPPORT FOR FACULTY PROPOSALS

- Obtain academic approvals and provide institutional approval for the proposal.

- Complete the final submission package, upload final documents and forms, and submit to the sponsor.

Colleges and universities can also provide programs and funding that assist scholars who want to branch out in new areas and methodologies. For example, UNC-Chapel Hill offers a semester long seminar for faculty who want to develop along the lines of engaged scholarship and participatory research. See Figure 4.2.

The action point for enhancing programs for SFD in research is benchmarking current efforts against peer institutions, assessing needs of senior faculty for research support, and targeting scarce resources toward the most beneficial ways of strengthening the set of current offerings. So, if science faculty members seem to be able to get good grant support for late career research, but humanities professors cannot, then the IHE may seek to augment opportunities for that group. Supporting senior faculty research efforts is not only a retention and renewal strategy; it can also have the benefits of raising faculty productivity, increasing the unit's reputation, and generating additional revenue.

Exhibit 4.2: Thorp Engaged Scholars Program (UNC-Chapel Hill)

Source: https://ccps.unc.edu/fes/
(This excerpt has been edited for brevity.)

The Thorp Faculty Engaged Scholars program (FES) brings together selected faculty from across campus to engage in a two-year experiential, competency-based curriculum designed to advance their engaged scholarship. Scholars participate in sessions in community settings to learn from Carolina faculty and their community partners. While developing individual projects, each class of scholars forms a learning community along with the faculty and community course directors to support one another's projects and community partners. The growing network of Thorp Faculty Engaged Scholars reports outcomes including new inter-disciplinary collaborations, successful grant applications and both traditional and non-traditional products of scholarship. The program provides a stipend of $5,000 per year, for each of the two years ($10,000 in total), supports interactions with like-minded colleagues and more experienced faculty from a variety of disciplines around issues related to engaged scholarship. Information on engaged scholarship is provided via a series of workshops, panels and case studies by leading UNC faculty, community and national experts and funding program officers and community partners.

Providing teaching assistance for senior faculty

There is also a long tradition in academia of support for improving teaching. Some of the grant programs mentioned above also support scholars who seek a leave to design or re-design a course. There are hundreds of Centers for Teaching and Learning across the U.S. They offer faculty assistance on many elements of effective teaching: syllabus construction, classroom management, course design, evaluation, grading, leading discussions, using technology, blended learning, and many other topics. These centers may also provide funds for faculty developing new courses and curriculum. Vanderbilt's teaching and learning center provides extensive inform-ation on how faculty members may gain funding to improve teaching methods. (14).

Often these programs focus on faculty in their early career stages. However, we should give more attention to the needs of senior faculty who may be behind the curve in new trends of instruction, such as large class participation methods and use of technology. Chairs and deans are instrumental in finding ways to engage their faculty with such programs and to bring such programs in-house:

- The University of Washington's Provost News-letter presents case studies of several senior faculty members on multiple campuses who are tackling new technologies to improve teaching.

- Northeastern University in Boston provides an Academic Technology Services unit to support faculty who are introducing new classroom tech-nologies such as "clickers" and Poll Everywhere, web conferencing, videos, etc.

- The SUNY system is experimenting with technology that can promote international classroom connections.

As technological capabilities expand, efforts to get senior faculty up-to-speed should include an assessment of how well older faculty are served by the instructional development resources that currently exist, what senior faculty might be interested in, and what services that will help faculty the most. (15)

Tying senior faculty pedagogy development to institutional initiatives is another effective strategy. At UNC-CH, the Chemistry department participated in an NSF grant-funded program to improve introductory courses in STEM subjects. They hired an early career faculty member who was a pedagogy specialist in chemistry and active learning methods. She began to co-teach the introductory courses with some of the most highly regarded researchers and teachers in the depart-ment.

The junior-teach-senior model turned out to be a success for the older faculty members, the early career faculty members, and the students—who did better on tests, enjoyed the classes more, and dropped out at lower rates. (16) The provost's letter at the University of Washington, cited above, reports a similar project at UW, so this kind of development is occurring coast-to-coast.

Providing opportunities for senior faculty to become involved in leadership

I have argued elsewhere that leadership development, particularly at the mid-level, is critical for enhancing the ability of an institution of higher education to adapt to change. Gmelch and Buller (2015) have shown that institutions of higher education at all levels across the country are developing leadership programs to support faculty and academic administrators. (17)

It is important to understand, however, that this trend toward leadership development in post-secondary institutions also provides an important resource for SFD. Many leadership roles fall disproportionately upon senior faculty members. These include:

- Leading search and selection committees

- Chairing departments

- Heading graduate and undergraduate studies programs

- Leading and participating in study and recommendations task forces

- Being active in and leading national and international disciplinary and professional organizations

- Heading and participating in faculty senate committees

- Leading in shared governance

In some universities, excellence in service along with excellence in research and teaching are part of the consideration for promotion to full professor. Yet, senior faculty members may be thrust into these positions with little training or support. Sometimes the negative experiences in leadership become a de-motivator rather than a source of renewal of faculty vitality. For this reason alone, it is important to help faculty members be successful when they take on these important service and leadership positions.

Programs to support teaching and research are more common and extensive than programs to support faculty leadership development; however, institutions of higher education are providing a variety of programs to address leadership development needs, including:

- Training programs for new chairs

- Orientations to leading academic units, including centers and institutes

- Skills training on leading meetings, supervising, planning, and other managerial duties

- Programs that emphasize broad leadership perspectives and career development

- Programs that provide coaching and advice for faculty new to leadership

- Programs that support the advancement of women into academic leadership ranks.

Such programs not only provide information, methods, and skills that faculty leaders need to be successful, they also provide support and colleagueship. Being a department chair or a center director is often a lonely task, and this isolation intensifies the stress of such difficult jobs. Participation in a formal program of training or consultation that is sponsored by the university or college's leadership helps the faculty leader know that the institution "has their back" and that they have colleagues who are dealing with similar situations and who they can talk with informally and confidentially.

Specific Programs to Support Senior Faculty at the *Institutional* Level

Implementing a program for SFD is a natural extension of the impulse to support faculty development at early and mid-career levels, but the key is the willingness of chairs, deans, and more senior leaders to conceptualize faculty development as a comprehensive and career-long process.

To take this final step, institutional leaders need to take actions at seven different levels. In this section of the chapter, I will discuss these 7 "Ps" of SFD:

Principles: What we as leaders believe about senior SFD.

Policies: What we will actually do to enact our beliefs and values about SFD.

Positions: Whom we will empower and support to implement programs for SFD. And how those positions will be defined, how incumbents will be prepared, and how actions will be coordinated.

Plans: How we will set priorities for scarce resources to invest in SFD.

Programs: What services are essential and needed, up to and including retirement.

People: How we will assure that all receive the benefits of faculty development regardless of gender, ethnicity, race, sexual orientation, disability, or other difference.

Provision: How we will pay for needed programs, positions, and policies.

1. Principles

It is important for the institution, the school, and the department to state that it believes that senior faculty are an important resource for the institution and that senior faculty also deserve opportunities for further development and assistance they need to reach their full potential. The absence of such statements on relevant websites or in policy documents may play into myths and beliefs that the institution does not care about senior faculty, that senior faculty are expected to develop themselves in isolation, or that the institution is just waiting for them to retire. It is much better to have clear statements about institutional beliefs and intent than for the IHE to leave it to the most pessimistic and critical members of the faculty to "fill in the blanks" with negative rumors and stories of past neglect or lack of support.

Here are two examples of the statements of the type I am advocating.

"The Institute for the Arts and Humanities (IAH) hosts programs for faculty at every stage of their career ... We do this from the moment new professors arrive for the first semester, through the tenure process, leadership opportunities, service, and retirement. IAH faculty programs support Carolina

233

scholars and artists because we believe that our faculty are crucial to the UNC goal of service." See:

https://iah.unc.edu/faculty-resources/join-faculty-lifecycle-program/

"Faculty members are at the heart of Penn's mission—not only educating our students but also creating a vibrant campus climate of interdisciplinary intellectual activity. See:

https://provost.upenn.edu/faculty/current

2. Policies

Each campus, school, and department or center with which faculty are affiliated should back up its statement of principles by developing and publicizing general policies supporting faculty development at all levels including senior faculty. At the institutional level, this needs to be articulated, perhaps in cooperation with the appropriate committees of the faculty council or senate and with the endorsement of senior administrative leaders. At the campus or school level, it needs to be worked through the relevant faculty committees. Such a policy would articulate the roles of centrally managed specialized faculty development programs, departments, and individuals. Such a policy would also identify a vision for the institution and what this development would be like when built out. Such a vision could assist in fundraising. In particular the policy should stress the value of faculty members of all age cohorts, and make clear the particular resources that older, retiring, and recently retired faculty represent to the institution. In previous mentoring policy statements, I have introduced departmental and school level policies. Here are a couple of institution level examples. (18)

Iowa State devotes 20 pages in its faculty handbook to identifying policies related to faculty recognition and development, including: professional development leaves, other leaves, fellowship programs, distinguished professorships, study opportunities, and research awards.

Simmons College's faculty handbook makes the following statement: "Faculty are encouraged to participate in and avail themselves of professional development opportunities … It is generally expected that the College shall provide faculty with resources for developmental opportunities. Developmental activities include, but are not limited to, travel to meetings and conferences, participation in workshops and short courses, development and incorporation of new teaching styles and methodologies, advanced certification, professional membership dues, disciplinary and interdisciplinary retooling efforts, preparation of manuscripts, access to major scholarly publications and databases, and purchase of research materials that are otherwise unavailable. Each School shall develop implementation guidelines for the criteria and process by which faculty professional development funds shall be awarded." The handbook goes on to provide seven pages (pages 42-49) of specific programs and opportunities for faculty related to the policy statement.

3. Positions

Institutions need to designate the units and individuals in charge of carrying out faculty development policies. For example a freestanding faculty development (e.g., Center for Faculty Excellence or Center for Teaching and Learning) unit is a logical administrative unit to be charged with the mission to develop and house faculty development programs including those for senior faculty. Sometimes a special unit of the Provost's Office manages or houses these types of organizational resources. Sometimes these functions can be located in an interdisciplinary center that serves the humanities, social sciences, natural sciences, or professional programs in architecture, agriculture, engineering, food sciences, health sciences and the like.

The following announcement by Old Dominion University's provost includes an illustration of what I mean (see: https://www.odu.edu/facultydevelopment):

> "I am pleased to announce the opening of Old Dominion University's Center for Faculty Development. As a university dedicated to innovation in research, teaching, and scholarly activities, the Center furthers Old Dominion University's commitment to educational excellence. Faculty at all ranks will find resources at the center to enhance their career planning and advancement. The center provides opportunities for faculty to develop effective teaching and learning strategies, participate in workshops aimed at promoting collegial conversations, and engage in forums to highlight faculty accomplishments."

At the department level, we see associate chairs for faculty development or mentoring coordinator positions. Many larger schools and colleges within institutions of higher education are now seeing the need for dean positions that carry titles like Associate Dean for Faculty Development. Responding to the call for institutions of higher education to become more diverse and to have faculty composition that better mirrors the student body, there are also Offices of Diversity and Inclusion, Inclusive Excellence, and other similar titles. These units also have specialized staff members that provide assistance to faculty members (including senior faculty) in regard to teaching, research and service, or help search committees in terms of being more inclusive, or provide programs for faculty leadership development and coaching. (19)

In addition to the role of the provost's office, the roles of the deans and department chairs also need to be articulated. For faculty development to be sustained effectively, those responsible need to understand what is expected of them and these expectations need to be regularized by clear job descriptions and performance standards. St. Lawrence University posted a job description for the Dean for Faculty affairs that includes: mentoring, seeking grants for faculty, administering awards for research and travel and teaching, diversity, and hiring. (20)

These responsibilities may be carried out differently in smaller departments and schools than in larger ones. In larger departments and schools, one could imagine a vice chair or associate dean for faculty development, or specific faculty development responsibilities that are assigned to leaders at these levels. (21)

Once faculty and administrators have been identified that have faculty development assignments in their portfolios, it then makes sense to offer them professional development opportunities related to the faculty development function. Workshops for departmental and school level faculty development officers would include topics such as:

- Understanding the career cycle of faculty, with special attention to the sub-phases of older faculty members and programs and services that might be offered at each stage.

- How to assess when faculty members are getting "stuck;" how to prevent faculty "stuckness" and "burnout."

- Strategies for helping senior faculty expand into new areas: How to assess whether faculty members are candidates for renewal of research effort or need a new emphasis on teaching, mentoring, leadership or service, or an alternative career.

- Profiling the developmental needs of the faculty in your unit.

- How to create a departmental climate that supports faculty vitality.

- How to raise departmental and school level funds for faculty development.

- Creating and maintaining unit level faculty development policies and programs.

- Using senior faculty as mentors.

- Diversity and inclusion considerations in addressing needs for SFD.

- Best practices for post-tenure review.

- Improving pre-retirement planning.

- Administering early retirement programs.

- Legal considerations in retirement.

- Working with retired faculty.

Finally, once SFD positions are established and incumbents prepared, actions need to be coordinated. Hopefully, a "community of practice" will emerge, including academic leaders at the dean, associate dean, chair, and assistant chair levels, who see themselves in the business of faculty development. These leaders would meet periodically to exchange information, develop new ideas, and provide continuing support for this effort. An associate provost could coordinate this effort, or a council of faculty development officers could oversee the effort at coordinating and maintaining this community. The faculty development or teaching and learning center (or other appropriate unit) could offer a space for these groups to meet, facilitate their efforts, and create a website where information is shared. (A prominent section of the website would be devoted to success stories, program resources, and tools for SFD.)

If working coordination can be achieved for the multiple actors and interested parties related to faculty development, then there can be synergies in programming, useful division of labor, and leveraging of scarce resources. While I was working at UNC-CH, I found that a program (i.e., bringing in a coach for senior faculty leaders) that cost $5,000 was not affordable for one unit, but when three units pitched in, we were able to provide the service to senior leaders who were developing strategic plans.

4. Planning and priority setting

Once achieved, such institutional coordination can be beneficial for planning and priority setting. Planning is key to the institutionalization of faculty development at all levels. Many of the services I have discussed in this chapter are expensive and complex, and success in one approach may serve as a prerequisite for success in others (e.g., creating institutional policies and mandates may facilitate the establishment of unit level programs and positions). Therefore, planning and sequencing faculty development initiatives over a period of several years are spurs to development. Plans, particularly strategic plans, are important aids to fundraising because they inform and inspire donors as to what their gifts will do for the faculty, the students, and the institutions they support.

A good institutional, school, or department level plan contains:

- An assessment of the strengths and weaknesses of what is already in place for development for faculty of various levels and statuses.

- A statement of possible actions at each level.

- An analysis of actions that can be taken with current authority and resources.

- A set of priorities for implementation.

- A plan to develop future resources to address additional priorities.

- An aspirational timetable for implementation with assignments of who is responsible.

Having said this, it is important to realize that the best way to get things done in a university is to respond to opportunities as they arise. Such opportunities may include finding an individual or group that is enthusiastic about an area of improvement and will work to make it happen, receiving a gift from a prominent donor, or capitalizing on an immediate crisis that can show the need for faculty development policies, programs, or positions.

So, planning is important in order to identify needs and priorities and to create the resources that will make implementation possible. However, opportunity may determine the order in which the many differing needs are addressed. The most important thing is to proceed with a comprehensive view of the needs and to persist until the most pressing needs are addressed.

Nevertheless, it is reasonable to expect that it will take a decade of continuous effort to implement the comprehensive program I have set out here. In pursuit of a long-term vision, it is also reasonable to have the goal to make progress for some groups of faculty each year, e.g., extend mentoring, improve policies, add mid-career and senior faculty programs, increase training opportunities and faculty learning communities, etc. so as to make steady progress toward the comprehensive program that I have set out as the gold standard.

5. Programs of particular importance to senior faculty

I have suggested that the senior faculty career trajectory may be divided into three broad periods:

- Peak performance (50-58)

- Last hurrahs (59-65)

- Pre-retirement (66-75)

Rick Reis summarized the results of several national studies of SFD needs. (22) Readers can use this framework as a checklist to see if their institution provides some or all of these programs for their senior faculty. See Figure 4.3. Programs listed combine all three levels: personal, functional, and institutional.

EXHIBIT 4.3: PRIORITY SERVICES FOR SENIOR FACULTY DEVELOPMENT

1. Career development planning and life planning, e.g., career development and goal-setting workshops.

2. Support for career development:

    a. Targeted grant monies to present at scholarly conferences and to network with colleagues within and across disciplines.

    b. Increasing graduate assistant support for teaching and/or research.

---

3. Improvement of recognition:

   a. Department-wide recognition of faculty accomplishments related to research, teaching, and service.

   b. Recognition of faculty service roles and accomplishments in newsletters, on web sites, and through interdepartmental correspondence.

   c. Explicit recognition of career accomplishments within the department and across the institution at the point of retirement.

4. Life balance programs and policies:

   a. Time management workshops, as well as workshops on handling email, scheduling, and stress management.

   b. Flexible and updated workload policies, e.g., allowing individual faculty members to "stack" teaching into one semester, allowing more uninterrupted time in the other semester for research or for new course development.

5. End of career services:

   a. Retirement planning workshops.

   b. Phased retirement programs.

6. People

In addressing inclusion issues for senior faculty who are women and/or under-represented minorities, sensitivity is the key.

The main message for chairs, deans, and institute heads who lead academic units is that they should show appreciation for all faculty at this stage and be conscious of what might be helpful to them at this stage of the career. But what is valuable for the typical professor at this stage will be doubly valuable for the senior faculty member who is a woman or under-represented minority. Given all the obstacles they may have faced in their careers, these individuals "have fought the good fight," they have persevered, and some will have been scarred along the way.

It is sobering to reflect on the experiences of under-represented faculty members I have known who are now in late career. Some have been extraordinarily successful and seem to be exemplars of what is possible when there is a truly inclusive climate and how both the institution and the individual benefit. Some have taken their hits but continued in spite of difficulties and continue to make contributions up to and beyond retirement. However, I have also seen: faculty members of color and women who have achieved full professor status but never felt accepted by the institution; very talented faculty who gave of themselves to serve students and the institution but never got full professor status; and some who have become embittered and resentful because of what they have had to endure.

As senior faculty members, many may be in a position to make their greatest contribution in the next decade or so.

Given the importance of diversity and inclusion goals, it makes sense for deans and chairs to work closely and collaboratively with their senior faculty of color, senior women faculty, and other senior faculty members who represent a dimension of difference that has been historically subject to discrimination. They are potential role models for faculty at lower ranks and how they are treated will be seen as a marker of inclusive the climate really is.

Helpful measures for these faculty members include:

- Mark the transition to full professor.

- Have the serious career conversation.

- Provide guidance on next steps that are possible, e.g., distinguished professorships.

- Provide opportunities for leaves, conferences, and workshops that may lead to new directions and accomplishments.

- Link to peers with whom senior faculty can share experience.

- Tap their expertise as mentors.

- Provide paths and guidance for academic leadership positions for those interested.

- For those who want it, provide counseling or coaching to enable them to come to terms with their career journey so far and to move to the next stage of their life.

I think the most important thing is that these activities be carried out with respect and appreciation for the individual and sensitivity to their career experience and their perspective on their career and accomplishments. Some will have been pioneers and activists and will want that recognized. Others will consider themselves as faculty members who happened to be female, black, or Hispanic and will not want minority status emphasized in any recognition. Each person will have their own perspective on the journey and what the next stage might hold.

7. Provision

Change usually involves incurring costs. Part of the reason change is needed in the first place is because we systematically underfunded certain functions, such as faculty development, and we are now paying the piper. Some of these costs are incurred in terms of time spent, emotional energy, dealing with conflict and the like. On the other hand, some costs are of the traditional variety, i.e., in dollars and cents. I have talked about the need for additional programming, for staff to implement that programming, and for additional policies and senior administrators who have it in their job descriptions to implement these policies. Institutions will need to allocate scarce resources to bring about change and improvement in faculty retention.

There are limits to funding that can be diverted to other priorities, constraints on raising tuition, and also increasing limits on governmental allocations either from legislatures or from federal grant sources. So, to the extent these funds can be raised through work with outside donors, the institution's financial position will be strengthened.

Accordingly, we must have institutional advancement and development staff who will take the time to understand the importance of faculty development through the career cycle, and we will need chairs and deans who will work closely with them to make faculty development programs a priority for fundraising. Donors already understand the importance of distinguished professorships and targeted awards for particular faculty achievements. It is also possible to educate them about the importance of funding faculty development initiatives at all levels including senior faculty. These include outside funding for each category of programming I have talked about in this chapter: individual programming, functional programming, and institutional level supports.

With respect to individual programming, funds could be raised to recognize and reward faculty mentors, or to provide career workshops for planning. With respect to functional programming, outside funds could support research leaves and travel, seminars in engaged scholarship and public service for faculty, and teaching and learning support programs. With respect to institutional level programs, external funding could go to support new positions and institutions that provide faculty development services.

During my years at UNC-CH, advancement officers, the senior administration, and committed faculty leaders were very successful in bringing in private funds to support faculty programs. (23) These included:

- $50,000,000 over 25 years to support an interdisciplinary Humanities Center that provided research leaves to faculty members.

- Several programs that provided tens of millions of dollars to health scientists for startup innovative research projects.

- Discretionary funds for department chairs to provide small amounts to support a variety of faculty initiatives.

- Funds to support and recognize faculty mentors.

- Funds for senior faculty leadership development programs.

No doubt you can identify similar examples on your campuses where enterprising faculty leaders and supportive donors have built partnerships around the needs to recruit, retain, and develop the best faculty and to support faculty through the career cycle. Academic Impressions and various professional associations and consulting groups have developed numerous resources to support the advancement efforts at institutions of higher education. If your institution has not already done so, this may be the time to make faculty development one area of focus for your institution's advancement efforts.

No robust plan of faculty development can be truly successful unless it is supported by substantial resources. Donor funding may be the key to realization of many efforts discussed in this chapter.

Summary

I have covered a lot of ground in this chapter, including a discussion of the needs of senior faculty members for late stage career development services—one that builds on programs and policies that have assisted faculty at various stages of the career ladder. I am now in a position to summarize the main argument of this book: That institutions of higher education should address the entire faculty career in the design, creation, and implementation of mentoring and faculty development programs, including tenured, tenure-track, and fixed-term.

In Chapters 1-4, I have described in detail the components of such a comprehensive effort. Exhibits 4.4 and 4.5, which will conclude this chapter, pull all of this together in outline form—in an attempt to summarize a comprehensive approach to faculty development throughout the faculty life cycle.

> ### EXHIBIT 4.4: CHECKLIST FOR INSTITUTIONAL EFFECTIVENESS IN FACULTY MENTORING AND FACULTY DEVELOPMENT—DEAN AND CHAIRS LEVEL
>
> - Does your school or department:
>
>   o Articulate clear principles about the support for faculty development throughout the life cycle? Include faculty of all statuses: fixed-term, adjunct, tenure track, part-time and full?
>
>   o Have policies that make that support tangible and specific?
>
>   o Locate responsibility for carrying out those policies in specific associate deans, chairs, or faculty committees?
>
>   o Encourage and support meaningful career conversations for all levels of faculty including senior faculty?

**EXHIBIT 4.4, CONTINUED:
CHECKLIST—DEAN AND CHAIRS LEVEL**

- o Actively work to help faculty obtain resources needed to achieve goals that come out those career conversations?

- Are there some school or department leaders who clearly have faculty development as part of their job descriptions?

- Is there a way for these leaders to get information about latest research and trends in faculty development?

- Is there some way for your faculty development leaders to connect to institution level groups who are thinking about and planning faculty development campus-wide?

- Do your faculty development leaders at the unit level have a clear understanding of the needs of faculty at each stage of their career and the needs of the tenure track, fixed-term, as well as adjunct faculty who have specialized roles?

- Are there processes in place to monitor the satisfaction, morale, and development needs of each level and status of the faculty in your school or department?

- Is there a long-term plan for faculty development for the school or department that seeks to develop solutions and improvements for each level of faculty member?

- Is faculty development a key component of any institutional fundraising efforts by the school or department?

EXHIBIT 4.4, CONTINUED:
CHECKLIST—DEAN AND CHAIRS LEVEL

- Does your unit plan include:

  o   Faculty mentoring for early career faculty of all statuses?

  o   A robust program to help mid-career faculty address the challenges they typically face?

  o   Programs to address senior faculty needs at peak career (age 50-57); late career (age 58-65); transition to retirement (age 65-75), and post- retirement?

  o   Faculty mentoring and faculty development programs?

- Does your school or unit make provision for identifying and addressing the particular needs and issues of women, under-represented minority faculty, LBGTQ+ faculty, international faulty, and faculty with disabilities?

- Do you have ways to continually assess the effectiveness of your programs and gauge the satisfaction of senior faculty members?

EXHIBIT 4.5: CHECKLIST FOR INSTITUTIONAL EFFECTIVENESS IN FACULTY MENTORING AND FACULTY DEVELOPMENT— INSTITUTIONAL LEVEL

- Does your institution articulate clear principles about the support for faculty development throughout the life cycle? And for faculty of all statuses: fixed-term, adjunct, tenure track, part-time and full?

    o Do you provide institutional policies that make that support tangible and specific?

    o Does your institution locate responsibility for carrying out those policies in specific, capable organizations and officials?

    o Do those officials clearly have faculty development as part of their job descriptions?

    o Is there a program of education and training in place for all who have faculty development in their portfolio?

    o Is there some kind of central coordination or community of practice in existence for these officials?

- Do the leaders of the institution and faculty leaders have a clear understanding of the needs of faculty at each stage of their career on the tenure track, fixed-term, as well as adjunct faculty who have specialized roles?

- Are there processes in place to monitor the satisfaction, morale, and development needs of each level and status of the faculty?

EXHIBIT 4.5, CONTINUED:
CHECKLIST—INSTITUTIONAL LEVEL

- Is there a long-term plan for faculty development that seeks to develop solutions and improvements for each level of faculty member?

- Is faculty development a key component of any institutional fundraising campaign?

- Does your institutional plan include:

  o Faculty mentoring for early career faculty of all statuses?

  o A robust program to help mid-career faculty address the challenges they typically face?

  o Programs to address senior faculty needs at peak career (age 50-57); late career (age 58-65); transition to retirement (age 65-75), and post-retirement?

  o Faculty mentoring and faculty development programs?

- Does your institution make provision for identifying and addressing the particular needs and issues of women, under-represented minority faculty, LBGTQ+ faculty, international faulty, and faculty with disabilities?

- Do you have ways to continually assess the effectiveness of your programs and gauge the satisfaction of senior faculty members pre- and post-retirement?

- Is the institutional advancement staff fully educated about and sufficiently motivated to make faculty development a key focus of external fundraising efforts?

Notes

1. Quoted in Rick Reiss, "Understanding Senior Faculty Needs," *Tomorrow's Professor* (blog), https://tomprof.stanford.edu/posting/793. Reiss summarizes a study of faculty in three large university systems: Berberet, J., et al. "Planning for the generational turnover of the faculty: Faculty perceptions and institutional practices." Clark, R. and J. Ma (Eds.), *Recruitment, Retention, and Retirement in Higher Education: Building and Managing the Faculty of the Future*. Cheltenham, UK: Elgar, 2005, p. 80-100.

2. See "Report of the Task Force on Senior Faculty Development," Johns Hopkins University School of Medicine, Nov. 1, 2017:

    https://www.hopkinsmedicine.org/fac_developm ent/sr-faculty-retirement- resources/_documents/senior-faculty-task-force- report.PDF

3. See Bland, Carol J. and Berquist, William H. "Conclusions and Themes to Guide Approaches to the Vitality of Senior Faculty," *The Vitality of Senior Faculty Members: Snow on the Roof--Fire in the Furnace*. George Washington University Press, 1997, pp. 83-118. Bland and Berquist take the position that senior faculty are highly productive and that this resource should be nurtured and developed. In Roger Baldwin and Carol Chang's Fall 2006 article in *Liberal Education*, "Reinforcing Our Strategies To Support Faculty During The Middle Years Of Academic Life," they call these faculty members the "keystone."

4. At the time of this book's publication, a copy of their report is available for download at: https://www.rit.edu/academicaffairs/facultydevel opment/sites/rit.edu.academicaffairs.facultydevel opment/files/images/FCDS_Mid-CareerRpt.pdf

5. See Benevino, David, and Davis Attis, *Supporting the Productivity of Faculty After Tenure*, University Leadership Council, 2012.

   See also June, Audrey Williams. "Most Professors Hate Post-Tenure Review. A Better Approach Might Look Like This," *Chronicle of Higher Education*, February 11, 2018.

   See also Vance, Erik. "President of Missouri State U. Threatens to Shut Social-Work School After Scathing Report," *The Chronicle of Higher Education*, April 20, 2017.

6. See page 4 of this report from the University Leadership Council (2012), which can be accessed at:

   http://cte.tcu.edu/wp-content/uploads/Supporting-Faculty-Productivity-After-Tenure_EAB.pdf

7. See the Johns Hopkins School of Medicine's Task Force on Senior Faculty Support and Transition, "Summary Report to Dean Paul Rothman": https://www.hopkinsmedicine.org/fac_developm ent/sr-faculty-retirement-resources/_documents/senior-faculty-task-force-report.PDF

   Also, see the Carnegie Mellon faculty handbook:

https://engineering.cmu.edu/faculty-staff/policies-procedures/faculty-policies.html

8. See "Getting and Giving Career Advice," prepared by the Advance Program at the University of Michigan: https://advance.umich.edu/resources/

9. For examples, see the following sites:

https://www.whatsnext.com

https://academiccoachingandwriting.org/about-acw/our-coaches

https://www.facultydiversity.org/meet-our-coaches

https://www.huffingtonpost.com/david-goldberg/5-times-in-a-career-when-b_3347761.html

10. See Robinson, S., and C. Gray, "Agents of Transformational Change, Coaching Skills for Academic Leaders," *Journal on Excellence in College Teaching*, vol. 28, no. 4, 2017, pp. 5-28.

11. In *Career Dynamics* (Addison Wesley, 1978), MIT Professor Ed Schein has pointed out that there are predictable crisis points in careers when family issues, physical and psychological developmental stages, and career stages (e.g., tenure, promotion, retirement) all intersect.

12. See Canale, Anne Marie, et al. "Mid-Career Faculty Support: The Middle Years of the Academic Profession" The Wallace Center, Rochester Institute of Technology, 2013.

13. For a sampling of how universities are supporting senior faculty research efforts see the following websites.

    http://arts-sciences.buffalo.edu/faculty-staff/faculty-staff-resources/faculty-funding.html

    https://faculty.dartmouth.edu/dean/research-teaching-support/internal-awards-and-fellowships/tenured-and-tenure-track-faculty-funding/senior-faculty-grants

    http://www.elon.edu/e-web/academics/teacsch.xhtml

    https://www.elon.edu/u/faculty/funding/

    https://maincampusresearch.georgetown.edu/senior-faculty-research-fellowship

    http://www.ou.edu/research-norman/about/research-council/funding-opportunities/arts-humanities-faculty-fellowship-program

14. See: https://cft.vanderbilt.edu/guides-sub-pages/grant-funding/

15. For detail on issues and opportunities in linking senior faculty to technologies to improve teaching, see the following articles:

    Carey, Jennifer. "How to Get Hesitant Teachers to Use Technology," *Powerful Learning Practice Network*, March 27, 2013. http://plpnetwork.com/2013/03/27/hesitant-teachers-technology/

"Innovators Among Us: Using Technology to Engage Students," *Provost's Letter*, University of Washington, November 2014.

http://www.washington.edu/provost/files/2012/11/edtrends-Innovators_Among_Us_Using_Technology_to_Engage_Students.pdf

Winston, Hannah. "Helping Professors Use Technology Is Top Concern in Computing Survey," *The Chronicle of Higher Education,* October 17, 2013. https://www.chronicle.com/article/Helping-Faculty-Members-Use/142377

St. Martin, Greg. "Tips, Resources to Bring Technology to Teaching," *News@Northeastern*, September 6, 2017. https://news.northeastern.edu/2017/09/tips-resources-to-bring-technology-to-teaching/

Redden, Elizabeth. "Teaching with Tech Across Borders," *Inside Higher Ed,* July 9, 2014. https://www.insidehighered.com/news/2014/07/09/faculty-use-internet-based-technologies-create-global-learning-opportunities

16. For more detail see:
https://college.unc.edu/2014/05/01/stemclass/

17. See Kiel, David. "Creating a Faculty Leadership Development Program," Academic Impressions, December 2015. https://www.academicimpressions.com/blog/creating-a-faculty-leadership-development-program/

See also Gmelch, Walter H., and Jeffrey L. Buller, *Building Academic Leadership Capacity: A Guide to Best Practices*, Jossey Bass, 2015.

18. See the following faculty handbooks, available online:

    https://www.provost.iastate.edu/faculty-and-staff-resources/faculty-handbook

    https://internal.simmons.edu/~/media/Simmons/Academics/CAS/Internal/Documents/Faculty-Policy-Manual.ashx?la=en

19. For examples of leadership development programs that support senior faculty members, see the following sites:

    Case Western Reserve:
    http://case.edu/facultydevelopment/career-path/faculty-leadership-development/

    Iowa State:
    https://www.provost.iastate.edu/faculty-and-staff-resources/development/fellowship

    Michigan State:
    https://msutoday.msu.edu/news/2017/msu-leaders-named-academic-leadership-program-fellows/

    Stanford University:
    https://facultydevelopment.stanford.edu/programs/leadership-development

    University of Illinois Chicago:
    https://faculty.uic.edu/files/2016/11/FALP-Description.pdf

    Virginia Tech:
    https://advance.vt.edu/content/dam/advance_vt_edu/documents/presentations/faculty_leadership_development_outcomes_presentation.pdf

20. See this Associate Dean for Faculty Affairs job description at St. Lawrence University:

    https://www.stlawu.edu/sites/default/files/resource/PositionDescriptionAssocDeanFacAffairs.pdf

21. For a sampling of how these positions are structured and advertised, see:

    https://www.indeed.com/q-Associate-Dean-For-Faculty-Affairs-Faculty-Development-jobs.html

    https://www.glassdoor.com/Job/assistant-dean-of-faculty-development-jobs-SRCH_KO0,37.htm

    https://www.higheredjobs.com/admin/search.cfm?JobCat=148

22. At the time of this book's publication, this report may be accessed at: https://tomprof.stanford.edu/posting/793

23. For detail on gifts to UNC that provide faculty development opportunities, see:

    https://pharmacy.unc.edu/news/2014/12/03/100-million-eshelman-gift-to-fund-innovation-is-largest-ever-to-a-pharmacy-school/

    https://college.unc.edu/2014/12/deangift/

    https://socialinnovation.unc.edu/spaces/gillings-innovation-labs/

CHAPTER 5
TO GET STARTED AND KEEP GOING: 10 EFFECTIVE PRACTICES

This chapter is addressed directly to academic leaders who are charged with program implementation. The introduction and the previous four chapters have mostly provided the *why* and the *what* of faculty mentoring programs with multiple case examples and options to choose from. This chapter—and the extensive workbook that follows in Appendix B—are intended to provide the "how."

NOTE TO THE READER

The message of this chapter is: build for the long-term, build for genuine and lasting impact, build on the foundation of internal motivation and commitment, and build in a way that suits your institution. This effort may take 2-3 years to really embed and become self-sustaining. However, the result will be a shift in the institutional culture toward more intentional support and activity for faculty development. Each step recommended in this chapter builds awareness, creates involvement, and installs effective programs.

In this chapter, I will introduce and illustrate ten important practices in implementing effective faculty mentoring practices on your campus:

1. Be mindful of existing policies and directives at higher levels

2. Assess your existing assets and build from you have in place

3. Set priorities based on peer research related to faculty recruitment and retention

4. Involve faculty in the planning

5. Establish policies that produce action at your level

6. Provide support for implementation

7. Centralize or de-centralize mentoring services to fit your situation

8. Address needs of smaller units

9. Invest in the time of staff and faculty to implement mentoring activities

10. Follow through on implementation with clear, supportive, and continuing leadership

Taken together, these ten practices constitute a roadmap for initiating, implementing, and sustaining effective faculty mentoring efforts. (1)

These ten practices apply equally whether you are a program director, chair, dean, or head of a cross-campus center, or in the provost's office. In the following pages, I will give examples for readers who have a variety of positions on campus but want to make a sustainable change in mentoring practices and culture in the unit, school, or campus-wide.

1. Be Mindful of Existing Policies and Directives

As a mentoring program leader or department chair, your role is to design a new program or strengthen an existing one. In all cases, you have the task of motivating busy people to do more or do things differently. If you are a chair or program director, it makes sense to have a detailed understanding of the policies and directives that exist at the school, campus or university system level, even to the extent of talking with the administrators of those programs so you can speak with your colleagues with firsthand knowledge of what the higher-ups are thinking and planning. As a consequence, you will be able to realistically state the consequences for the unit of not acting and the external benefits for the unit (in terms of its political positioning) of moving forward on the mentoring issues, while emphasizing the intrinsic benefits. Similarly, if you are a dean who or associate dean who is contemplating school-wide action, it is good to understand the plans and preferences of the provost and communicate them to your chairs or division leaders so they also know the degree to which participation in any program is required or voluntary. This understanding will shape the parameters of the program that you design.

2. Assess Current Practices and Existing Resources—Build from What You Have in Place

Assess current practices

Almost all campus change is resisted in some quarters, but the arguments of naysayers are undermined when you can show that several units on your campus or other colleagues in the department have already implemented the changes you are suggesting and that they have experienced positive results. Organizational leaders, it turns out, particularly when their institutions are large and complex, often lack knowledge of all the good practices that are taking place in various units. This is also true at the department level since much faculty work is so individual. But how do you know "who is doing what," when there are multiple departments, schools, and other units on campus?

One way is to do a systematic assessment of existing faculty mentoring practices. This could be at the department level, the school level, or the campus level.

If working campus-wide from the provost's or president's office, a personal phone interview with deans and chairs is arguably the best approach, though it is time consuming. There are so many surveys people are asked to fill out and there is no guarantee that the information that is desired will actually be collected in an anonymous survey. But, if someone from the provost's office calls each dean or department chair and asks them to share their best practices in mentoring that are now going on, that accomplishes several purposes:

- It lets the mid-level leader know this is of interest to the senior leadership.

- It gives the provost a chance to "catch someone doing something right."

- It provides a fine-grained understanding of the diversity of situations that units face relative to mentoring.

- It uncovers good practices that can be shared with others and used to show skeptics that what is wanted not only can be done but has been done.

- It might show that the main effort needs to be in certain parts of campus or certain levels of faculty.

- It can uncover problems that might be encountered in implementation and what assistance might be needed for implementation.

In Exhibit 5.1, I share an example of such a survey protocol and the type of results achieved. Critical to the success of this strategy is a good write-up of any interview, checking back with the person interviewed for accuracy, and approval that the results can be shared with others on the campus.

Q. Please tell me about your department's approach to faculty mentoring? What is it, what are the goals and tell me a little bit about the history of how it got started. My task is to document departmental and school practices for the provost. I will let you review the notes from this interview.

A. We used to be "just let it happen," but now we have a well-defined program. Several years back we had one tenure case bounced back at the college level, and this was a wake-up call that pushed us to better define and structure our effort. We currently have three assistant professors in a department of about 20 full-time faculty, about half of whom are full professors. We just promoted three to associate professor.

We felt a new approach to our mentoring program was needed because our faculty was growing. In our field there are wide differences between the training and methodologies in each subfield. We no longer all speak the same technical language or publish in the same journals, and thus a diverse committee model is necessary.

Q. Please describe how it works in some detail: who mentors, how are mentors chosen and linked with those they mentor, etc.

A. For each assistant professor, we have two people who serve on the mentoring committee and are appointed by the department chair. One person, usually the mentoring committee chair, is very close to the new faculty member (NFM) in terms of research interest, and another person is deliberately chosen to come from an unrelated subfield.

EXHIBIT 5.1, CONTINUED: INTERVIEW WITH A STEM DEPARTMENT CHAIR AT A PUBLIC UNIVERSITY, PROVIDING A PROGRAM DESCRIPTION

The rationale is that when it comes to third year review and promotion review, the NFM should have an advocate outside the field who has taken the trouble to understand what the NFM is doing, at least at the level of whether peers in the field see it as strong work. If all things go well in the first several years, then the new faculty member will have two advocates when the case goes to the whole faculty.

In setting up the mentoring committee, I meet with the person who is going to be the chair and confirm their willingness to serve, then I also make sure that person is OK with my second appointment, and then I go ahead and talk with the second person.

Q. How often do mentors and mentees meet, and how do you keep track of progress, if at all?

A. The two-person committee meets twice a year with the mentee, at least once per semester. This is not necessarily a long meeting, but it permits the mentors to check with the mentee about how he or she is following up on past advice relative to papers, conferences and professional visibility, teaching, etc. The goal here is to make sure there are no surprises when the three-year review comes around. We hope the relationship will be one of trust and that a good relationship will build. I require the committee to send me an email confirming the meeting took place, that is all.

In the spring all the senior faculty review the progress and then the two-committee members take the perceptions of the senior faculty and translate them into feedback for the candidate.

Exhibit 5.1, Continued: Interview with a STEM Department Chair at a Public University, Providing a Program Description

I use that feedback to structure my annual review. We have a written template for this that covers the main issues. The committee sits in on the review so they can follow up with the mentee. In this way, the whole senior faculty is involved with the progress of the candidate, not just the chair or the committee.

Q. How satisfied are you with your program, how might you improve it?

A. We are hopeful this process will prove to be valuable in the long run and our early experiences with the new approach have been positive.

Once this data is collected and collated from a number of units (by whatever method), it is important to share it with deans and chairs so they can see who is doing what currently. This may be enough of a "word to the wise" to get something going in some units. For those slow on the uptake, there is a strong basis for saying: "If they can do it, why can't you?" See Exhibit 5.4 for a summary report that demonstrates that there is progress already being made, with the implication that it can be built on.

If, on the other hand, we are talking about a small department, then the person charged to set up a mentoring program—perhaps a chair or vice chair—might be better off holding informal conversations. See Exhibit 5.3 for a sample script for such an informal conversation.

EXHIBIT 5.2: SCRIPT FOR A CONVERSATION ABOUT MENTORING NEEDS WITH JUNIOR & SENIOR FACULTY

You may know the chair has asked me to gather information and make a report at a faculty meeting of what we might do in response to the dean's request that we do more to "formalize our faculty mentoring programs." Here are a few things I would like to talk to you about and take some notes as we talk. I want to use your ideas but I won't quote you in the report.

To what extent have you benefitted from mentoring by colleagues in the department? How did that come about?

What are you aware of that we are doing for our faculty in terms of mentoring or general assistance?

What do you think are the unmet needs, if any, for early career faculty or associate faculty in the department, and for non-tenure-track faculty?

Which of these should be addressed first, assuming we have to set priorities, and why?

Would you be interested in participating in any new mentoring initiative that we set up? If so, how?

For a larger group, such as the faculty of a school or the faculty of an especially large department, it may be more efficient to deploy a well-crafted survey using Likert-scaled items. (See Exhibit 5.3 for an example.)

EXHIBIT 5.3: SAMPLE NEEDS ASSESSMENT SURVEY

Circle the number that best corresponds to your view. Please use the following scale:

> 5 - strongly agree
> 4 - agree
> 3 - neither agree nor disagree
> 2 - disagree
> 1 - strongly disagree

1. The arrangements in the department for mentoring faculty on the tenure track are working well.

> 5   4   3   2   1

2. The arrangements in the department for mentoring contract early career faculty who want to advance to the associate level are working well.

> 5   4   3   2   1

3. Associate professors who are tenured but not yet full professor need better mentoring.

> 5   4   3   2   1

4. Associate professors who are not tenured need better mentoring.

> 5   4   3   2   1

5. Developing new mentoring programs and practices should be a high priority for the department in the coming year.

> 5   4   3   2   1

In one paragraph below, please give the rationale for your answers to these questions. (Your answers will be kept anonymous, and any identifying comments will be removed.)

Any survey that arrives via an email will need to have been prefaced by discussion at a faculty meeting and should be accompanied by a note from the dean or chair explaining the context.

One consideration is that unless there is a large number of potential respondents, it may be difficult to assure anonymity. For example, it may be difficult to ask the respondents to reveal their ranks if there are only five or six faculty members at each level.

EXHIBIT 5.4: SAMPLE SUMMARY REPORT

Preliminary Presentation of Findings of Unit-Based Mentoring Program Surveys in 2015-16 at a Public Research University: 12 Program Dimensions.

Seventeen interviews and profiles have been completed to date. Those interviewed were mentoring program leader units with established faculty mentoring programs. Six were Health Science Units. Seven were in the College of Arts and Sciences, including each of the four divisions, and four were in other professional schools.

1. **Goals:** Most of the 17 unit-based programs profiled have the goal of supporting early career faculty through the tenure and promotion process. All address the needs of tenure track faculty in this regard, though some include fixed-term faculty, and make mentors available to interested associate professors.

2. **Size:** Most involve mentoring committees with as few as two mentors and as many as five mentors serving.

3. **Program models:** Two units rely on a single mentor, and two units rely on an associate dean as the primary mentor and address other needs through a group mentoring program or through a series of career development activities for early career faculty that are distinct from the mentoring effort.

4. **Role in faculty evaluation:** Some units exclude mentor information from evaluation processes, while other units seek input from mentoring committees. However, in all cases the formal evaluation of the faculty member's progress or promotion rests with the relevant chair, division head, or dean.

5. **Budget:** Most unit-based programs have little or no budgets or expenditures. Only one provides a stipend to the mentor (through a special endowment). For all others, mentoring is considered a form of departmental service.

6. **Costs:** Mentoring costs consist largely of time spent in the mentoring process.

7. **Required participation:** Participation of early career faculty is required or strongly encouraged, and according to reports, almost all faculty are happy to participate.

8. **Frequency of mentoring meetings:** In units where there are mentoring committees, these are required at least once a year and as many as three times a semester. Informal meetings often occur more frequently between faculty members and mentors.

9. **Who initiates:** Four units place the responsibility for calling meetings on the early career faculty members. Other units expect mentoring committees to take a lead role in initiating meetings and discussions.

10. **Reporting:** Seven units require an annual written report of mentoring progress and eleven do not. Some units think documentation is essential for an effective program, and some others think it gets in the way of a supportive relationship.

11. **Additional activities:** Ten units have topical seminars, social events, or peer sessions as a part of their programs to support early career faculty.

12. **Administration:** Larger units appoint a mentoring program director since there may be a score or more committees to keep track of. Some support staff time is dedicated to tracking and administration in larger units. Smaller units may rely on an associate dean or vice chair to manage the mentoring program.

Assess existing resources

On many campuses, academic units do not have to provide all the mentoring resources their faculty need from within their own walls. Those developing department and school-based mentoring programs should investigate other resources that may be available on campus, such as the Center for Teaching and Learning, the Office of Research, the Campus Mental Health Services, the Campus Writing Center, the Ombuds Office, the Campus Diversity Program, and the Office of Human Resources. Some of these programs can be excellent referral sources for mentoring committees when particular needs arise, such as deficits in teaching or research, health problems, conflicts, etc.

Sometimes faculty members affiliate with strong inter-disciplinary centers. In my conversation with one chair about their mentoring approach, he said that while he provided the new faculty members guidance on promotion and tenure rules and process, the substantive guidance in research often came through their affiliation with one or more of the strong interdisciplinary centers on campus. In the medical school and in health sciences, often research training may be obtained through programs set up to mentor faculty in translational and other forms of research. At UNC-CH's School of Medicine, the NIH funded Clinical Translation Science Program will match young health science researchers with more senior researchers in their field as a starting point for mentoring relationships.

3. Set Priorities Based on Peer Research Relative to Faculty Recruitment and Retention

Mentoring programs for faculty are primarily justified on the basis that they help in recruiting and retaining faculty by increasing chances for promotion and retention, and by accelerating faculty productivity. If you know where you stand with respect to peer institutions, then you will better understand whether your mentoring effort has the potential of making your campus a peer leader, helping your campus stay competitive, or correcting a serious deficit.

Understanding this can help in setting priorities for program development and allocating resources. Institutions can gather this information by cooperative agreement, by review of websites, by informal sleuthing, and by sharing results of surveys such as the COACHE program, operated by the Harvard School of Education. COACHE provides faculty exit surveys and faculty satisfaction surveys that can be compared with results of a selected group of peer institutions. (2)

When North Carolina State University (NCSU) compared results with its peers (Iowa State University, Purdue University, University of Arizona, UC-Davis, and Virginia Tech); on the 2015 COACHE survey, it found that NCSU scores on most dimensions were in line with their peers, though it lagged in the quality of benefits. There were several areas, though, in which NCSU stood out positively, e.g., quality of interdisciplinary programs. This suggests that the strategic function of NCSU's mentoring efforts might be to make NCSU a great place for faculty to work, compensating for the lag in benefits. (3) (Benefits is an area the university has relatively little control over since, in NC, they are determined by state benefit policies.)

When a University of Minnesota team compared their early career faculty scores on a variety of dimensions, they found a need to improve on a number of dimensions: expectations for teachers, assistance in seeking grants, work-life balance, and opportunities for interaction with junior and senior faculty. Their study went on to do best practice benchmarking for mentoring programs at five aspirational peer institutions. (4) This initiative identified specific areas where faculty development efforts could be focused to improve faculty satisfaction and, arguably, retention.

It would probably make the most sense for chairs and deans to benchmark departments' and schools' mentoring approaches against those of peer institutions but also other comparable departments and schools on the same campus. So, when the chair of History at UNC-CH determined that the History department could improve its already relatively effective mentoring program, the chair appointed a committee of faculty who benchmarked what UNC was doing against peer departments at Emory and Michigan to determine what additional components could be added to the program. It would also be a relatively simple project to compare the department's program with other units of the same size and comparable disciplines (e.g., a history department would compare its approach to other comparable humanities or social science units on campus).

4. Involve Faculty in the Planning

At the school or department level, a tried and true method of involvement is to appoint a faculty committee to look into the adequacy of current mentoring practices and the potential for improvement. The key to success is to appoint a faculty member who has the confidence of the department and to thoughtfully consider the composition so various perspectives are represented. Any committee would be helped by a clear description of the charge and a date by which to report. (See Exhibit 5.5.)

EXHIBIT 5.5: SAMPLE "CHARGE TO THE MENTORING COMMITTEE"

From: The Chair
To: The Faculty Mentoring Committee
Re: Charge to the committee

During the fall, the mentoring committee will survey all members of the department to assess their views about how well the department's current mentoring practices are working and what, if any, improvements are needed. Specifically, the committee will recommend whether mentoring services should be extended to contract faculty and how this should best be accomplished. In making their recommendations, the committee should take into account the relevant experience of other departments in the division and peer units around the country.

The mentoring committee will provide a written report by Feb. 1, and its recommendations will be discussed at the March faculty meeting.

Change at the campus level is a bit more complicated but the same principles apply. In many universities and colleges, there is a traditional and often wise reluctance of administrators to impose demands upon already strapped and sometimes struggling faculty units, even when these demands "are for their own good." Instead, it is important to prepare the ground and to generate broad campus support for any faculty development initiative. Here is where the faculty committee comes in.

If there is a strong tradition of faculty governance, the faculty senate or council should be involved. The key is to assure that this group is well led and adequately staffed. Any such faculty group that reviews the literature or campus practice will likely conclude there is a need for both policy and tangible support for faculty mentoring and faculty development. Senior leaders can then proceed to implement with clear support from faculty. This faculty group (with staff support) could conduct an assessment of existing mentoring practices on campus, highlight effective practices, and evaluate the level of mentoring support relative to peer institutions.

Faculty mentoring efforts at UNC-Chapel Hill received a big boost when a faculty sub-committee with representation from nine units (five departments and four schools) recommended establishing mentoring programs in each unit. The committee was one of five task forces and subcommittees studying promotion and tenure policies. Over forty faculty members served on the task force overall, including many respected faculty leaders from all parts of the campus. Exhibit 5.6 shows how the structure of a university-wide mentoring effort can be outlined in a faculty recommendation.

EXHIBIT 5.6: EXCERPT FROM THE UNC-CH PROVOST'S TASK FORCE ON FUTURE PROMOTION AND TENURE POLICIES AND PRACTICES

Jan 25, 2010. Subcommittee on Mentoring.

The full report may be accessed at:
https://provost.unc.edu/taskforce-future-promotion-tenure-policies-practices/

Recommendation #5: Ensure good mentoring of faculty.

1. All academic units that grant tenure and promotion should have a mentorship plan in place that is filed with the provost's office.

2. Mentorship training for promotion and tenure should be provided to all department chairs and school deans.

3. Senior faculty should be provided regular university-wide workshops on mentoring.

4. Mentorship should be part of the post-tenure review evaluation. In the provost's document, "Dossier: Format for Tenure Track or Tenured Faculty Review," the section that provides guidelines for the formatting of the chair's letter should be revised to instruct the chair to address the faculty member's mentorship as part of his or her service to the academic unit or larger university community.

5. Mentoring awards should be instituted by the University, College, Schools and departments.

6. A regular survey of early career faculty (perhaps in their fourth or fifth years) should be conducted to determine the state of mentorship on campus as well as the mentorship needs and expectations of early career faculty.

In the example given in Exhibit 5.6, the provost accepted the recommendations of the task force and assigned responsibility for implementation to the Center for Faculty Excellence, which reported to the executive vice provost. A new staff member was assigned responsibility for working with units to bring about the changes approved by the provost.

5. Establish Policies That Produce Action at Your Level

Once chairs or deans have studied the situation and engaged the faculty, they are in a position to craft tailored policies and programs for their campus. Leaders who get results do two things: 1) they communicate high expectations; and 2) they provide assistance and encouragement that helps those they lead to meet those expectations. If they have prepared the ground by involving faculty as recommended above, then setting high expectations will be seen as strong leadership and being "supportive" will be seen as responsive leadership.

Senior leaders, of course, have a major role in setting campus-wide policies that support adoption of faculty mentoring programs. They can also set the tone by requiring that academic units have written policies in place that provide for faculty mentoring appropriate to the units' needs and situations. Examples of leadership statements that define the institution's requirements for mentoring programs are readily available on the Internet. In Exhibit 5.7, I give give three examples from public universities that show how leaders at department, school and campus levels state minimum requirements for acceptable mentoring programs.

Example 1: A Health Sciences Department

The chair of a health science department I worked with issued new guidelines to govern the department's newly revised mentoring program in October 2013. These are the guidelines (edited for brevity).

Overview: We are piloting a new process for reviewing faculty progress toward promotion and/or tenure that incorporates the mentoring system recently put in place; this includes both tenure track and fixed-term faculty. A change in process is proposed in order to: 1) provide a more structured approach and support for departmental mentoring of our assistant and associate professors; 2) increase efficiencies within the department's operations related to our APT review process; and 3) provide more structured advice to faculty being reviewed. …

[The review will utilize existing standards and measures.]

Fall faculty review will occur sometime between October and December of each year. Faculty to be reviewed include all tenure track assistant and associate professors as well as fixed-term assistant or associate professors who have expressed interest in consideration for promotion. The reviewers will be the departmental APT committee that includes all tenured faculty members. The faculty being reviewed will not be present for the review and discussion. Their assigned mentor will provide feedback to the mentee after the meeting.

Prior to each Fall Faculty Review meeting, a set of materials will be assembled for each faculty member being reviewed and a primary reviewer will be assigned. The faculty member's assigned mentor will be present for the review but will not be assigned as the reviewer. …

**EXHIBIT 5.7, CONTINUED:
EXAMPLES OF LEADERSHIP GUIDANCE
FOR UNIT MENTORING PROGRAMS**

The chair's office will be responsible for the following tasks:

1. Scheduling the fall review and assigning reviewers.

2. Preparing an updated grant spreadsheet and asking for confirmation or correction of the information by the faculty being reviewed.

3. Assembling all of the documents and providing them to the faculty assigned to do the review at least three days prior to the scheduled review.

4. Making copies of these materials available prior to and at the review meeting for other faculty who would like to review the documents.

5. The chair will moderate the Fall Review meeting.

Prior to the meeting the faculty reviewer should review the assembled documents provided by the chair's office. ... To assist in the review, the faculty reviewer should examine the department's and the School's guidelines for faculty promotion.

At the meeting the reviewer should be prepared to briefly (in less than 10 minutes) recap the faculty's progress toward promotion/tenure with regard to:

1. Research (publications and research funding).

2. Teaching and mentoring.

3. Service and community engagement.

4. Special considerations and responsibilities as a fixed-term faculty.

5. The faculty's timeline for progress toward tenure and or promotion goals.

After the meeting, the mentor, who is an observer but not participant in the review, will write up and report the results of the review incorporating any additional comments from the chair. The mentor will provide the written report or the review to the faculty member being reviewed in a face-to-face discussion.

Example 2: A University System

The University of Colorado System and the Office of the President have issued a new Administrative Policy Statement (APS) on mentoring. This APS requires that all units with tenure-track faculty must create a formal mentoring process. We have provided information and models to help you in creating a process that works for you. All units should move to create mentoring procedures; reporting on mentoring practices has become a required part of program review, where units should either describe their mentoring process or describe how they are going about creating one. (5)

Example 3: A College of Natural Sciences

Michigan State University, College of Natural Sciences: ...
The structure of mentoring programs may also vary among units but must include the following elements:

EXHIBIT 5.7, CONTINUED:
EXAMPLES OF LEADERSHIP GUIDANCE
FOR UNIT MENTORING PROGRAMS

- A description of the mentor selection process, including the potential for mentors from outside of the department.

- Expectations for confidentiality and the role of the mentor(s).

- The duration of mentoring responsibilities and the process for changing mentors, including a provision for faculty members to choose not to have mentors.

- A description of expected mentoring activities, with elements addressing research, teaching, and leadership development.

- A description of how mentoring activities will be reported and evaluated.

- One or more senior faculty mentors for each early career faculty member, in addition to the unit executive officer. The mentors need not necessarily be from the unit. ... (6)

6. Provide Support for Implementation

If senior level leaders ask chairs and deans to establish new mentoring programs or strengthen existing programs according to new guidelines that set high expectations, then they should also provide support and assistance to implementing units. This assistance may include any of the following activities:

- Publishing and circulating exemplary policy statements.

- Providing models of exemplary programs via websites.

- Presenting panels and discussions that disseminate best practices.

- Supporting visitation to comparable universities and colleges that are farther along.

- Providing technical assistance and consulting to leaders who are trying to innovate in their units.

- Offering recognition and rewards for exemplary programs.

- Surveying and reporting on effective campus practices.

One of my jobs while working at the Center for Faculty Excellence was to support mentoring program development. Since the CFE was under the provost's office, I could work with any faculty unit. Working as a consultant to departments, I monitored the national literature, kept records of best practices, conducted surveys and assessments for various units, organized internal workshops, designed helpful forms and checklists for mentors and mentees, and consulted with chairs and deans about program designs. I also organized campus-wide education seminars and panels on mentoring topics. Having someone like myself in that position meant that any unit could get significant help in creating, extending, or improving their mentoring or broader faculty development services.

What deans can do

Deans can hold workshops for their department chairs or division heads in which they present guidelines for mentoring and discuss how they would adapt them to their units. Later, they can monitor how the process of implementation is going, to assure that the school's implementation is consistent with general guidelines.

What chairs/heads can do

They can assign a mentoring program coordinator and relieve that person of other service duties. They can also provide training and orientation sessions for mentors and mentees focused on the new guidelines. They can assure that evaluation occurs after the pilot year.

What leaders in general can do

Leaders at the campus, school, and department levels should assess their situation and consider what supports will make the most difference at their levels and implement those supports once the new policy has been set and distributed.

7. Centralize or De-centralize Mentoring Services (to Fit Your Situation)

Throughout this chapter, I have talked about the roles of chairs, deans, and senior faculty in implementing mentoring programs. Those roles will certainly vary depending on the size and nature of the campus. On campuses where departments are quite small, it probably makes sense to have mentoring programs centered in the provost's office or a faculty development unit, since small departments may not have the resources to develop their own programs. In larger universities, it may make the most sense for each of the larger schools to have their own faculty development support staff and for responsibility for programming to be fixed at the department level. The provost's office may retain standard-setting and monitoring functions.

In smaller colleges and universities, the deans may want to take on this responsibility themselves. In one College of Arts and Sciences at a prestigious mid-size private university I know of, the dean holds an annual meeting with all early career faculty members in each division (arts and humanities, natural sciences, and social sciences). She identifies the tenure track faculty's questions and concerns, and then the divisional deans follow up with the chairs that report to them.

Two-year colleges may organize by the same criteria: larger units may have their own programs, and centralized programs may serve smaller units—or in the case of a small campus, the entire institution.

However campus mentoring services are organized, they should provide access in several areas. These services should:

- Provide guidance for faculty members so that they fully understand the processes for promotion and tenure.

- Have a way to direct faculty to the guidance and training they might need to perform the functions required by the institution in terms of teaching, research, service, and leadership.

- Attend to the special needs of particular faculty groups who have historically faced unique challenges in navigating traditional academic cultures: e.g., under-represented minority faculty, women in STEM disciplines, international faculty, and LGBTQ+ faculty.

8. Address the Needs of Smaller Units

Small units in departments or colleges may have to get creative to address faculty needs. They may need to:

- Establish interdisciplinary peer mentoring groups with access to senior faculty advisors from multiple departments.

- Access off-campus resources (e.g., create small college consortia for faculty mentoring).

- Access resources across the discipline on other campuses.

- Make the most of web-based resources.

- Create campus-wide or school-wide orientation programs.

To the extent that smaller campuses lack programs that are targeted to each discipline, it becomes more important that the programs they do create equip faculty to advocate for mentorship on their own behalf and to reach out to resources outside their home units.

Peer mentoring groups is one possible solution. Interdisciplinary units such as centers for teaching and learning can be an important resource on small and large campuses. Susan L. Phillips and Susan T. Dennison give clear and detailed directions about how such units are able to set up peer mentoring groups in Chapter 2 of their mentoring manual. (7) In their model, effective peer mentoring groups meet about once a month for an academic year, and are composed of a diverse group of faculty members of the same rank but from different units. There are two facilitators for each group, and they say eight is the maximum effective size.

The facilitators are effective group leaders and knowledgeable about mentoring and promotion processes. Participants volunteer for the program and are interviewed by the group leaders before coming into the group. In their model, facilitators plan each session and front-load the program with informational and team building activities during the first semester. In the second semester, the group evolves into a support group with members expressing concerns and participants responding and with the facilitators serving as a reality check when necessary. Facilitators may meet one-on-one with a faculty member who needs special help. In the UNC-Greensboro program showcased in Exhibit 5.8, the sponsor is the University Teaching and Learning Center (UTLC).

EXHIBIT 5.8: UNC-GREENSBORO PEER FACULTY MENTORING PROGRAM

Source: https://utlc.uncg.edu/teaching/faculty-mentoring/about
(Edited for brevity.)

Since its inception (in 2008-9) the New Faculty Mentoring Program (NFMP) has brought senior and junior colleagues together for the purpose of supporting faculty development and enhancing the likelihood that our faculty community members would consistently choose to stay at UNCG in increasingly productive career paths. Program evaluation indicates a significant "holding power" effect of the program, with a 91% retention rate among faculty who complete the program. The 2015-16 academic year cohort of mentees is the first to include both non-tenure-track and tenure-track faculty…

The program aims to:

- Provide a variety of mentor-mentee and group-based interactions that nurture faculty through mutually appropriate knowledge sharing in teaching, research, community engagement, and academic leadership.

- Aid…the university in competitively recruiting and retaining excellent faculty, especially with attention to the needs of colleagues from historically under-represented groups.

...Participants will be offered the following opportunities:

- Individual mentoring with an experienced faculty member outside your department.

- Participation in a series of topical discussions comprised of new faculty members and two experienced faculty members (co-facilitators).

- Opportunity to apply for a stipend for a teaching or research project of your design.

Senior Faculty who serve as mentors will:

- Receive early fall training in mentoring.

- Meet with Senior faculty mentors 2-3 times per semester for topical discussions.

- Receive a small budget for travel/lab support.

- Meet with their mentee monthly.

Selected Group Facilitators will...

- Receive early fall training in group facilitation.

- Receive a small budget for travel/lab support.

How to get involved:

- Have a conversation with your department chair.

- Applications are available at https://utlc.uncg.edu/teaching/faculty-mentoring

> **EXHIBIT 5.8, CONTINUED: UNC-GREENSBORO PEER FACULTY MENTORING PROGRAM**
>
> - Mentee self-nomination process takes place in March of the year prior to the NFMP year.
>
> - Mentor self-nomination process takes place in May of the year prior to the NFMP year.

9. Invest in Faculty and Staff Time to Implement Mentoring Activities

Creating and maintaining faculty mentoring programs is time-consuming and sometimes costly. In large schools (e.g., Medicine, Engineering, or a College of Arts and Sciences) an Associate Dean for Faculty Affairs might be the individual who is assigned this responsibility. In cross-disciplinary or cross-campus faculty development units (e.g., Centers for Teaching and Learning or Centers for Faculty Excellence) the director of that unit would be assigned that responsibility (which he or she might delegate to one of the specialists on staff.) It is very important to fix responsibility for implementation and hold these individuals accountable, or it is unlikely that much will get done: "Everybody's job is nobody's job."

In Exhibit 5.9, I show the typical elements of such a job. The description is excerpted from a current posting at a regional university.

Exhibit 5.9: Defining the Job

The following sample job description illustrates key elements of key faculty development roles that have responsibility for implementing mentoring initiatives.

"The Associate Dean for Faculty Development (ADFD) has responsibility for leading the planning, implementation and evaluation of activities within the Office of Faculty Development, to ensure that faculty needs are met and that programs are effective in increasing academic productivity and career longevity. ... Faculty development programs are based on needs assessment data and in response to national trends. ... ADFD will design, develop, and implement programs around the concepts of skills development and mentorship including faculty development sessions with well-defined objectives, small group learning formats, and faculty performance of designated skills ... engaging in scholarship, and other professional development needs. ..." (8)

As in many other areas, the dean or department chair also has a crucial role to play in establishing formal systems of mentoring support. In small departments, he or she may take on the role of designing and implementing a program. However, in many departments and schools the chair or dean is so overloaded already that it would be better to assign the job to an associate chair or dean or to a faculty committee. Yet, there is no getting away from the fact that this will be a big job if done right, and it will come at the expense, probably, of other activities those individuals or the unit would have done. Those sacrificed activities are the "opportunity costs" of the initiative.

The rationale, though, is that if we don't "pay the piper" in establishing a robust faculty mentoring program and mentoring culture, the faculty will suffer in terms of turnover, retention, and limited overall productivity. There never was a more classic case of "giving to get" then in establishing programs to assist faculty along the course of their career development.

My experience with mentoring programs suggests that robust faculty mentoring programs at the unit level are time-consuming but do not require big budgets. On the other hand, putting in the time required is essential for producing quality programs.

10. Follow Through

Follow through on implementation with clear, supportive, and continuing leadership.

Get it in writing

When leaders provide reasonably detailed guidance documents, this fosters clarity. At the unit level (i.e., departments, divisions, and schools), leaders can produce documents to support programs, such as:

- A statement of standards for promotion of tenure track and non-tenure-track faculty.

- A clear description of the tenure and promotion process of the specific school and department.

- A definition of the roles and responsibilities of staff and mentoring program faculty leadership in carrying out the department's program.

- A declaration of the department's commitment to helping faculty at all levels achieve their potential through faculty development.

- Specific expectations of the duties of mentors and the responsibilities of mentees.

Make it valued

Deans and chairs can promote a culture of faculty development in their units by:

- Speaking in support of mentors and mentoring activity on a frequent basis.

- Establishing programs of recognition and reward for good mentoring.

- Creating opportunities for faculty to learn and grow as mentors through training and discussions.

- Ensuring there is regular review and continuous improvement of the mentoring programs in place.

- Talking about how they were or could have been helped by mentors in their own careers, their current experiences in mentoring others, and the benefits they gain from those involvements.

The USC Mentoring Awards (University of Southern California)

https://faculty.usc.edu/mentoring/awards/

[These awards] honor individual faculty members for helping to build a supportive academic environment through faculty-to-student mentoring and faculty-to-faculty mentoring. Distinguished mentoring for academic and professional success occurs at USC through formal and informal channels, and may vary in style and substance from discipline to discipline.

- Faculty Mentoring Faculty, Postdoctoral Scholars, Medical Residents, and Fellows

- Faculty Mentoring Graduate Students

- Faculty Mentoring Undergraduate Students

Provost's Award for Excellence in Faculty Mentoring (Rhode Island Institute of Technology)

https://www.rit.edu/academicaffairs/facultyawards/provost-mentoring-award.php

This award recognizes a RIT faculty member who has demonstrated an outstanding commitment to faculty mentoring by actively helping less experienced faculty in developing their career(s) at RIT by offering advice, feedback and guidance that reflects a deep understanding of their department, college and university. The faculty member receiving this award embodies the spirit of RIT's values, honor code and diversity statement, actively engages in research and/or related scholarly activities possesses a publication record that meets College standards (if applicable), and receives consistently satisfactory/acceptable teaching eval-uations. He or she also connects mentees to relevant internal and external networks, preserves their intellectual independence, and consistently maintains confidentiality.

Women's Leadership Council Awards (UNC-Chapel Hill)

The Women's Leadership Council bestows three Faculty Mentoring Awards each year, one for faculty-to-undergraduate student mentoring, one for faculty-to-graduate student mentoring, and one for senior-faculty-to-early-career faculty mentoring. Each recipient will receive $5,000.

With more than 200 members, the Carolina Women's Leadership Council is a network of women from across the country who are committed to supporting the University and students' educational experiences. Members support Carolina's mission by volunteering their time, sharing expertise, championing Carolina in their regions, providing financial support, and serving on boards that further the University's mission.

Make it work

Units should provide ongoing support for mentoring, mentors, and mentees. Mentors need to understand the specific mentoring role they are being asked to play in their units and mentees need to understand how they can make the best use of their mentors. Effective mentoring programs will provide written guidance, targeted trainings, and good orientations about how the mentoring program is supposed to work.

EXHIBIT 5.11: ASSISTANCE FOR MENTORING IMPLEMENTATION, UNC-CHAPEL HILL

Academic Year 2014-15, UNC-CH Center for Faculty Excellence Series on Mentoring.

All sessions will be from 12:00 - 1:30 p.m. in 308 Wilson Library and lunch will be served.

Finding a Mentor and Making the Most out of the Mentoring Relationship (Friday, Oct. 24)
A discussion on how to find mentors, build relationships, and avoid missteps.

Becoming a More Effective Mentor to Early Career Faculty (Thursday, Nov. 13)
Effective practices in mentoring will be discussed. This is a great opportunity to learn and trade tips about how to be a good mentor to early career faculty.

Developing Effective Mentoring Programs for Early Career Faculty (Friday, Jan. 23)
CFE will share preliminary results from its survey of mentoring practices across campus.

**Strengthening Mid-Career Faculty
Development: Promising Practices and
Programs** (Friday, Feb. 27)
A wide-ranging discussion of faculty development
at mid-career. CFE will share promising post-
tenure development practices that were identified
in a survey of peer institutions.

Keep it on track

In addition, effective mentoring programs will have good
evaluation mechanisms and will learn and improve with
experience. This includes checking to see how individual
mentoring relationships are going on an annual basis,
making adjustments where needed, and assessing through
surveys and discussions how effective the particular
features of the unit's mentoring program have been (i.e.,
committees, orientation, incentives, discussions, plans,
etc.).

EXHIBIT 5.12: 2012 HEALTH SCIENCE DEPARTMENT
FACULTY DEVELOPMENT SURVEY RESULTS

This survey was distributed to the faculty in the division by David Kiel, Center for Faculty Excellence, on behalf the Chair at the March 7 meeting, and these results will be discussed at the May 15 faculty retreat, which will focus on mentoring.

---

1. What topics/issues would you like to see covered in the session on mentoring on May 15?

Results:

- How to distinguish between too much and too little mentoring

- How to balance the needs of the individual with the needs of the research group

- Are there commonly accepted "principles" for mentoring?

- How often should you meet? In what context?

- Developing national visibility in professional organizations

- Transparency regarding confidential information

- Mentoring students/ trainees in extracurricular skills—presentation, interviewing, teamwork, communication, etc.

- Identifying mentors outside the school/ discipline (for faculty)

- Compare different mentoring styles/strategies and discuss pros/cons of each (what works well, what does not)

- Transition from junior to senior trainee, and how mentoring styles/strategies should/can evolve

2. What faculty development topics might be of interest in future sessions? (For example, list topics related to: teaching methods and approaches; research and research funding; mentoring at any level, e-learning, distance education, and classroom technology; or aspects of faculty leadership, such as planning, leading meetings, problem-solving, negotiation, communication, project management, fundraising, etc.)

Results:

- Running effective meetings

- Developing a business plan for the lab

- Use of e-learning to classroom teach and facilitate active learning

- Negotiation, especially in transitions (e.g., faculty to director, faculty to dean level, etc.)

- Transitions and changes in responsibilities

- Entrepreneurship/consulting opportunities

- Networking

- Financial planning (finance for managers)

EXHIBIT 5.12, CONTINUED: HEALTH SCIENCE DEPT
FACULTY DEVELOPMENT SURVEY RESULTS

- Student mentoring and development of communication

- Skills regarding communicating with professional and graduate students

- General comment: "All of these topics are excellent and very useful. I would place the 'leadership' topics at the top of the list."

Conclusion—Implementation is a Team Effort

Implementation of mentoring services requires a team effort. The chairs or deans must create the policy framework and show strong continuing support. Program leaders must do their best to establish the programs on a sound basis, continually evaluate, and improve. Individual mentors must step up and those mentored need to take responsibility for their own development using the prescribed mentoring service as one of several resources to assure their advancement.

Undergirding all this effort is the belief that mentoring and faculty development is important work and necessary to advancement of the department or school and that extending a helping hand to highly motivated junior and mid-career faculty members is an important value.

As in almost all human endeavor, persuasion is a key element, but faculty by nature are skeptical and analytic. Therefore, at every step it makes sense to demonstrate results through assessment and measurement, but then to talk about those results, and collectively and incrementally adjust the mentoring programs to better reflect departmental and school needs.

Notes

1. For additional references on this topic, see "Advice for the Director of a Faculty Mentoring Program," Chapter 6 in Phillips and Dennison (2015), p. 41-46, cited earlier, and Appendix A, "Checklist for Developing, Implementing and Assessing Mentoring Programs," in Bland et al. (2009), p. 163-165.

2. For a comprehensive view of the COACHE model and its results, see Trower, Cathy Ann, *Success on the Tenure Track: Five Keys to Faculty Job Satisfaction.* John Hopkins University Press, 2012. You can also see a description of the COACHE project at: https://coache.gse.harvard.edu/about

3. You can review NCSU's 2015 COACHE Survey results at:

   https://oirp.ncsu.edu/wordpress/wp-content/uploads/2017/04/COACHE.AY14_15. NCSU_.TTonly.Peers_.pdf

4. See "Faculty Mentoring at the University of Minnesota," a Report of the President's Emerging Leaders Program 2006-7, accessed at:

https://conservancy.umn.edu/bitstream/handle/
11299/5487/facmenreport.pdf?sequence=2&isAll
owed=y

5. For the full report from the University of Colorado, go to:

   https://www.colorado.edu/facultyaffairs/faculty-support/professional-development/mentoring-resources

6. For Michigan State University's full policy, see: https://natsci.msu.edu/faculty-staff/policies-procedures/faculty-mentoring-policy/

   Six of the 11 points of the MSU policy are listed in this excerpt.

7. See Phillips, Susan L., and Susan T. Dennison. "Guidelines for Setting Up, Planning, and Facilitating a Mentoring Group," Faculty Mentoring: A Practical Manual for Mentees, Mentors, Administrators and Faculty Developers, Stylus, 2015, p. 11-20.

8. This is excerpted and slightly edited from a job description posted to *Inside Higher Ed* by the School of Medicine at East Carolina University on July 14, 2017:

   (https://careers.insidehighered.com/job/1413055/associate-dean-for-faculty-development/

APPENDIX A: MENTORING AND SUPPORT FOR FULL-TIME, NON-TENURE-TRACK FACULTY

There is a large group of faculty who at some, but not all, campuses are excluded from mentoring and faculty development programs. This group includes both the full-time and part-time faculty who are neither tenured nor tenure track, sometimes called "contingent faculty." Often these faculty members have poorly structured jobs which are not conducive to the professional commitment needed to fuel faculty development. In the worst cases, these jobs do not pay a living wage or benefits, and teachers work without any promise of continued employment or meaningful participation in their units.

This creates significant problems for their morale, effectiveness, and for student outcomes. As a consequence, across the country at every level of institution, there have been protests, union drives, and stories in the press decrying the situation of contingent faculty. The largest part of this group are part-time faculty (PTF).

I believe most of these PTF need better structured jobs before efforts in faculty development will have much of an impact. Many of these PTF are so overworked and underpaid that, while they contribute mightily to their institutions, they are so stretched that it will be hard for many to make the additional effort required to utilize faculty development services. While there are institutions that are making an effort to improve these conditions and while notable success stories are available for emulation, I think the best opportunity for improving faculty development in the short-term is to work to improve the status of full-time, fixed-term faculty (FTF), who after PTF are the fastest growing faculty group. (1)

The reason that FTF are more likely to benefit from job improvement efforts that include access to faculty development and mentoring programs is that the IHE already is investing a full-time salary in these individuals. In many cases, they are looking for a closer connection to the institution. What we need to do is remove the barriers to greater engagement.

Many of the problems that FTF experience (e.g., lack of the opportunity for multi-year contracts, unclear employment policies, lack of participation in governance, and lack of access to professional development) are more immediately fixable than those of PTF—some of whom are in positions that do not meet the minimum standards of decent jobs and for whom solutions are much more expensive for the institution.

Accordingly, in this appendix, I will discuss research findings and case examples that focus on the FTF component of contingent faculty—mostly, but not exclusively, at research institutions. While the articles and cases cited speak about non-tenure-track faculty (NTTF) in general, it should be understood that FTF are mostly targeted. PTF who would be affected by these suggestions are mostly those who have a chance to move toward FTF status in several years.

Defining FTF Needs and Identifying Directions for Improvement of Jobs and Working Conditions

Organizational behavior theorists (2) have argued that there is a hierarchy of needs that is activated when a person seeks employment. Basic or existence needs include such elemental dimensions as job security, physical safety, compensation, benefits, adequate work space and equipment, and decent hours. Failure to meet these needs leads to dissatisfaction but meeting these needs does not necessarily motivate the individuals involved to do their best work.

However, once basic job needs are fulfilled, then meeting the need for relationships on the job *does* motivate people to participate actively. The bonds they build generate the desire to be contributing members of the team or unit. Also, by providing work that is meaningful and that allows employees to use their abilities in creative ways, we create the conditions for higher levels of job satisfaction and productivity.

These theories have informed a lot of the research related to FTF. A team of researchers studied contingent faculty at 12 research institutions. (3) About 74% of their sample were FTF. Their goal was to identify those actions that would make the most positive difference in faculty motivation and commitment to the institution. Their research supported the idea that, failing basic job security, it will be hard to create an optimally motivated and productive work force. So, in their conclusions, they emphasized the primary importance of improving the length and dependability of employment contracts, including:

> ...the creation of two- or three-level career ladders, with multiple-year contracts for each level. For example, an Instructor I might be on a two-year contract; Instructor II, a five-year contract; and so on. In some cases, institutions have implemented even longer contracts or other means of establishing the expectation of continued employment for non-tenure-track faculty (NTTF) who have met institutional review standards—along with clear title systems and procedures for evaluation and contract renewal. At institutions where these policies were not present, the focus group participants named them as the ones they would most like to see. (pp. 431-32)

They also concluded that once job security was enhanced,

> ... administrators could significantly improve the level of job satisfaction and institutional commitment of NTTF—and thus optimize their contributions to their institutions—by supporting their teaching efforts, enacting policies that (permit) advancement opportunities, and creating inclusive climates.

They go on to say that:

> Deans and upper-level administrators need to be reminded that in addition to the policies they implement, the manner in which they are implemented and communicated down the institutional hierarchy can have a profound impact on the volitional autonomy and perceived relatedness of NTTF faculty, which in turn can impact their well-being.

> Specifically, administrators need to implement policies designed to foster a greater sense of relatedness for NTTF. This could include ensuring adequate represent-

ation of NTT faculty in faculty governance and on relevant committees, providing department chairs with the ability to offer longer term contracts to senior NTTF and making explicit commitment to NTTF wellness and work–life balance.

At the department level, department chairs need to voice that NTT faculty are valued members of the department, recognize NTTF for contributions to the department's mission and excellence in teaching/service, and ensure NTTF are supported in navigating the contract renewal and promotion processes (e.g., mentoring).

Finally they say it is important for NTTF to be active on their own behalf:

Perhaps most important is that NTTF cannot isolate themselves or be passive in pursuing well-being. To the extent it is possible, NTTF need to be active participants in their departments and in institutional governance. If barriers do exist, it behooves NTTF to join together for support and to form a collective voice to advocate for their needs through the proper channels. An equally important implication is the simple fact that, as this sample demonstrated, NTTF can attain well-being in their positions....

Other recent research (4) supports the proposition that compensation and benefits and job security, as represented by longer-term contracts, are key to NTTF satisfaction and well-being—but emphasizes that what the researchers call "environmental supports" are also important. The study team concluded that NTTF want reasonable spaces to teach and work, and the tools they need to do their jobs. NTTF want to have positive relationships with their chairs and senior administrators, as well as be recognized and valued for what they contribute. Finally, NTTF want to feel a part of the units in which they work. They want to contribute to governance, represented on committees, and have their opinions respected. There is also evidence that NTTF want flexibility in their job requirements and recognition of the need for work life balance.

Elizabeth Simmons, then a senior administrator at Michigan State University, writing in *Inside Higher Ed,* summed up NTTF needs by using the terms "Valued," "Rewarded", "Included," and "Consulted" (5).

Exhibit A.1 offers a list of promising practices, drawing both from Simmons' article and other research on meeting the needs of NTTF.

EXHIBIT A.1: PROMISING PRACTICES THAT ADDRESS THE NEEDS OF NON-TENURE TRACK FACULTY MEMBERS

1. Provide basic job security and work conditions

- Provide a full-time job with benefits whenever possible and practical and convert part-time to full-time positions when long-term staffing was needed.

- Work to improve the rate of pay so as to retain best faculty.

- Create and publicize career tracks and paths for promotion of faculty of all ranks; provide mentoring for those who want to work toward promotion.

- Encourage part-time faculty to apply for full-time positions that make sense for them.

- Provide a title that reflects their actual work and expertise.

- Assure good office and meeting spaces.

2. Include NTTF in governance activities:

- Attending faculty meetings and participate in discussions.

- Participating in searches, e.g., attending job talks, giving impressions of candidates, etc.

- Voting where appropriate.

- Membership on committees relevant to their roles and expertise.

- Input decisions about space, personnel, curriculum, and other matters relevant to them.

3. Recognize them as contributing members by:

- Nominating NTTF Faculty for awards and small grants for which they are eligible.

- Providing opportunities for NTTF to make their expertise known to tenure track colleagues via presentations and talks.

- Inviting them to join in multi-investigator research initiatives when qualified.

- Offering them opportunities to serve, e.g., leading study abroad groups and mentoring junior colleagues.

Case Studies: Improving FTF Jobs at Research Universities

The Delphi Project (6) provides examples of case studies of improving FTF status and working conditions from several research universities including Virginia Tech, Villanova, and University of Southern California (USC):

- At Virginia Tech, a proposal put forward by English Department faculty was discussed with department heads across campus with support of the Provost's Office. Criteria for promotion of full-time teaching faculty were developed. Current FTF were invited to submit their portfolios for review and several rounds of promotion then ensued. A similar process was then created for FTF who had research appointments.

- At Villanova, FTF worked with the Department of Institutional Research to compile a data-rich report on the status of FTF, conducted a benchmarking study of peer and aspirational peer institutions, and surveyed FTF about needs and concerns. Through a series of processes including revision of the faculty handbook and participation in the accreditation process the group was able to bring about significant reforms. These included: requiring departments to comply with existing policies to include FTF in governance, changing toward longer contracts, providing more lead time to prepare courses, increasing advocacy for improving salaries, and instituting more inclusive leave policies.

- At USC, the faculty senate created a white paper that documented the variety of practices at USC's various schools and conducted a benchmarking study of FTF practices at 11 other elite institutions. These studies were shared with the deans of the various schools resulting in changes in several areas. These changes were adopted on a school-by-school basis. They provided more professional leave opportunities, released time for public service, and new paths to promotion. They moved toward multi year contracts and they also reformed FTF titles and made provisions for greater FTF participation in governance.

These examples and the one presented in more depth below represent change efforts driven by faculty governance leaders in faculty senates or faculty councils in concert with FTF themselves and with the support of institutional leaders.

Changing the culture for FTF at one institution

Campus level and system change

While I was at UNC-CH working as a faculty developer, the Fixed-Term Committee of the Faculty Council led a similar change project. (7) UNC-CH has a particularly high ratio of full-time faculty relative to part-time faculty in its contingent workforce, therefore the focus on full-time non-tenured faculty, called "fixed-term faculty" (FTF) made sense relative to the numbers of faculty affected. In 2014, they surveyed 1400 FTF across the 13 schools and Colleges of the institution (44% of the faculty overall) and received over 800 responses. They found that 63% were satisfied or very satisfied with their jobs, but they also found that slightly over half (including many with five or more years of service) had one-year appointments. They reported that the "top issues concerning Fixed-Term Faculty are salary equity, length of contracts, valuation, promotion criteria, retention, and growth opportunities." They also said some FTF are not well supported by their departments, resulting in their feeling less valued."

Having worked with that committee, I can report that the satisfaction scores varied a lot by academic unit, with some units having a relatively satisfied group of FTF and some with a very dissatisfied group. (It was a delicate matter deciding how to report and use these data.) Clearly, this suggests that improvements in the conditions for FTF have to do both with policies (e.g., length of contracts) and unit level practices such as whether FTF are included, consulted, and respected by their colleagues and senior leadership.

What is useful to note about the UNC-CH experience is not the specific findings (they are consistent with other campus studies and job satisfaction theory) but how a targeted study of the campus also provided guidance of for next step improvements in a fairly rapid but incremental process. The committee recommended to the faculty council that they adopt a "best practice list" for fully integrating NTTF in all departments. The list included:

- Increasing length-of-contracts as the years of service increases, up to five years.

- Requiring a non-renewal notice at least six months in advance or 12 months in the case of a multi-year contract.

- Providing a clear path for promotion with transparent and widely communicated standards and processes.

- Offering mentoring, access to training, travel funds, competitive leaves, and internal grants and awards.

- Encouraging participation in faculty meetings and discussions with voting rights in accordance with departmental and university by laws, and listing on all rosters and websites.

- Provide salary levels consistent with responsibilities, and policies to provide regular salary increases.

In their 2016-17 report to the Faculty Council, the FTF Committee reported that they were successful in getting the Campus Trustees to regularize titles for FTF and to convince several schools to adopt polices that resulted in multi-year contracts—though they said that not all schools cooperated to the same degree. In 2017-18, the committee reported additional progress:

- New titles and ranks of fixed-term faculty were approved by the UNC System Board of Governors and went into effect July 1, 2017. (The campus has seen quick and widespread adoption of the new titles.)

- More Faculty awards were opened up to FTF.

- The Committee updated the "Best Practices" document to include integrating FTF in departmental mentoring programs and inclusion in faculty meetings with voting privileges consistent with their ranks.

- Listing of names in University academic catalogs, faculty building directories, and departmental websites consistent with school policy.

- Inclusion in all routine departmental and university mailings.

- Inclusion in curriculum discussions.

- Consideration for leadership development and service opportunities within the department.

They also reported that the College of Arts and Sciences had recommended that chairs adopt contract lengths based on years of service and that the College was pushing to have all units adopt written practices governing FTF. (8) One can see in the sequence of events how the norms and standards for treating FTF are changing through information, advocacy, and persuasion. Needless to say, this effort would not have been very successful without the support of deans and other senior academic leaders.

Department level change initiatives

As I have noted, improving the status of FTF requires action at the department level as well. In one area studies department I worked with, about half the faculty were FTF. The tenured and tenure track faculty (TTF) were more traditional scholars (e.g., anthropologists, art historians, scholars of comparative literature, and political historians) who were both teaching and pursuing interdisciplinary scholarship. The FTF faculty provided instruction in eight different languages.

The chair thought the FTF were poorly represented in faculty forums and had little opportunity to identify common problems and make suggestions for improvement. She also thought that as a group they were not well integrated into the department and, as a result, the department was diminished. Accordingly, she appointed two of the more senior FTF to be coordinators for the language faculty and gave them a one-course release to perform those duties. As a consequence, this large group of faculty in that department gained representation and had a channel to bring their concerns to the chair. She also worked to involve NTTF in reviews of their colleagues, in voting on appointments, to advise on curriculum, and, in general, to make them into fuller citizens of the department.

At UNC-CH's medical school two large departments, Pediatrics and Psychiatry, developed extensive mentoring programs for their faculty including committees, annual reviews, goal setting, and accountability mechanisms. Significantly for the purposes of this discussion, they also included FTF. While the time frame for review and appointment varied between TTF and FTF, mentoring opportunities are extended to both groups.

School level change initiatives

In addition, faculty leaders conducted a self-assessment of mentoring resources available at the UNC-CH Medical School in 2018. They concluded that about half the faculty had access to mentors and that mentoring was associated with faculty member accomplishment, satisfaction, and insti-tutional commitment. They discussed gaps in current mentoring efforts and the need to extend mentoring, and they reported on a pilot project to extend peer mentoring to early career faculty, both NTTF and TTF. (9) By publishing progress in some units, faculty leaders are exerting pressure on their colleagues to address issues of concern to FTF.

Conclusion: Charting a Way Forward for FTF

The research suggests that institutions that want to improve the lot of FTF on their campuses have clear pathways to do so. These include:

- Developing an institutional commitment to improve FTF working conditions.

- Doing an assessment of the institutional needs of FTF on the campus.

- Engaging senior administrators and faculty in reviewing internal data.

- Benchmarking against peer institutions and exemplary institutions.

- Developing a set of recommendations/best practices.

- Incrementally (but systematically) implementing recommendations.

- Assessing results and addressing areas where problems may persist.

Since most of those affected are already full-time, the immediate impact on costs is not so great as migrating many PTF to full-time status in a short period of time. However, improving FTF jobs does require structural and culture change in the form of uniform titles, multi-year contracts, inclusion in governance forums at the institutional and departmental levels, and inclusion in mentoring and faculty development initiatives.

None of these things are easy to implement. However, these changes seem straightforward and, frankly, long overdue, given that in some institutions FTF are more numerous than TTF.

What may be a limiting factor is the bandwidth of deans and department chairs to work in a systematic and sustained way to manage changes. Such efforts may require actively facilitated discussions with faculty at all levels if they are to be really embraced rather than grudgingly implemented.

The implication is that by involving FTF to take action on their own behalf, using internal data and benchmarking, building allies among the TTF, creating infrastructure for the change effort (e.g. faculty committees, associate deans), and by gaining the support of senior academic leaders, positive changes are eminently possible.

Notes

1. For analysis of the situation with full and part-time non-tenure-track faculty, see *One Faculty Serving All Students*, Coalition on the Academic Workforce, February 2010:

    http://www.academicworkforce.org/Research_reports.html

    See also "Report on the Project Working Meeting," The Changing Faculty: The Delphi Project on Student Success, May 2012, p. 14:

    http://www.thechangingfaculty.org

    See also *Trends in the Academic Labor Force 1975-2015*. Accessed at:

    https://www.aaup.org/our-work/research

    The Delphi Project is sponsored by the Pullias Center for Higher Education Research in Rossier School of Higher Education at the University of Southern California.

    Also see: http://www.aera.net/Newsroom/News-Releases-and-Statements/AERA-Issues-Recommendations-for-Supporting-Non-Tenure-Track-Faculty

    and

    https://www.aacu.org/publications-research/periodicals/why-are-we-hiring-so-many-non-tenure-track-faculty

Researchers have also looked at why institutions are increasingly employing NTTF. Gappa, Austin, and Trice (*Rethinking Faculty Work*, 2007, Jossey-Bass) cited cost and flexibility as drivers of the current shift. Through interviews with administrators and NTTF, Cross and Goldenberg (*Off-Track Profs*, 2009, MIT Press) found that the increase in NTTF hires at elite research universities is "not always the result of conscious policy but instead often emerges as a by-product of other initiatives." For example, NTTF instructors are often hired to "fill in" teaching assignments in highly specialized disciplines, and they bring real-world knowledge and expertise that student's enjoy See Waltman, Jean, et al. "Factors Contributing to Job Satisfaction and Dissatisfaction Among Non-Tenure-Track Faculty," *The Journal of Higher Education,* vol. 83, no. 3, 2012, pp. 411-434.

See also Kezar, Adrianna, et al. "The Imperative for Change: Understanding the Necessity of Changing Non-Tenure-Track Faculty Policies and Practices," Pullias Center for Higher Education, University of Southern California, 2014. This is a whitepaper prepared as part of the Delphi Project. Its production was supported by grants from the Teagle, Carnegie, and Spencer Foundations.

Many contingent faculty members are on year-to-year contracts. In 2010, CAW reported that "a third of full- and part-time faculty members teaching off the tenure track in the humanities, social sciences, and natural sciences have been in their current teaching position longer than six years; a fifth or more have held their current position longer than ten years." In situations like this, the institution has the benefits of flexibility, but the faculty member absorbs the cost of uncertainty.

2. The "classical" theorists of contemporary workplace motivation are Frederick Herzberg (Hygiene Theory), Abraham Maslow (Hierarchy of Needs) and Clayton Alderfer (Existence, Relatedness, Growth Theory: ERG).

3. Waltman, Jean, et al. "Factors Contributing to Job Satisfaction and Dissatisfaction Among Non-Tenure-Track Faculty," *The Journal of Higher Education*, vol. 83, no. 3, 2012.

4. Seipel, Mathew T., and Lisa M. Larson. "Supporting Non-Tenure-Track Faculty Well-Being," *Journal of Career Assessment*, vol. 26, no. 1, 2018, pp. 154-171. The authors provide an extensive review of the research on NTTF satisfaction. This literature supports the following propositions: a) that satisfaction with compensation is the single biggest predictor of NTT overall satisfaction; b) satisfaction with benefits is a significant correlate of overall satisfaction and the reverse is also true; c) that recognition by the chair and deans including individual consideration, offering rewards, and positive relationships is a predictor of FTF faculty satisfaction; d) unclear, inconsistent, or non-existent policies related to contract renewal and promotion are a source of dissatisfaction; e) work-life balance is a significant predictor of overall satisfaction, and this is related to scheduling flexibility; and f) that if FTF faculty feel connected to colleagues and the department this moderates the effect of other areas of dissatisfaction.

5. Simmons, Elizabeth H. "Supporting Academic Staff," *Inside Higher Ed*, March 2, 2017.

6. See the Delphi Project Path to Change Archive:

   https://pullias.usc.edu/download/path-change-campus-communities-worked-change-non-tenure-track-policies-practices/

7. The complete report of the Fixed-Term Committee may be viewed here:

   https://facultygov.unc.edu/committees/appointed-committees/fixed-term-faculty-committee/committees-recommended-best-practices-related-to-fixed-term-faculty/

   (At UNC-CH, full-time faculty not on the tenure track are called "fixed-term faculty" and so I use the acronym "FTF" for both in this section.)

8. See the 2017 and 2018 annual reports of the Fixed-Term Faculty Committee to the UNC-CH Faculty Council. PDFs are available at:

   https://facultygov.unc.edu/files/2017/04/FXT2017.pdf

   https://facultygov.unc.edu/files/2018/04/FXT2018.pdf

9. These reports may be accessed at:

   https://www.med.unc.edu/pediatrics/about/faculty-development/promotions-and-tenure-1/dop-promotions-policy

   and

   https://www.med.unc.edu/aoe/files/2017/12/Girdler-and-Colford-AOE-November-2017.pdf

APPENDIX B: WORKBOOK

Assessments, Examples, Lists, Tips, and Tools to Assist Deans, Chairs, and Other Academic Leaders in Implementation of Faculty Mentoring Programs

HOW TO USE THE WORKBOOK

Each of the first five sections of this workbook follows the corresponding chapter of the book and supplements the chapter with step-by-step worksheets. By working through this material, you can do the thinking needed to design and implement a comprehensive mentoring and faculty development program that fits your unit.

Section 6 is a bonus section and contains training and orientation material for first time mentors and early career faculty mentees.

LIST OF WORKSHEETS

1 Design the Mentoring Program Your Unit Really Needs

1.1   Worksheet to Clarify Responsibilities for Pairing Mentors and Mentees

1.2   Worksheet for Making Sure the Mentoring Program is Working Correctly

1.3   Example of a Year-End Program Evaluation Survey of Mentees

1.4   Gathering Data on the Four Key Design Criteria

1.5   Clarifying the Broad Goals of Your Mentoring Program

1.6   What Services Will Your Mentoring Program Provide?

1.7   Specifying Who Will Participate in Your Mentoring Program

1.8   What Format Should Your Mentoring Program Have?

1.9   Operational Decisions Worksheet

1.10   Getting the Faculty Involved: Sample Charter for a Faculty Committee

1.11   Faculty Study Committee Assessment Tool for Mentoring

2   What Services Are Needed to Support Early Career Faculty?

2.1   Improving Clarity of Standards and Processes: Survey of Tenure Track Faculty

2.2   Improving Clarity of Standards and Processes: Fixed-Term (Contract) Faculty

2.3   Unit Self-Assessment of Activities to Clarify Promotion Standards and Processes

2.4   Survey of Individual Needs for Teaching Assistance Services

2.5   Departmental Self-Assessment: Mentoring Needs of Early Career Faculty in Teaching

2.6   Survey of Faculty Needs for Support with Research and Writing Skills

2.7   Departmental Self-Assessment: Mentoring Needs of Early Career Faculty in Research

2.8   Survey of Faculty Needs for Professional Development

2.9   For an Early-Career Professor: Assessing My Support Network for Academic Productivity

2.10   Assessment: Inclusive Policies and Practices

2.11   Creating an Inclusive Climate

2.12   Examples of Initiatives and Programs to Improve Diversity and Inclusion

2.13   A Department Chair's Self-Assessment: Next Steps in Improving Mentoring Services

3   Designing and Implementing Programs for Mid-Career Faculty

3.1   Self-Assessment for Recently Tenured or Recently Promoted Faculty

3.2   A Chair's Interview Guide for Newly Tenured/Promoted Faculty

3.3   Mid-Career Planning Template

3.4   At the Academic Unit Level: Self-Assessment of Mid-Career Mentoring and Faculty Development Services

3.5   Checklist for Improving Promotion Processes for Associate Professors

3.6   A Guide to Interviewing a Mid-Career Professor Who Has Been 10 Years in the Rank

3.7   For a Mid-Career Professor: Assessing My Support Network for Academic Productivity

3.8   At the Academic Unit Level: Assessment of Unit Support for Under-Represented Mid-Career Faculty

4   Senior Faculty Development (SFD): Tools for Academic Leaders

4.1   An Academic Leaders' Confidential Assessment of Senior Faculty Productivity

4.2   A Self-Assessment for Senior Faculty

4.3   A Guide for a Conversation about Senior Faculty Development

4.4   Senior Faculty Development Needs/Readiness Assessment Guide

4.5   What Are the Best Options for Career Conversations with Senior Faculty?

4.6   Senior Faculty Self-Assessment: What Resources Might Be Most Helpful for Me?

4.7   Unit Leader's Assessment of Resources Needed for Senior Faculty Development

4.8   Quick Assessment: Support for Under-Represented Faculty and Women Faculty at the Senior Level

5   Worksheets for Leading the Development of Mentoring Services

5.1   Worksheet to Assemble Information Needed for Planning Mentoring Services

5.2   Worksheet to Identify Specific Needs that Your Unit Should Address

5.3   Worksheet to Identify Opportunities to Involve Faculty in Discussion and Planning

5.4   Checklist for Drafting an Effective Mentoring Policy for Your Unit

5.5   Worksheet for Identifying Faculty Role Models and Mentors

5.6   Checklist for Supporting Your Faculty Mentors and Mentees

5.7   List of Steps to Ensure the Program Leadership Role Is
        Adequately Supported

5.8   Worksheet: What Funds Can You Raise From Alumni to Support
        Faculty Development?

6   Tools, Tips, Checklists, and Other Resources For First-Time Mentors and Early-Career Faculty

6.1   What Makes a Good Mentor?

6.2   Seven Tips for First-Time Faculty Mentors

6.3   Checklist to Help Determine Topics for Mentoring

6.4   What to Say to New Faculty Members

6.5   Helping New Faculty Members Think About the First Year

6.6   Practical Tips for Mentoring Faculty

6.7   Sample Mentoring Agreement

6.8   Developmental Survey: How Would You Assess Yourself as a
        Mentor?

6.9   Tips for Mentees for Finding Success Through Mentoring

6.10   Tips for Mentees from Experienced Mentors

6.11   The Work Plan: Sample Checklist for a New Faculty Member

6.12   On Being a Good Protégé

6.13   Assessing the Culture of Your Department and How You "Fit
        in"

6.14   Advice: How to Find the Right Mentor and How to Manage
        Your Mentor

1. Design the Mentoring Program Your Unit Really Needs

1.1. Worksheet to Clarify Responsibilities for Pairing Mentors and Mentees

1. Who is the formal head of your mentoring program? What are their duties?	
2. Who identifies and qualifies mentors in your unit?	
3. What criteria are used to qualify mentors to serve in the program?	

4. Is mentoring voluntary or required? If voluntary, how are mentors recruited? If required, under what circumstances can ment-ors "opt out" with unit approval?	
5. Who matches mentors to mentees in your program (if not already indicated above)?	
6. When does this happen? Immediately after hiring? Early in the first semest-er? Some other point in the first months or years after hiring?	

1.2. Worksheet for Making Sure the Mentoring Program is Working Correctly

Individual Mentoring Relationships
1. In your program, who is responsible to follow up to make sure individual mentoring relationships are working correctly?
2. When is this follow up required to occur (e.g., in the first few months, after a year?)
3. Who is empowered to change or terminate formal mentoring relationships in your program?

4. What formal documentation is there of the follow up and resultant action, if any, and who keeps the records?

How the Program as a Whole is Functioning

5. Who is responsible for leading the program assessment?

6. What form is assessment expect to take: e.g., survey, interview, focus group, or some combination?

7. How often is the formal assessment and review? (E.g., annually, every 2-3 years, some combination?)

8. How does the faculty participate in the assessment, review, and revision of the program?

1.3. Example of a Year-End Program Evaluation Survey of Mentees

Adapted from a mentoring program at a large Health Sciences Department.

1. Please indicate whether you are a fixed-term or tenure track faculty member.

Answer	Fixed-Term	Tenure Track	Total
Fixed Term	16	0	16
Tenure Track	0	17	17
Total			33

2. Which of the following best describes the nature of your face-to-face interaction with your Mentor?

Answer	Fixed-Term	Tenure Track	Total
We only meet regularly as part of a standing (e.g., weekly, monthly, etc.) research group meeting.	5	3	8
We only meet regularly as part of a standing (e.g., weekly, monthly, etc.) one-on-one meeting.	0	0	0
We meet regularly as part of both a standing (e.g., weekly, monthly, etc.) research group meeting and a standing (e.g., weekly, monthly, etc.) one-on-one meeting.	9	7	16

Answer	Fixed-Term	Tenure Track	Total
We do not have a standing meeting. All of our face-to-face interactions are "as needed."	2	6	8
Total	16	16	32

3. Which of the following options best describes your preference for a face-to-face/one-on-one meeting with your Mentor?

Answer	Fixed-Term	Tenure Track	Total
I prefer to meet as needed.	5	8	13
I prefer a regularly scheduled/standing meeting.	11	7	18
I do not need to meet one-on-one with my major advisor (i.e., our group meeting and/or electronic correspondence is sufficient, etc.).	0	1	1
Total	16	16	32

4. Please explain:

[open-ended responses]

5. What would be the optimal frequency of such a meeting with your mentor?

Answer	Fixed-Term	Tenure Track	Total
Daily	0	0	0
Multiple Times a Week	0	2	2
Weekly	6	5	11
Every Other Week	9	6	15
Monthly	0	1	1
None of the Above	1	1	2
Total	16	15	31

6. Please explain:

[open-ended responses]

7. Overall, how satisfied are you with the frequency of your face-to-face/one-on-one meetings with your mentor?

Answer	Fixed-Term	Tenure Track	Total
Very Satisfied	8	11	19
Somewhat Satisfied	4	3	7
Neither Satisfied or Dissatisfied	1	0	1
Somewhat Dissatisfied	3	1	4
Very Dissatisfied	0	1	1
Total	16	16	32

8. How could this be improved?

[open-ended responses]

9. Overall, how satisfied are you with the quality of the collective interactions/meetings with your mentor(s)?

Answer	Fixed-Term	Tenure Track	Total
Very Satisfied	8	13	21
Somewhat Satisfied	6	2	8
Neither Satisfied or Dissatisfied	0	0	0
Somewhat Dissatisfied	2	1	3
Very Dissatisfied	0	0	0
Total	16	16	32

10. Have you had a negative mentoring experience?

Answer	Fixed-Term	Tenure Track	Total
Yes	4	3	7
No	12	13	25
Total	16	16	32

11. Please explain. How could it have been improved?

[open-ended responses]

12. Rate the effectiveness of the mentor orientation session.

Answer	Fixed-Term	Tenure Track	Total
Highly effective – it really helped prepare me to start in the program	3	6	9
Effective, but room for improvement	6	5	11
Neutral	5	3	8
Ineffective- needs significant improvement	2	2	4
Total	16	16	32

13. How could the mentor orientation session be improved?

[open-ended responses]

14. Is your mentoring program exceeding, meeting, or failing to meet your expectations as a useful step forward in your career development?

Answer	Fixed-Term	Tenure Track	Total
Far exceeds my expectations	0	6	6
Meets my expectations	11	5	16
Adequate	4	4	8
Failing to meet my expectations	1	0	1
Total	16	15	31

15. Please explain.

[open-ended responses]

16. What should be changed or added so that the program better prepares you for the next phase of your career?

[open-ended responses]

Note: A parallel instrument could be distributed to the mentors.

1.4. Gathering Data on the Four Key Design Criteria

NUMBERS
1. What is the estimated number of new hires into our faculty on an annual basis?
2. How many faculty members do we have who could serve as mentors?
3. What, therefore, is the ratio of mentors to mentees we need to serve?

SPECIALTIES
4. What are the specialties that exist in the unit whose promotion requirements/competencies are fundamentally different? (E.g., in Art: Studio vs. Art History or in Anthropology: Archeology vs. Cultural Anthropology)
5. What differences in qualification of mentors are required for these varying competencies and experiences?
HISTORY
6. Have there been recent problems in tenure and/or promotion of early career faculty in the department that need to be corrected? If so, what are these?

7. Are there particular unit strengths in mentoring that your program should incorporate in some way? If so, what are these? (E.g., a faculty member who is particularly knowledgeable about the professional association, a staff member who is an extraordinarily knowledgeable and effective statistical consultant.) See also worksheet 5.6.

8. Are there successful, ongoing activities that need to be part of your program? If so, what are these? (E.g., a peer mentoring group on teaching, the process for conference paper review, engagement with the Center for Teaching on campus.)

CULTURE
9. Does your department need to have some discussions to resolve differing beliefs and attitudes before your program can be successful? E.g., do some believe people should "make it on their own" while other believe that a supportive department is a best practice? Do some believe that under-represented faculty are at an inherent disadvantage and their concerns should be given special consideration to create a "level playing field" while others think that true fairness involves "treating everyone just the same?" Do some believe that the new faculty members should play a major role in forming his or her own mentoring committee, convening, and seeking help, but others believe the best program is pre-structured, systematic, and prescribed for all?
10. If so, what is needed to help faculty members discuss and resolve these differences?

It may be that filling out the worksheet that follows (1.5) will help determine which attitudes toward mentoring are most important for discussion in your unit.

1.5. Clarifying the Broad Goals of Your Mentoring Program

In this worksheet, prioritize the broad goals of your mentoring program, using the following scale:

A   Most important

B   Next most important

C   Nice to have

D   Not important

Note: Do not select more than three "A" priorities.

Broad Goal	Priority (A,B,C, or D)
1. Increasing transparency and clarity about tenure and/or applicable promotion standards and processes for tenure track and/or fixed-term faculty members.	
2. Better preparing candidates for the tenure/ promotion process by providing regular feedback on progress.	
3. Assuring that each new faculty member has a point-person they can go to with questions.	

4. Making sure that the unit's program meets campus-wide standards and policies.	
5. Promoting improvement of teaching skills and performance.	
6. Promoting improvement of research and writing skills and performance.	
7. Increasing clinical, public service, or administrative skills and performance.	
8. Deepening the engagement with the discipline.	
9. Building connections with industry or relevant agencies.	
10. Strengthening citizenship or engagement with the campus or in the unit.	
11. Bringing the unit into compliance with new standards for mentoring.	
12. Extending mentoring services to fixed-term faculty/adjuncts.	
13. Extending mentoring services to mid-career.	

14. Extending mentoring services to late-career.	
15, Supporting the special needs and concerns of minority and under-represented faculty members.	
16. Providing support for faculty members who may experience stress or conflict.	
17. Creating interdisciplinary contacts for the mentee.	
18. Additional goal: _____	
19. Additional goal: _____	

1.6. What Services Will Your Mentoring Program Provide?

Based on how you prioritized the broad goals of the mentoring program in worksheet 1.5, now use worksheet 1.6 to select which services you should include in a new mentoring program or add to your existing mentoring program.

Once again, use the following rubric:

A   Most important

B   Next most important

C   Nice to have

D   Not important

Note: Do not select more than three "A" priorities.

Service Provided By Mentors/Unit	Priority (A,B,C, or D)
1. Matching each mentee with a mentor or group of mentors.	(This is assumed.)
2. Mentors clarifying expectations of mentees for promotion.	
3. Providing feedback on progress toward promotion.	

4. Helping each individual set annual goals.	
5. Creating multi- year career plan.	
6. Teaching observation and feedback, coaching on teaching issues, referral to specialist resources.	
7. Review of research and research proposals; advising on submissions to journals or other publications.	
8. Clinical, service, or administrative coaching (e.g., lab management).	
9. Guidance about which national meetings to attend and how to get involved with the discipline.	
10. Making connections with industry or relevant agencies.	
11. Facilitating interdisciplinary contacts for research and/or teaching projects.	
12. Coaching about engagement on the campus or in the unit.	
13. Coaching about time management; constraining engagements that are not relevant for promotion or tenure.	

14. Providing advice about personal and work habits that may get in the way of performance.	
15. Making a professional referral when serious health issues or personal problems arise.	
16. Supporting the special needs and concerns of minority and under-represented faculty members, either via unit mentoring or through additional resources.	
17. Providing support for faculty members who may experience stress or conflict.	
18. Additional service: _____	
19. Additional service: _____	

1.7. Specifying Who Will Participate in Your Mentoring Program

A. Considering the goals you have prioritized and the services you want to offer, who will be eligible to mentor in your program? What ranks and statuses of faculty may participate? Check all that apply.

Can be a...	Mentor	Mentee
Part-time adjunct professor		
Fixed-term full-time junior professor or equivalent title like "lecturer"		
Fixed-term full-time associate professor or equivalent title like "senior lecturer"		
Fixed-term full-time professor or equivalent title		
Assistant professors on the tenure track		
Tenured associate professors		
Tenured full professors		

B. Will department or IHE staff serve in auxiliary mentoring capacities? If so, how?

C. Will mentees be required/permitted to have at least one mentor from outside the department or division? Or will unit members deliver all formal mentoring?

D. Will there be mentors who are outside the university? (E.g., in industry, or in other universities?)

1.8. What Format Should Your Mentoring Program Have?

How might each of the following models fit—or *not fit*—with your situation?

One-to-one mentor to mentee model. The key is that a new faculty member has a designated, publicly known, single, "go to" person for questions and a first line of assistance.

The mentoring committee model. 3-5 persons are formally designated to help the faculty member.

Division of labor models (e.g., one mentor for teaching and one for research).

Group model (i.e., one assigned mentor for a group of mentees—and often the mentee cohort meets as a group).

Designated mentors "on call" or a mentor "pool" (i.e., There is a defined pool of mentors all new faculty members may call on. They are not a committee and do not meet as a group).

Mixed and match models (e.g., have a single member as a research mentor and participate in a group for improvement of teaching methods).

1.9. Operational Decisions Worksheet

Use the following worksheet to identify key operational decisions.

1. What will be the duration of your mentoring program for each faculty member? (e.g., one year, until promoted, etc.?)
2. When and how are potential participants informed about the program? During candidacy or after they are hired? Who has responsibility for this?
3. What written materials (if any) are distributed in hard copy or via electronic means?

4. Do you expect the candidate to assemble his or her mentoring committee/approach the mentor, or do you expect the unit to assign the mentors? If the former, what assistance is provided to the faculty member? If the latter, to what extent are the mentees and mentors consulted in advance? Who is responsible for seeing that all mentors and mentees are connected? (Review worksheet 1.2.)

5. What are the expectations for documentation (if any) of a) required mentoring activities, b) that other activities have occurred, or c) regular reports from mentoring pairs or mentoring committees? What are the deadlines for reports being received, if any, and who administers any records kept of mentoring activity?

6. Who has responsibility for checking on how mentoring relationships are going and making any needed adjustments? Who has responsibility for carrying out a periodic review of the program as a whole? (Review worksheet 1.2.)

7. Is it expected that the mentor will participate in the formal assessment of progress of the mentee or remain entirely in a supportive and guiding role? What are the confidentiality agreements that should exist between mentor and mentee? What process will exist for discussing these agreements?

8. How will mentors be rewarded, recognized, and supported? Who will be responsible for carrying out recognition, reward, and support activities?

1.10. Getting the Faculty Involved: Sample Charter for a Faculty Committee

SAMPLE CHARTER

Memorandum

From: Department Chair

To: Faculty Committee for Recommending a Mentoring Program Design to the Department

CC: Full-time faculty in the Department

A faculty committee consisting of Professors Smith, Jones, Brown, and Black will study the department's need for updating and revising of our approach to mentoring and will provide a written report of their study and recommendations at the first faculty meeting of the spring semester.

The recommendations will be discussed and adopted by the voting members of the faculty during the spring semester and implemented in the following academic year. Professor Smith will serve as chair and will serve as the author of the recommendations with the advice of the other committee members.

The committee will review the guidelines recently published by the Office of the Provost for recommended mentoring approaches and consider what similar size units are doing in the Division and across peer institutions and recommend changes for the full faculty to consider. Additional specific questions that the committee might ask include but are not limited to:

SAMPLE CHARTER

- Are revisions in our mentoring programs needed in light of recent experience of our early career faculty coming up for tenure decision?

- What, if any, mentoring services should be extended to the various groups of fixed-term faculty who serve in the department?

- What, if any, mentoring services should be extended to recently tenured faculty?

In making their recommendations, the committee should assess the views of the faculty and particularly the needs and concerns of early career faculty on the tenure track and the fixed-term full-time faculty. The committee should also consider current best practices. The committee will share an interim report of its findings and preliminary recommendations with the executive committee of the department by November 15.

The department staff will assist the committee in any logistical, scheduling matters.

1.11. Faculty Study Committee Assessment Tool for Mentoring

This worksheet template can be used for individual reflection and also to guide a discussion of a mentoring study committee:

Area of Mentoring Program Design and Operation	What we do now? (who, what, how, when?)	How is it working?	How might we improve?	What we can do right now vs. do later	Expected benefit
1. Written statement of our mentoring program					
2. Sharing our mentoring program with candidates					

	What we do now? (who, what, how, when?)	How is it working?	How might we improve?	What we can do right now vs. do later	Expected benefit
3. How mentors are matched with mentees					
4. How mentors are oriented					
5. How the mentoring relationship is initiated					

	What we do now? (who, what, how, when?)	How is it working?	How might we improve?	What we can do right now vs. do later	Expected benefit
6. How we check to see if individual mentoring relationships are working					
7. How we assess the program on a regular basis					
8. How we make changes in individual mentoring arrangements					
9. How we adjust the overall program based on a systematic review					

2. What Services Are Needed to Support Early Career Faculty?

2.1. Improving Clarity of Standards and Processes: Survey of Tenure Track Faculty

This survey could also be adapted for use to assess the needs of a group of early career faculty or as a discussion guide to set an agenda for a specific faculty mentor-mentee relationship.

Which of the following services would be most helpful to you in terms of gaining clarity about tenure standards for your unit? Please use a 1-5 scale to indicate your response:

5 = This is very much needed.

3 = This would be helpful but not essential.

1 = This has already been done to my satisfaction.

Area for needed clarification or additional assistance:	Your rating (1-5)
1. Clarify what is expected in order to qualify for tenure and promotion (e.g., expectations for research, teaching, service, or clinical performance).	

Area for needed clarification or additional assistance:	Your rating (1-5)
2. Clarify how much various teaching evaluations count in the decision (e.g., student evaluations, review by senior faculty).	
3. Clarify how many articles, books, and other written products might be expected—and the indicators of quality that are most important in the tenure decision.	
4. Clarify how much generating funded research or other revenue counts in the tenure and promotion decision.	
5. Clarify what, if any, essential departmental or university service should be performed prior to tenure.	
6. Would appreciate an annual review of progress toward tenure and promotion and feedback about how I could strengthen my case.	
7. Would appreciate seeing the CV's and recommendation letters for recent successful tenure candidates.	
8. Would like more detailed guidance about what I need to submit for my tenure dossier and the timeline (when I need to submit it).	

Area for needed clarification or additional assistance:	Your rating (1-5)
9. Would like guidance about what I might be expected to do in terms of being engaged in our national or regional professional organizations prior to gaining tenure.	
10. Would be interested in a discussion of how tenure track faculty are expected to participate in faculty meetings and faculty committees.	
11. Would be interested in a discussion of any activities that early career faculty should avoid or minimize pre-tenure.	
12. Would be interested in how the department might describe "the ideal" candidate for tenure in this unit.	
13. Additional item: _____	
14. Additional item: _____	

2.2. Improving Clarity of Standards and Processes: Fixed-Term (Contract) Faculty

This survey could also be adapted for use to assess the needs of a group of early career faculty or as a discussion guide to set an agenda for a specific faculty mentor-mentee relationship.

Which of the following services would be most helpful to you in terms of gaining clarity about promotion standards for your unit? Please use a 1-5 scale to indicate your response:

5 = This is very much needed.

3 = This would be helpful but not essential.

1 = This has already been done to my satisfaction.

Area for needed clarification or additional assistance:	Your rating (1-5)
1. Clarify what is expected in order to qualify for promotion (e.g., expectations for research, teaching, service, or clinical performance).	
2. Clarify how much various teaching evaluations count in the decision (e.g., student evaluations, review by senior faculty).	
3. Clarify how many articles, books, and other written products might be expected—and the indicators of quality that are most important in the promotion decision.	

Area for needed clarification or additional assistance:	Your rating (1-5)
4. Clarify how much generating funded research or other revenue counts in the promotion decision.	
5. Clarify what, if any, essential departmental or university service should be performed prior to promotion.	
6. Would appreciate an annual review of progress toward promotion and feedback about how I could strengthen my case.	
7. Would appreciate seeing the CV's and recommendation letters of recent fixed-term candidates who were promoted to the next rank.	
8. Would like more detailed guidance about what I need to submit for my promotion application and the timeline (when I need to submit it).	
9. Would like guidance about what I might be expected to do in terms of being engaged in our national or regional professional organizations prior to gaining promotion.	
10. Would be interested in a discussion of how fixed-term faculty are expected to participate in faculty meetings and faculty committees.	

Area for needed clarification or additional assistance:	Your rating (1-5)
11. Would be interested in a discussion of any activities that early career faculty should avoid or minimize prior to promotion.	
12. Would be interested in how the department might describe "the ideal" fixed-term faculty candidate for promotion in this unit.	
13. Additional item: _____	
14. Additional item: _____	

2.3. Unit Self-Assessment of Activities to Clarify Promotion Standards and Processes

This worksheet is for use by a faculty planning committee to self-assess the current quality of its services to support mentoring efforts that are directed toward clarifying the promotion and tenure process and toward providing needed coaching.

How would you rate following services that your unit provides to help either tenure track or fixed-term early career faculty in your unit with the promotion process?

A = This is an area we should prioritize for increased effort.

B = This is a second priority.

C = We do a good job already in this area.

D = Action is not really needed in this area.

Area to assess	Tenure Track	Fixed-Term
1. Clarity of written statements of what is expected in order to qualify for promotion (e.g., expectations for research, teaching, service, or clinical performance).		
2. Clarity about how much various teaching evaluations count in the decision (e.g., student evaluations, review by senior faculty).		

3. Clarity how many articles, books, and other written products might be expected, and what are the indicators of quality that are most important in the promotion or tenure decision.		
4. Clarity about how much generating funded research or other revenue counts in the promotion decision.		
5. Clarity about what, if any, essential departmental or university service should be performed prior to promotion.		
6. Clarity about the relative importance of teaching, research, and service for promotion as a faculty member in this unit.		
7. Provide candidates for promotion or tenure with a review of progress and with feedback about what could strengthen the case for promotion or tenure.		
8. Provide more detailed guidance about how to prepare the promotion/tenure dossier and application.		
9. Provide better guidance about what faculty might be expected to do in terms of being engaged in national or regional professional societies prior to gaining promotion or tenure.		

10. Provide guidance about how early career faculty are expected to participate in departmental activities.		
11. Provide guidance on activities that are frowned upon for early career faculty seeking promotion.		
12. Additional item: _____		
13. Additional item: _____		

2.4. Survey of Individual Needs for Teaching Assistance Services

This survey could be adapted for use to assess the needs of a group of early career faculty or as a discussion guide to set an agenda for a specific faculty mentor-mentee relationship.

Which of the following services would be most helpful to you in terms of addressing your needs as an instructor <u>in the next year</u>? Please use a 1-5 scale to indicate your response:

> 5 = This is very much needed.

> 3 = This would be helpful but not essential.

> 1 = This has already been done to my satisfaction.

Area that might be helpful to learn more about:	Your rating (1-5)
1. Guidance on a general philosophy of teaching that would fit for my courses and on drafting a teaching philosophy statement.	
2. Understanding of the criteria for good teaching that are reflected in my institution's teacher evaluations.	
3. Understanding what my unit considers to be excellent teaching and any preferred methods and approaches.	

Area that might be helpful to learn more about:	Your rating (1-5)
4. How to design an introductory, intermediate, or advanced course.	
5. How to write learning objectives. How to measure those objectives.	
6. How to design learning activities that fit my learning objectives.	
7. How to use technology in the classroom for student engagement.	
8. How to use the specific teaching tools provided by my institution (e.g. Blackboard, Sakai, etc.) to improve the student learning experience.	
9. How to be a better lecturer.	
10. How to be a better discussion leader.	
11. How to be a better advisor and mentor of students.	
12. How to assess the meaning of course evaluation results.	

Area for needed clarification or additional assistance:	Your rating (1-5)
13. How to design a syllabus.	
14. How to deal with problem students and student behavior.	
15. How to make sure my classroom is inclusive and welcoming.	
16. How to accommodate different learning styles in my instructional methods.	
17. How to use quizzes and other assessments to track student learning.	
18. How to grade efficiently, fairly, and effectively.	
19. Additional item: _____	
20. Additional item: _____	

2.5. Departmental Self-Assessment: Mentoring Needs of Early Career Faculty in Teaching

1. Based on data from student evaluations and recent observation of early career faculty teaching, what, if any, are the typical deficits in the teaching skills of early career faculty members?
2. Based on any campus, school, or unit-wide initiatives, what are the desired directions for innovation in teaching? What skills are needed by faculty members to implement these directions?
3. What skills should our mentoring program focus on to address the concerns identified in answer to 1 & 2 above?

4. Who are the faculty members in the department who demonstrate strengths in various areas of teaching? How do these strengths match up with needed skills for our early career faculty?

5. What programs or initiatives do we currently have in place to strengthen teaching? How might these be expanded to address early career faculty needs?

6. What's the best way to address these skills in our mentoring program:

A) Include in one-on-one mentor or committee mentoring arrangements?
B) Have an organized skill building effort in our unit (e.g., a seminar/support group on effective teaching)?
C) Make it a mandatory or voluntary referral to the campus teaching and learning center (or equivalent)?
D) Other? _____

7. Do we expect too much of teachers in their first year? Should we require fewer new preparations? Should we offer a reduced teaching load during the first semester or until new faculty demonstrate more comfort in the classroom?

8. What are the next steps in implementing identified mentoring program improvements, as indicated in the answers above? Who will be responsible for carrying out these changes?

2.6. Survey of Faculty Needs for Support with Research and Writing Skills

This survey could be adapted for use to assess the needs of a group of early career faculty or as a discussion guide to set an agenda for a specific faculty mentor-mentee relationship.

Which of the following services would be most helpful to you in addressing your needs as a researcher and writer, in <u>the next year</u>? Please use a 1-5 scale to indicate your response:

5 = This is very much needed.

3 = This would be helpful but not essential.

1 = This has already been done to my satisfaction.

Area that might be helpful to discuss with a mentor or advisor:	Your rating (1-5)
1. Guidance on a general philosophy of research that would fit for my interests.	
2. Understanding of my unit's preferred criteria for good research.	
3. Defining significant, yet manageable, research questions to launch a productive series of inquiries.	
4. Mapping out a research program based on these areas of inquiry.	

Area that might be helpful to discuss with a mentor or advisor:	Your rating (1-5)
5. Defining and designing specific studies to implement my research program.	
6. Opportunities to join a lab or research project that is ongoing or about to get started.	
7. Opportunities to partner with a more senior faculty member on a writing or research project.	
8. Getting further training in a new (to me) methodology.	
9. Carving out time to work on the research; establishing a routine and a discipline for blocking out research time.	
10. Identifying needed supports for writing productivity, (e.g., a writing group).	
11. Developing a good outline for an article or book.	
12. Identifying and using campus resources that can assist me in my research.	
13. Getting and using feedback on early drafts of an article or book chapter.	

Area that might be helpful to discuss with a mentor or advisor:	Your rating (1-5)
14. Clarifying which journals/presses are the best venues for publication, in the view of the department.	
15. Submitting an article/book for publication.	
16. Identifying sources of funding for my research (e.g., travel funds).	
17. Clarifying which sources of funding are worth my time applying for and which are likely to be a waste of my time.	
18. Writing funding proposals.	
19. Identifying research funding sources relevant to my discipline (e.g., NSF, NIH, NEH, NIE, etc.).	
20. Getting guidance on how to approach funding sources.	
21. Identifying possible research partners or collaborators.	
22. Getting help in organizing my laboratory and/or supervising graduate students and post-docs.	

Area that might be helpful to discuss with a mentor or advisor:	Your rating (1-5)
23. Additional item: _____	
24. Additional item: _____	

2.7. Departmental Self-Assessment: Mentoring Needs of Early Career Faculty in Research

1. Based on data from promotion applications and from recent experience of observation of early career faculty research, what, if any, are the typical deficits in their research skills?
2. Based on any campus, school, or unit-wide initiatives, what are the desired directions for innovation in research? What skills are needed by faculty members to implement these directions?

3. What skills should our mentoring program focus on to address the concerns identified in the answers to 1 & 2 above?

4. What's the best way to address these skills in our mentoring program?

A) Include in one-on-one mentor or committee mentoring arrangements
B) Have an organized skill building effort in our unit (e.g., a seminar/support group on effective writing)
C) Provide funds for off campus workshop on research methods
D) Other _____

5. What are the next steps in implementing identified mentoring program improvements, as indicated in the answers above? Who will be responsible for carrying out these changes?

2.8. Survey of Faculty Needs for Professional Development

This survey could be adapted for use to assess the needs of a group of early career faculty or as a discussion guide to set an agenda for a specific faculty mentor-mentee relationship.

Which of the following services would be most helpful to you in addressing your needs for assistance in professional development, in <u>the next year</u>? Please use a 1-5 scale to indicate your response:

5 = This is very much needed.

3 = This would be helpful but not essential.

1 = This has already been done to my satisfaction.

Area that might be helpful to discuss with a mentor or advisor:	Your rating (1-5)
1. Guidance as to what professional meetings it makes sense for me to attend.	
2. Guidance as to how involved to become in my professional organizations at this stage of my career.	
3. Introduction to individuals who might help me navigate or get involved in professional organizations.	
4. Facilitation of contacts with faculty in the department or on campus who share my interests.	

Area that might be helpful to discuss with a mentor or advisor:	Your rating (1-5)
5. Linking me to campus resources for faculty related to teaching, research, or public service.	
6. Opportunities to participate in professional development courses on topics such as: time management, stress management, goal setting, career planning, organizational skills, etc.	
7. Finding additional informal mentors and building my network of professional contacts.	
8. What service activities, if any, are good to be involved with in my unit, in my school, and on campus? How to get engaged?	
9. Getting help to withdraw from or decline offers of activities that might take time away from priority activities at this stage of my career.	
10. Additional item: _____	
11. Additional item: _____	

2.9. For an Early-Career Professor: Assessing My Support Network for Academic Productivity

A. RESEARCH AND WRITING
1. The individuals with whom I can talk over the most important conceptual issues in my research are:
2. The individuals with whom I can discuss the most important methodological issues in my research are:
3. The individuals who can advise me where to publish and help me make contact with potential publishers are:

4. The individuals who can connect me to those on campus or in my field who would be good collaborators or advisors are:

5. Individuals who can connect me with funding sources, resources for research leaves, travel funds and other resources are:

6. Individuals who will read and comment on my drafts are:

7. Other needs for research support not listed above are:

8. Based on my assessment of this area, I need to extend my network in the following way:

B. TEACHING AND WORKING WITH STUDENTS

1. Individuals with whom I can discuss the design of a course are:

2. Individuals with whom I can discuss the use of new technologies in the classroom or creating online courses are:

3. Individuals who can advise me when I run into problems with the class are:

4. Individuals who can advise me when I run into problems with individual students are:

5. Other needs for teaching and working with students not listed above are:

6. Based on my assessment of this area, I need to extend my network in the following way:

C. SERVICE AND LEADERSHIP

1. Individuals who can advise me about leadership development opportunities on the campus and in the school are:

2. Individuals who could advise me on what departmental service roles to take on and tips in performing these roles (e.g. director of undergraduate studies) are:

3. Individuals who could advise me about the next steps to take in advancing in my professional association are:

4. Other needs for service and professional development not listed above are:

5. Based on my assessment of this area, I need to extend my network in the following way:

D. CAREER PLANNING AND DECISION MAKING

1. Individuals who could help me develop a career plan might be:

2. Individuals who would be good advisors on creating better work life balance could be:

3. Individuals who could guide me about departmental, campus, or professional association politics might be:

4. Individuals who could help me with personal or family problems that might arise are:

5. Other needs for career planning and decision-making not listed above are:

6. Based on my assessment of this area, I need to extend my network in the following way:

2.10. Assessment: Inclusive Policies and Practices

Please use the following scale to indicate your response:

A = This is very much needed.

B = This would be helpful but not essential.

C = This has already been implemented well / is not needed.

To what degree does your unit need to implement the following practices?

Inclusive policy or practice	Priority for improvement (A, B, or C)
1. Create and adopt a written statement about commitment to non-discrimination and inclusive policies.	
2. Review how minority perspectives are represented in the curriculum, in class discussions, and in recruitment and retention of students, faculty, and staff.	
3. Make a plan to recruit and retain under-represented minority faculty members that includes best practices in hiring.	

4. Conduct training on such topics as discrimination, microaggressions, implicit bias, and sexual harassment. Make sure the training is accessible to students, faculty, and staff.	
5. Provide outside-of-unit coaching and mentoring options for faculty members who identify with groups that are traditionally under-represented in the faculty (e.g., African American, women in certain STEM disciplines, LGBTQ+, non-US-national faculty members).	
6. Use feedback from under-represented faculty members to improve the climate of inclusion and support.	
7. Self-assess and discuss the ways our unit is welcoming/unwelcoming to people of color and other minority groups.	
8. Make it clear that our mentors are willing to talk about issues related to the faculty member's minority status if that would be helpful.	
9. Show sensitivity to how current events on campus and in the broader society might impact members of under-represented groups in the unit and find a way to have constructive conversations.	
10. See that resources for new faculty (e.g., mentoring, travel funds, research leaves, teaching assistance, etc.) are fairly distributed.	

2.11. Creating an Inclusive Climate

While some items in this inventory do not directly relate to faculty recruitment and retention, the literature shows that a general positive climate for diversity issues across the board is a factor in minority faculty satisfaction and retention.

(This exercise could be adapted as a group activity for faculty members.)

Please use the following 1-5 scale to indicate the level at which your unit implements the following effective diversity practices:

5 = We do a good job with this.

3 = We could do better with this.

1 = We are not active in this area.

Indicate whether you are rating your (circle one):

System | Campus | School | Unit

Work that we do to create an inclusive climate	Your rating (1-5)
1. We create an inclusive climate by actively recruiting minority faculty through such means as conducting targeted searches, employing and then hiring minority post-docs, using promising recruiting channels for under-represented minority (URM) faculty, assuring that each search includes diverse candidates, etc.	

Work that we do to create an inclusive climate	Your rating (1-5)
2. We create an inclusive climate by steadily increasing the number of URM students, so as to achieve a class that represents the diversity of the communities we serve.	
3. As a faculty, we recognize and acknowledge the special challenges that URM faculty face (e.g., serving on an excessive number of committees, being the victim of microaggressions, etc.), and we are able to talk about those problems openly and supportively.	
4. As a faculty, we have looked at the issue of implicit bias and how it might impact our processes of hiring, recruitment, and retention.	
5. We have discussed issues of race, gender, and sexual orientation among ourselves and are working toward a truly diverse and inclusive community.	
6. We have worked at our campus to make sure that URM faculty members have the option to participate in peer mentoring and support groups.	
7. We create coaching, counseling, or mentoring options for URM or women faculty who are trying to address the problems and stresses associated with being somewhat isolated on the faculty.	

Work that we do to create an inclusive climate	Your rating (1-5)
8. As appropriate to our discipline, we offer a curriculum that reflects concerns of URM and women.	
9. As appropriate to our discipline, we support research agendas that address URM and women's concerns.	
10. We recognize and reward faculty members who contribute to building a friendly and welcoming climate across differences of color, ethnicity, national origin, gender, or sexual orientation.	
11. We make it possible for faculty members to learn about issues related to inclusion and diversity and to identify helpful practices.	
12. We have someone who is formally designated as a champion for diversity and inclusion issues.	
13. We have opportunities for URM mid-career faculty to meet together to share issues of concern.	
14. We have annual events exploring aspects of diversity and inclusion.	
15. Diversity and inclusion is identified as a formal goal.	

Work that we do to create an inclusive climate	Your rating (1-5)
16. There is a diversity and inclusion strategy in place.	
17. We keep track of metrics about our progress in diversity and inclusion.	
18. We have financial aid policies that support our diversity goals and that help students graduate with minimal debt.	
19. We have programs in place to help increase graduate rates of URM students.	
20. We provide faculty guidance on how to conduct inclusive classes that support the achievement of URM and first generation college students.	
21. There is effective training and orientation for new and continuing staff on diversity and inclusion issues, and this training aims toward a climate of mutual respect.	
22. We address how changing expectations (e.g., childcare, work-life balance, etc.) might create tensions in tenure and promotion processes for women and URM of younger generations, and how these might place barriers to a reasonably paced advance through the ranks.	

Work that we do to create an inclusive climate	Your rating (1-5)
23. We make a special effort to retain URM faculty who receive offers from other institutions.	
24. Additional item: _____	
25. Additional item: _____	

Once you have completed this assessment, go back and **circle three areas** for priority action. Discuss why you have chosen these three as priorities.

2.12. Examples of Initiatives and Programs to Improve Diversity and Inclusion

The following information has been excerpted and reorganized by topic from the University of Southern California Academic Senate's November 2016 preliminary best practices report on diversity and inclusion, which drew upon information from 16 universities. You can access the full report here:

> https://academicsenate.usc.edu/files/2015/08/Clima
> te-Committee-Annual-Report-2016-2017.pdf

The information below has been presented in order of direct impact on faculty inclusion. Some material less relevant to faculty inclusion has been deleted, and some entries have been edited for brevity.

1. Examples of inclusive faculty mentoring initiatives

Carnegie Mellon University—Jr. Faculty Program. This is a mentoring program focused on promotion, inclusion, and assisting new faculty in acclimating to the university setting.

https://www.cmu.edu/faculty-office/faculty-
development/Mentoring/index.html

Columbia University's Office of the Vice Provost for Faculty Diversity and Inclusion provides a best practices guide for faculty mentoring, clear articulation of career goals/departmental priorities, and technical and psychological support. The site also identifies mentor models, resources needed, roles and responsibilities, and oversight and evaluation.

http://facultydiversity.columbia.edu/

The University of Notre Dame's Office of the Provost sponsors faculty participation in the Faculty Success Program, a 15-week mentoring experience offered by the National Center for Faculty Development & Diversity. The online program, facilitated by tenured faculty, is designed to equip faculty with the skills and strategies necessary to increase research productivity, promote effective time management, and maximize work-life balance. http://diversity.nd.edu/take-action/

UC Berkeley provides faculty mentoring (both formal and informal). Each department tailors its own program to address department-specific needs. Department planning toolkits are available.

http://diversity.berkeley.edu/programs-services/faculty

2. Examples of faculty hiring/onboarding initiatives

Dartmouth University's Experience Dartmouth Ed Program provides the opportunity for a newly hired staff/faculty member to meet with a more senior staff/faculty member of the Dartmouth community regarding career advice and community adjustment.

https://www.dartmouth.edu/~ide/programs/

Duke University's Office for Institutional Equity supports the faculty recruitment process by assisting in the development of recruitment plans, reaching out to a diverse applicant pool of qualified candidates, and discussing best practices for conducting equitable searches that are also compliant with legal and regulatory requirements. https://web.duke.edu/equity/toolkit/

The University of Notre Dame's *Hiring Game Changers Workshop.* This recruiting workshop provides leadership and staff involved in hiring with a framework for using multicultural awareness, skills, and knowledge to reduce bias in the hiring process, from prospect identification and recruitment to interviews and onboarding. To date, more than 400 new employees at the university have also participated in the multicultural competencies training during new hire onboarding. This training segment includes awareness, skills, knowledge, attitudes, behaviors, and beliefs developed to interact with and better serve diverse populations.

http://diversity.nd.edu/take-action/

Stanford University's "Best Practices for Creating a Diverse Search Plan" includes guidelines for determining opportunities for diversifying staff, evaluating job descriptions for alignment with commitment to diversity and inclusive language, diversifying the applicant pool, establishing diverse search committees, etc.

https://diversityandaccess.stanford.edu/diversity/diversity-facts

Yale University. In 2015, Yale allocated funds for faculty positions focusing on unrepresented and/or under-represented communities; established a five-year initiative to support diversity (including supporting faculty recruitment, appointments, and pipeline development); created a dean position for diversity and faculty development; and began providing course offerings that reflect an inclusive perspective. http://ritm.yale.edu/

3. Examples of trainings on implicit bias, microaggressions, etc.

Carnegie Mellon University's Plaidvocates. Carnegie Mellon College of Engineering's Center for Faculty Success has established a series of "Plaidvocates" workshops on how to be aware of and minimize the effects of unconscious bias.

https://engineering.cmu.edu/faculty-staff/professional-development/center-faculty-success/index.html

Cornell University. Staff groups provide professional, educational, and social outlets for staff to learn and grow together. Cornell has annual Multicultural Staff Group celebratory events as well as monthly professional, social, and learning events—including a Multicultural Springfest Complimentary lunch, art exhibits, live music.

https://living.cornell.edu/live/community/studentcenters/intercultural.cfm

The University of Notre Dame's Project on Inclusive Curriculum for All. As part of this project, vice presidents and senior leaders in the Office of the Executive Vice President participate in training on cultural competency, microaggressions, and the benefits of diversity.

http://diversity.nd.edu/take-action/

University of Pennsylvania. Penn's Office of Affirmative Action and Equal Opportunity offers faculty programming in the form of a lecture series and workshops. One particular workshop, "Professional and Respectful Behavior in the Workplace," is a 60-minute training that looks at various forms of "disrespect" encountered in people's everyday lives.

http://www.upenn.edu/affirm-action/offerings.html

University of Pittsburgh. The Office of Diversity and Inclusion provides monthly, customized trainings on issues related to diversity and inclusion. The Diversity and Inclusion Certificate Program for university employees includes two required workshops—"Fostering a Diverse and Inclusive Environment: The Why and How" and "Preventing Sexual Misconduct: Understanding Your Responsibility") and four elective workshops.

https://www.diversity.pitt.edu/education-training/diversity-and-inclusion-certificate-program

4. Examples of Campus Climate initiatives

UC Berkeley offers a university-wide program to educate students, faculty, staff, and community members on the systemic roots of racism, sexism, ableism, and inequalities to create a better campus climate. The initiative includes diversity research from a range of institutes and academic units on campus, including the Haas Institute for a Fair and Inclusive Society, the Center for Latino Policy Research, the Department of Gender and Women's Studies, the Department of African American Studies, etc. Faculty Equity Advisors appointed by each school's dean assist in improving equity and inclusion across campus programs.

http://diversity.berkeley.edu/programs-services/faculty

University of Chicago. The Office of Diversity and Inclusion was created to support the diversity of ideas, beliefs, and ethnicities of the students, faculty, and staff affiliated with the University of Chicago Medicine, Pritzker School of Medicine, and the Biological Sciences Division. Programs supported by the Office include: Diversity Dialogues; Diversity speaker series; Diversity research and small grants programs (health disparities research); and the Distinguished Award in Diversity and Inclusion.

https://bsddiversity.uchicago.edu/page/signature-events-and-programs

Cornell University's Qualitative Study of Climate for Diversity at Cornell. You can read the executive summary and recommendations here:

https://diversity.cornell.edu/sites/default/files/uploaded-files/Qualitative-Study-of-Student-Climate-Full-Report.pdf

Dartmouth University's Diversity Reading Group is a program to empower faculty and staff to dive into deeper issues regarding identity.

https://www.dartmouth.edu/~ide/programs/readinggrou p.html

Harvey Mudd College has published its *Representations of Diversity on Campus Key Goals:*

https://www.hmc.edu/diversity/

Northwestern University has released a *Diversity and Inclusion Timeline and Report and Inaugural State of LGBT Health Symposium* (8.18.2016), "bringing together researchers, policy makers, community-based organizations, and members of the broader LGBT community to discuss the intersection of research and policy related to LGBT health." They also held a dance marathon (6.24.2016) to support "educational and therapeutic programming to individuals of all ages with Down syndrome to build their confidence and promote continuous improvement." They established a Native American Steering Group (6.3.2016); launched Institute for Sexual and Gender Minority Health and Well-Being, "the first research institute in the United States...that is focused exclusively on LGBT health"; and established a centralized fund "to support the hiring of employees with disabilities." See their *Embracing Diversity* brochure:

https://www.northwestern.edu/diversity/docs/diversity-inclusion-brochure.pdf

Purdue University's 2016 Program Guide details examples of events/programs/organizations that support diversity and inclusion (including safe space zones with times, panels, lectures, celebrations of holidays, etc.)

https://issuu.com/purduediverityandinclusion/docs/16_s pring_program_guide_0f1e7b2b5cad60/15?e=0/32126868

The University of Houston's Center for Diversity and Inclusion provides an computer lounge, study and meeting space "for students to study, engage in inter-cultural dialogue, and enhance their leadership abilities," as well as diversity education workshops and programs and a library of diversity-related resources. The office's work is fueled by extensive partnerships with other departments and organizations on campus. http://www.uh.edu/cdi/

Yale University. In 2016, Yale created the Center for the Study of Race, Indigeneity, and Transnational Migration, "an academic and research center that houses the undergraduate Ethnicity, Race, and Migration Program and the academic journal, *Social Text*." The Center hosts lectures, offers conferences, aligns with other student initiatives, and gives out an Award for Community Engagement.

http://inclusive.yale.edu/

Yale also created a new website for students that talks about university policies and procedures surrounding discrimination and harassment:

http://student-dhr.yale.edu/

Also, Yale established a committee to develop principles to guide the renaming of campus buildings:

http://president.yale.edu/advisory-groups/presidents-committees/committee-establish-principles-rena ming-0

5. Diversity Awards initiatives

Northwestern University. The Provost Office's created two new programs: Grants for Faculty Innovation in Diversity and Equity and the Daniel I. Linzer Awards for Faculty Excellence in Diversity and Equity. See:

http://www.northwestern.edu/provost/faculty-resources/career-development/diversity-and-equity-grants/index.html

and

http://www.northwestern.edu/provost/faculty-honors/award-for-excellence-in-diversity-and-equity/index.html

6. Examples of self-assessment, policy, and measurement initiatives

Cornell University. Since 2000, Cornell's Title IX coordinator has tracked biases that have been reported and has updated a list of incidents monthly and has created monthly incident summaries as well as mid-year and annual reports. Their 2013 *Quantitative Study of Climate for Diversity at Cornell* focused on engagement and inclusion and prompted further research.

https://diversity.cornell.edu/reports-and-data/assessing-campus-climate

Northwestern University. Starting in 2000, their diversity office began creating annual reports "to gauge the university's progress recruiting and retaining under-represented groups."

http://www.northwestern.edu/diversity/resources/reports/index.html

2.13. A Department Chair's Self-Assessment: Next Steps in Improving Mentoring Services

1. Based on your surveys and discussions, what are the mentoring services that early career faculty members believe are most needed?

2. Based on surveys and discussions, what are the mentoring services that more senior faculty believe are most needed to support early career faculty members?

3. Are there particular groups of faculty members in your department who have special pressing needs (e.g., fixed-term faculty, faculty of color, faculty in a particular specialty)?

4. What action, if any, might be needed to integrate the perceptions of more senior faculty with more early career faculty?

5. What are the next steps in implementing mentoring to address these needs? What are the additional services or improvements in existing services that are likely to be most supported by faculty at all levels?

6. To what degree can these improvements be implemented with existing resources?

7. Where might additional needed resources be obtained?

8. Based on the answers above, which improvements should be implemented now with current resources and which should be implemented later if additional resources are found?

3. Designing and Implementing Programs for Mid-Career Faculty

3.1. Self-Assessment for Recently Tenured or Recently Promoted Faculty

This self-assessment is to be completed six months after receiving tenure, or six months after receiving promotion to the next rank for a fixed-term faculty member.

Please use the following scale to record your responses:

    3 = This very much applies in my situation.

    2 = This applies to me somewhat.

    1 = This only applies a little, or not at all.

Since receiving tenure or promotion...	Your rating (1-3)
1. I find myself still somewhat exhausted from the effort it took to achieve that milestone.	
2. I do find myself being asked to take on significantly more administrative and service work in the unit.	

Since receiving tenure or promotion...	Your rating (1-3)
3. It's not at all clear to me what the path is to the next promotion.	
4. The transition to associate professor was not remarked on much in my unit.	
5. It's not clear yet what is expected of me as an associate professor.	
6. At home, it has been made clear to me that my significant others have sacrificed quite a bit for me to get to this point.	
7. I am expected to do more at home in terms of domestic responsibilities.	
8. I don't see additional opportunities associated with my promotion.	
9. I am not sure what my next major projects will be, and I am not clear how I will figure them out.	
10. I am surprised at how disoriented I feel currently.	
My Total Score (Add Scores from 1-10)	

If your total score on this intuitive and informal assessment is between **20** and **30**, it would be reasonable to assume that you may be suffering from a high level of post-tenure stress. This would be a good time to talk about this openly with a mentor.

3.2. A Chair's Interview Guide for Newly Tenured/Promoted Faculty

Suggested introduction: "I am making it a practice to meet with each new associate to check in and to identify actions that might be helpful at this stage."

Next, using the questions below, take some time to explore the experience of the newly promoted faculty member:

1. What have been the positive elements you have experienced in relation to your recent promotion? What has pleased you?

2. Have there been any negative elements? If so, what have they been? What has disappointed or upset you, if anything?

3. What has been surprising or unexpected?

If needed, reassure the faculty member that their experience is not so unusual.

Then ask:

4. Do you have a clear sense of what is expected of an associate professor that is different from what was expected of you in your previous rank? If so, what are your thoughts?

After listening to the faculty member's comments, confirm or correct their perceptions as needed. Take a minute to talk about the role of the associate professor (or the next rank for a fixed-term faculty member) in the department. When you are confident that you both have a shared understanding, proceed to the next question.

5. Might you need some guidance on any of the new duties and responsibilities we have talked about? (If so, I will try to direct you to a good source of help.)

6. What are your thoughts about where you might go from here in terms of teaching, research, or other areas that are emerging as interests for you?

Take a minute to explore the faculty member's thoughts about emerging interests (e.g., how might this lead to new articles, experiments, courses, or other activities?). Ask if he or she has colleagues or a community that shares this interest, etc. Ask what obstacles or problems they anticipate in going forward in this direction. Invite them to reflect on what help might they need along the way.

Then, offer to go over what resources the unit, school, or campus provides for faculty members post-tenure or post-promotion (e.g., research leave, travel funding, research assistant, mentoring program, etc.).

Close by reinforcing the suggestion that you and other senior faculty members are interested and supportive of their progress in this new phase of the career, and that you will be helpful as might be feasible and appropriate. If there is a mentoring option for mid-ranked faculty in your unit, explore that option with the newly promoted faculty member.

3.3. Mid-Career Planning Template

This template, developed for UNC-Charlotte, has been edited slightly for general use. The original may be downloaded at:
https://advance.uncc.edu/sites/advance.uncc.edu/files/media/mid_career_plan_2010_2011%20%283%29.pdf

Step 1. Assess your career goals

- What are your long-term career goals?

    o Promotion to Full? In what area of distinction?

    o Movement into an administrative position/role?

- What are your short-term goals that will ultimately take you there?

- How are these goals aligned with the needs and expectations of your department/unit?

Step 2. Seek understanding on the promotion criteria in your department or unit and in the institution.

- Examine both departmental and institutional criteria and seek clarity as needed. Discuss criteria and guidelines for promotion with your chair, dean, mentor, etc.

- Attend any unit or campus sponsored forums on promotion. Have expectations changed, and how have these changes coincided with your career progress?

- Ask to see samples of previous (and recent) successfully promoted candidates in your area.

Step 3. Conduct a Self-Assessment

Consider the trajectory of your career so far:

- How has its course changed, and why? How has it departed from your earlier plan/direction?

- Have these departures been intentional?

- Have they been aligned with your changing interests and opportunities?

- How has your course been affected by work-life balance issues? How has it been affected by the needs of the department/unit? What needs to be adjusted so that your course aligns with your goals as defined in Step 1 above?

- Examine your previous performance feedback.

- Assess your strengths and areas that need development.

- What resources/mentoring do you need?

- How is your current situation aligned with your department/unit needs and expectations? (Ask peers, mentors, and others for their input.)

Step 4. Write a Mid-Career Plan

This plan should incorporate the results of Steps 1-3 above and should include:

- A list of your skills and strengths that you can build on.

- Specific skills, strengths, etc., that you need to develop.

- Specific short- and long-term career goals and associated timeframes.

- A list of approaches, resources, strategies, and training that you will need to achieve your plan. That is, how will you go about implementing your plan?

Step 5. Discuss Plan with Mentor or Chair

Specifically, seek their input on how realistic the plan and timetable is.

- Do they have ideas for obtaining the resources needed and for implementing the plan?

- Do they see the plan as aligned with department or unit needs? Do they feel that the plan is aligned with the performance criteria?

Step 6. Implement the Plan

- Put your plan into action.

- Revise and modify the plan as necessary.

- Review the plan with your mentor(s) and chair regularly.

3.4. At the Academic Unit Level: Self-Assessment of Mid-Career Mentoring and Faculty Development Services

In the assessment below, refer to the unit appropriate to your role. Thus, if you are a dean, consider your school; if you are a chair, consider your department; if you are an institute director, consider your institute, etc. This assessment can also be used by participants to prepare for a discussion with your faculty.

Use the following rating scale to mark your answer.

A = We do a good job with this.

B = We need to improve in this area.

C = This is not a priority for us at this time.

Mentoring or Faculty Development Service	Your rating:
1. We have an appropriate and meaningful ritual or ceremony in our unit that marks the transition to associate professor or the next fixed-term faculty rank.	
2. We orient new mid-career professors as to how the expectations will now differ from the time they were in the more junior position.	
3. We provide a clear written explanation of the expectations for productivity required to advance to the next rank.	

Mentoring or Faculty Development Service	Your rating:
4. We provide a clear written explanation of the process and timelines for advancing to the next rank, and how to assess whether a faculty member is ready to apply for promotion to the next rank.	
5. We make available a planning template for mid-career faculty.	
6. We either offer a career planning workshop to our mid-career faculty under the auspices of our unit or support participation in a workshop outside our unit.	
7. We offer a mentoring option for mid-career faculty.	
8. We provide a variety of tracks for faculty to achieve the status of full professor or highest non-tenured rank.	
9. We provide an opportunity for faculty members to take a semester leave to develop a new research program or activity.	
10. Our campus, school, or unit provides an opportunity for faculty members to take a semester leave or get released time to develop a new course or improve an existing one.	
11. We provide opportunities for mid-career faculty to get training in a variety of academic leadership skills.	

Mentoring or Faculty Development Service	Your rating:
12, There is a resource on our campus, in our school, or in our unit where mid-career faculty can apply for funds to initiate or continue a research or teaching project.	
13. We recognize the additional challenges women faculty members may face in some disciplines, and we provide the resources (e.g., mentoring, coaching, special training and development opportunities, peer connections, etc.) these faculty members need to prevail over these challenges.	
14. We recognize the additional challenges that under-represented minority faculty face in the academy, and we have resources (e.g., mentoring, coaching, special training and development opportunities, peer connections, etc.) for these faculty members to get the help they need to prevail over these obstacles.	

3.5. Checklist for Improving Promotion Processes for Associate Professors

This checklist has been adapted from the Report of the Indiana University Northwest Task Force on Faculty Development and Career Success Planning. The full report can be read at:

https://www.iun.edu/aqip/docs/devcareerplanning.pdf

Based on faculty survey findings, the Task Force recommended the following actions steps to encourage mid-level faculty to seek the next career stage. Has your own academic unit, at your institution, implemented these or similar steps?

Exemplary practice	Doing this?
1. Notify the newly promoted faculty member of, or publicize, the salary increment between associate professor and professor rank.	
2. Seek additional funding to support two summer faculty fellowships reserved for associate professors.	
3. Institute a third year post-promotion review of associate professor, which includes a career plan or map (including proposed timeline) toward further promotion described more fully above.	
4. Offer information sessions (at least one per year) for associate professors, outlining resources and criteria for promotion.	

5. Increase chairs' and directors' sense of responsibility to focus attention on progress toward promotion (e.g., in the faculty annual report).	
6. Add questions in sabbatical/grants applications to identify how the proposed activity contributes to progress toward promotion.	
7. Increase the ceiling on the amount awarded for a grant in aid of research.	
8. Set up a fund to award supplemental travel grant money to enhance the ability of faculty to present their research at disciplinary conferences.	
9. Offer extended orientation workshops for assistant professors and open these sessions up to the rest of the faculty.	
10. Offer "How To" workshops on promotion and tenure.	
11. Display significant faculty publications or creative work in the unit or on campus.	
12. If a long-term associate professor revives her or his research agenda and is progressing well in terms of research, teaching, and service, we support this faculty member by assigning a reduced teaching load to aid the faculty member in achieving the rank of full professor.	

3.6. A Guide to Interviewing a Mid-Career Professor Who Has Been 10 Years in the Rank

Assessment of the Past

1. Please describe the most satisfying professional experiences you have had in teaching, research, and service since being promoted?

2. What made these experiences satisfying and meaningful to you?

3. What would you say have been your key accomplishments in the past ten years?

4. What helped you be as successful as you were?

5. What kept you from being as successful as you might have been?

6. Looking back, if you could do something differently over the past then years, what might that be?

Assessment of the Present

1. What is most satisfying about your work currently?

2. What might you want to change or improve?

3. What are your immediate plans?

Visioning the future

1. If you were looking back from ten years hence, how would you describe your last ten years,

assuming they would work out just as you hoped? Start with an imaginative statement about what you did over the first three years, the three after that, and in the final four years.

2. So, given that vision of a successful decade, what should be your specific goals for the next five years? For the next two years? What would you start doing differently right away?

3. Is part of your ten year vision being promoted? Why or why not?

   (The interviewer should explore the basis of the faculty member's answer for that last question. It is important to make sure their answer is not based on a faulty understanding of the academic unit's promotion criteria or on a lack of self-confidence. Ask these questions to dig deeper.)

4. What might you do differently to be even more effective in achieving your goals?

5. How might the campus, school, or department be of greater assistance to you?

6. How could I help in my role (e.g., as chair, mentor, colleague)?

3.7. For a Mid-Career Professor: Assessing My Support Network for Academic Productivity

A. RESEARCH AND WRITING
1. The individuals with whom I can talk over the most important conceptual issues in my research are:
2. The individuals with whom I can discuss the most important methodological issues in my research are:
3. The individuals who can advise me where to publish and help me make contact with potential publishers are:

4. The individuals who can connect me to others on campus or in my field who would be good collaborators or advisors are:

5. Individuals who can connect me with funding sources, resources for research leaves, travel funds, and other resources are:

6. Individuals who will read and comment on my drafts are:

7. Other needs for research support not listed above are:

8. Based on my assessment of this area, I need to extend my network in the following way:

B. TEACHING AND WORKING WITH STUDENTS

1. Individuals with whom I can discuss the design of a course are:

2. Individuals with whom I can discuss the use of new technologies in the classroom or creating online courses are:

3. Individuals who can advise me when I run into problems with the class are:

4. Individuals who can advise me when I run into problems with individual students are:

5. Other needs for teaching and working with students not listed above are:

6. Based on my assessment of this area, I need to extend my network in the following way:

C. SERVICE AND LEADERSHIP

1. Individuals who can advise me about leadership development opportunities on the campus and in the school are:

2. Individuals who could advise me on what departmental service roles to take on and tips in performing these roles (e.g., director of undergraduate studies) are:

3. Individuals who could advise me about the next steps to take in advancing in my professional association are:

4. Other needs for service and professional development not listed above are:

5. Based on my assessment of this area, I need to extend my network in the following way:

D. CAREER PLANNING AND DECISION MAKING

1. Individuals who could help me develop a career plan might be:

2. Individuals who would be good advisors on creating better work life balance could be:

3. Individuals who could guide me about departmental, campus, or professional association politics might be:

4. Individuals who could help me with personal or family problems that might arise are:

5. Other needs for career planning and decision-making not listed above are:

6. Based on my assessment of this area, I need to extend my network in the following way:

3.8. At the Academic Unit Level: Assessment of Unit Support for Under-Represented Mid-Career Faculty

Check all that apply.

Supportive practice	True of us?
1. We are aware that under-represented minority (URM) and women faculty may experience the transition to tenure and promotion differently than others, and we take the time to check in with them.	
2. We discuss their experiences as assistant professors to learn more about how to make the unit a more welcoming and inclusive place.	
3. Given that research shows that URMF and women tend to do more service work throughout their careers, we monitor that fact when assigning service jobs after tenure.	
4. We provide or support opportunities for URMF and women faculty to make contacts with colleagues who share their concerns in the unit or across the campus.	
5. We have career conversations, and we validate the person's experience as a UMRF or woman in the department, and we try to learn from them and from their experiences.	

6. We talk with UMRF and women to get their perspectives on the mid-career.	
7. We monitor that research leaves, course development grants, and other funding opportunities are distributed fairly.	
8. We participate in conversations with other leaders about how the campus can be a more welcoming place for URMF and women faculty members.	
9. We assess progress toward the next rank (e.g., full professor) and note if URMF and women tend to make slower progress, and we work to equalize time to promotion.	
10. We look at compensation patterns and give attention to situations where URMF or women are underpaid for work they do and work to create pay equity going forward.	
11. We have a good understanding of what it will take to retain our productive URMF and women faculty during mid-career.	
12. We ask our mid-career URMF and women how they think our unit could be more inclusive in terms of curriculum, recruitment of students, recruitment of faculty, policies, and programs.	
13. We explore whether URMF and women have aspirations to leadership positions in the unit, the campus, or the professional organization, and we direct them to opportunities for training and mentoring.	

4. Senior Faculty Development (SFD): Tools for Academic Leaders

4.1. An Academic Leaders' Confidential Assessment of Senior Faculty Productivity

1. How many of your faculty are 50 years or older?

2. List the number of faculty in each rank.
Group A: full-time, tenured, full professor   _____   Group B: full-time, tenured, associate professor   _____   Group C: full-time fixed-term full professor   _____   Group D: full-time fixed-term associate professor   _____   Group E: part-time associate and full professors   _____

3. How would you describe the members of each group above in terms of their productivity and engagement? Within each group, who are the most productive and the least productive? Who are the most engaged and who the least?
Group A:

Group B:

Group C:

Group D:

Group E:

4. Assuming you could have a frank and constructive individual career conversation with each of the most productive faculty members in the department, what might you say to them? What would you like to ask them? What does the unit need them to do? How do you think they might respond?

5. Assuming you could have a frank individual career conversation with each of the least productive and engaged, what might you say to them? What might you like to ask them? What does the unit need them to do? How do you think they might respond?

6. Assuming you could have frank career conversation with those in the middle in terms of productivity and engagement, what might you say to them? What questions would you like to ask them? What does the unit need them to do? How do you think they might respond?

7. Are there individuals in the unit (e.g., other departmental officers) with whom you could test your impressions about various individuals and get feedback?

8. Based on your thinking and the discussions you are able to have, what are your conclusions about where your unit needs to put its emphasis relative to senior faculty development?

4.2. A Self-Assessment for Senior Faculty

NOTE TO THE READER

This guide is based on the program I developed for the Academic Leadership Program Retreat at UNC-Chapel Hill. Leaders can make this guide available for senior faculty to complete as an individual exercise or as a prelude to a scheduled career discussion with the chair, head of the unit's mentoring program, or other advisor.

A. ASSESSING THE PAST

During the first two decades of your career, in what areas do you feel you have made significant achievements? List what comes to mind.

1. Research in my field:

2. Teaching and advising students:

3. Writing that is important for pedagogy in my field:

4. Writing that can generate significant income (e.g., a text book):

5. Writing that can be a guide for action related to my field of study:

6. Service to the department, school, or institution:

7. Activity that led to the development of new products, services, organizations, or for-profit companies:

8. Other areas of accomplishment:

9. Most significant honors or public recognition conferred:

10. Looking back on this list, what are you most proud of? Why?

11. Looking back on this list, do you think any area of endeavor has been under-attended to? Which ones and why?

B. LOOKING FORWARD BY LOOKING BACK

Conduct an imaginative exercise. Imagine that it is ten years hence, and you are asked to produce a similar list. Use the same categories below to list your desired future accomplishments. Be optimistic but also realistic in making your list.

1. Research accomplishments:

2. Accomplishments in teaching/advising students:

3. Writing that is significant for integrating and interpreting research in my field:

4. Writing that is important for pedagogy in my field:

5. Writing that can generate significant income (e.g., a text book):

6. Writing that can be a guide for action related to my field of study:

7. Service to the department, school, or institution:

8. Activity that might lead to the development of new products, services, organizations, or for-profit companies:

9. Other areas of accomplishment:

10. Most significant honors or public recognition conferred:

11. Looking back on this list of envisioned future accomplishments, what are you most proud of? Why?

C. TAKING OTHER FACTORS INTO CONSIDERATION

What other obligations or calls on your time might be competing with these potential accomplishments? Note any of the following that apply.

1. Raising children:

2. Health considerations:

3. Aging parents:

4. Spousal obligations:

5. Other professional obligations (e.g., I might be asked to be departmental chair):

D. SETTING TEN-YEAR GOALS

Taking all this into consideration (i.e., what you aspire to achieve and the other competing demands for your time and attention), what might be a few realistic and challenging future goals in your academic life for the next ten years?

1. Ten-year goals:

2. What would be the sequence of these academic goals? (Why this sequence?)

3. Given these goals what steps do you need to take in the next year? In the next 3 years?

4.3. A Guide for a Conversation about Senior Faculty Development

This is intended for use by a dean or chair (or other designated interviewer) with a senior faculty member. Set the stage for this conversation by first letting the faculty member know that this is a conversation you are having with all senior faculty. The purpose of the conversation is to give faculty members a chance to reflect on their careers and plan for the future. Have the faculty member complete the Senior Faculty Self-Assessment Guide (4.2) as a preparatory activity for this discussion.

During the discussion, ask the following questions and discuss the faculty member's answers together:

- What have been the professional activities that have been most satisfying to you in recent years?

- What about those activities has been positive for you?

- What factors have made these activities possible?

- Assuming anything was possible, and in an ideal world, what new areas of professional activity might you like to get involved in?

- What about those activities is attractive to you?

- What obstacles, if any, do you anticipate in being able to shape your activities in the way you want in the future?

- What help might you need from the department or the institution to overcome those obstacles?

- What is your next career milestone? (e.g., If you are an associate professor, would you like to get promoted to full professor? Or if you are a full professor, is there a distinguished chair or professorship you would like to attain?)

- To what extent are you clear about the criteria for such a step?

- What activities have you considered that might increase your eligibility for such a position?

- What support might you need from the department, school, or institution to pursue those activities?

4.4. Senior Faculty Development Needs/Readiness Assessment Guide

Use this form to assess how ready your unit is to launch a senior faculty development program. Check as many as may apply.

A. Unit Assessment	True?
1. A significant proportion of our faculty members are over 50 years of age.	
2. We provide mentoring and faculty development services at the junior and the associate level right after tenure but not yet for senior faculty members.	
3. In many cases, our senior faculty members are not sure what the next steps are in their careers.	
4. Some senior faculty may feel a lack of collegial support currently.	
5. Some of our senior faculty members seem to be drifting away from departmental engagement.	
6. Some of our senior faculty members have the potential to make greater contributions to their field than they are currently making.	
7. The unit needs senior faculty members to play a stronger role in the department as role models, mentors, and leaders in the unit, on campus, and in the field.	

8. Our school or institution is urging us to provide more development services at all levels of faculty.	
9. Most of our senior faculty would be receptive to discussing programs that would help them advance in their careers, if presented to them in the right way.	
10. Additional considerations related to the status and motivation of senior faculty, and to the readiness of the unit to engage in further development activities for senior faculty, which include the following: _____ _____ _____ _____ _____	

B. Action Planning

1. Based on your assessment above, what factors would indicate that greater efforts at senior faculty development would be beneficial or welcome?

2. What concerns, if any, would make you hesitate to raise the question of senior faculty development with your faculty?

3. Is there someone you might check your perceptions with to see if they agree with your assessment?

4. Is this a good time to start a conversation about senior faculty development in your unit?

5. If so, who might you discuss this with first?

6. If not, what might be done to better prepare the ground?

4.5. What Are the Best Options for Career Conversations with Senior Faculty?

Check as many as you think would be valuable and feasible for your division, institute, department, or school.

A. Options for Career Conversations	Valuable and Feasible?
1. The school or department could mandate a 5-year career plan, updated on a semi-annual basis.	
2. The chair or dean could offer a voluntary career planning conversation for each senior faculty member on an annual or semi-annual basis.	
3. We could make available online resources for career planning.	
4. We could make available an online template for a career plan.	
5. We could ask faculty members to put five-year career goals on their personal webpage.	
6. The unit could arrange a career planning conversation with an outside group on campus (e.g., the Center for Teaching and Learning).	
7. We could conduct a workshop for the department on the value of career conversations.	

8. The department or school could hire a well-regarded academic facilitator or coach to provide a career planning workshop for faculty.	
9. We could create an annual session of the senior faculty to discuss their career goals (e.g., an annual meeting with the unit head).	
10. We could provide an incentive (e.g., competitive leaves or departmental research/travel funding) for those who base their application on a well-formed career plan.	

B. Action Planning

Using any of the ideas above as a springboard for your own brainstorming, what do you think would be a series of steps that would result in senior faculty in your unit being more thoughtful and intentional about their career plans? List those steps below.

1.

2.

3.

4.

5.

4.6. Senior Faculty Self-Assessment: What Resources Might Be Most Helpful for Me?

What types of assistance would help you most right now? Check any items that stand out for you as particularly helpful at this time.

A. Assistance to support my teaching	Helpful?
1. Support for developing a new course, including some time off for thinking, study, and design work.	
2. Opportunity to work with an expert to introduce participatory and group methods into my classes.	
3. Training in using technology in the classroom.	
4. Support to develop online modules or courses.	
5. Coaching on creating a more inclusive classroom environment.	
6. Coaching and help for dealing with controversial issues in my courses.	
7. Other teaching assistance:	

B. Assistance to support my research	Helpful?
1. Opportunity for research leave.	
2. Opportunity to get training in a new methodology.	
3. Ability to hire research assistants.	
4. Funding for research-related travel.	
5. Funding for research expenses.	
6. Assistance in proposal writing.	
7. Assistance in grants management and reporting.	
8. Opportunity to meet with potential collaborators in other disciplines.	
9. Other research assistance:	

C. Assistance to support my institutional service	Helpful?
1. Training/mentoring in relevant areas of academic leadership (e.g., chairing a department, leading a university-wide task force, etc.).	
2. Opportunity to get involved in academic governance (e.g., faculty senate).	
3. Help in getting involved in institution-wide programs and initiatives.	
4. Other areas of assistance:	

D. Assistance to support my community engagement/entrepreneurship:	Helpful?
1. Training in working with community-based research or service projects.	
2. Mentoring in entrepreneurship as a part of teaching or in developing an innovative idea that I have for a product or service.	
3. Help in getting involved with state and national outreach programs related to my field.	
4. Other community engagement assistance:	

4.7. Unit Leader's Assessment of Resources Needed for Senior Faculty Development

Suppose that your unit could devote more resources to Senior Faculty Development.

Based on your assessment of faculty needs and unit goals, what would be the best use of these resources? Please check those uses that appear most valuable to you.

A. Assistance to teaching and advising students	A priority?
1. Support for faculty members developing new courses, including some time off for research and syllabus development.	
2. Mentoring and guidance on how to introduce participatory and group methods into classes.	
3. Training in using technology in the classroom.	
4. Support to develop online modules or courses.	
5. Coaching on creating a more inclusive classroom environment.	

6. Coaching and help for dealing with controversial issues in courses.	
7. Other teaching assistance:	

B. Assistance to support research, writing, and publication	A priority?
1. Opportunities for research leave.	
2. Opportunity to get training in a new methodology.	
3. Ability to hire research assistants.	
4. Funding for research-related travel.	
5. Funding for research expenses.	
6. Assistance in proposal writing.	
7. Assistance in grants management and reporting.	
8. Opportunity to meet with potential collaborators in other disciplines.	

9. Other research assistance:	

C. Assistance to support institutional service	A priority?
1. Training/mentoring in relevant areas of academic leadership (e.g., chairing a department, leading a university-wide task force, etc.).	
2. Opportunity to get involved in academic governance (e.g., faculty senate).	
3. Help in getting involved in institution-wide programs and initiatives.	
4. Other areas of assistance:	

D. Assistance to support community engagement/entrepreneurship:	A priority?
1. Training in working with community-based research or service projects.	
2. Mentoring in developing innovative ideas that faculty have for a product or service.	
3. Help in getting involved with state and national outreach programs related to their field.	
4. Other community engagement assistance:	

4.8. Quick Assessment: Support for Under-Represented Faculty and Women Faculty at the Senior Level

Check all that apply.

Exemplary practice	True of us?
1. We are aware that under-represented minority faculty (URMF) and women faculty may experience the transition to the senior role differently than others, and we take the time to check in with them about their experience.	
2. We discuss their experiences as faculty colleagues to learn more about how to make the unit a more welcoming and inclusive place.	
3. Given that research shows that URMF and women faculty tend to do more service work throughout their careers, we monitor that fact when assigning service jobs after tenure.	
4. We provide or support opportunities for URMF and women faculty to make contacts with colleagues who share their concerns in the unit or across the campus.	
5. We have career conversations, and we validate the person's experience as an UMRF or woman in the department, and we try to learn from them and from their experiences. We encourage senior faculty members to think positively about their next decade of scholarly activity.	

6. We talk with UMRF and women faculty to get their perspectives on the late career.	
7. We monitor the allocation of research leaves, course development grants, and other funding opportunities to ensure they are distributed fairly.	
8. We participate in conversations with other leaders about how the campus can be a more welcoming place for URMF and women faculty members.	
9. We assess progress toward the next rank (e.g., full professor) and note if URMF and women faculty tend to make slower progress and work to equalize time to promotion. However, if the person has achieved the full professor rank, we discuss opportunities (e.g., distinguished professorships, chaired professorships) that they might aspire to.	
10. We look at compensation patterns and give attention to situations where URMF or women faculty are underpaid for work they do and work to create pay equity going forward.	
11. We have a good understanding of what it will take to retain our productive URMF and women faculty during late career.	
12. We ask our late-career URMF and women faculty how they think the unit could be more inclusive in terms of curriculum, recruitment of students, recruitment of faculty, policies, and programs.	
13. We explore whether URMF and women faculty have aspirations to leadership positions in the unit, the campus, or the professional organization, and we direct them to opportunities for training and mentoring.	

5. Worksheets for Leading the Development of Mentoring Services

5.1. Worksheet to Assemble Information Needed for Planning Mentoring Services

Please review any previous worksheets you have completed before filling out this next one.

1. What are the most relevant policies on faculty mentoring at the level of your school, institution, or system?
2. Are there any areas in which your unit is out of compliance that should be addressed in any new mentoring program initiatives?

3. Which internal assessments of faculty mentoring needs have been completed? Which are still needed? Mark Y/N in the table below:

Faculty Group	Completed (Y/N)	Needed (Y/N)
Tenure Track Assistant Professors		
Non-tenure-track Assistant Professors*		
Tenured Associate Professors		
Non-Tenured Associate Professors*		
Tenured Full Professors		
Non-Tenured Full Professors*		
Under-Represented Minority Faculty (all ranks)		
Female Faculty (all ranks)		

* Titles may vary with institution (e.g., Lecturer, Research Professor, etc.).

4. For any priority internal assessments that are needed, who should carry them out, and when do they need to be completed?

5. What external assessments (i.e., benchmarking against peer institutions and organizations) have been conducted? Do you know how your mentoring program compares with programs at comparable units at peer institutions? If you do, how does it meet or exceed the quality of what is provided by peer institutions?

6. Do you know how your mentoring program compares with similar sized comparable units in your own institution? If so, how?

7. What external assessments, if any, do you still need to complete before finalizing your mentoring plans? Who will carry them out, and when do they need to be completed?

8. Based on what you now know about how your mentoring program measures up against your peers, are there certain services you need to add that might especially help with recruiting or retaining faculty at any level?

9. What mentoring or faculty development services currently exist in your units that should be continued or extended (e.g., a good informal mentoring system that could be built on; a good orientation for new faculty; a good workshop for preparing tenure dossiers, etc.)?

10. Which faculty mentoring or development services exist outside your unit (e.g., in the Teaching and Learning Center) that can be used as part of any programs you currently have or wish to develop?

5.2. Worksheet to Identify Specific Needs that Your Unit Should Address

Please review any previous worksheets you have completed before filling out this next one.

1. Based on your current assessments, what are the highest priority unmet needs for mentoring and faculty development, for each group of faculty? (E.g., Clarity of standards and processes for early career faculty? Opportunities for mentoring for mid-career faculty? Research support for late-career faculty?)

Faculty Group	Highest Priority Needs
For early career faculty on the tenure track	
For early career faculty *not* on the tenure track	
For associate professors recently tenured	
For associate professors (or comparable rank) who are *not* tenure track	

For professors of any rank with 20 years of service	
For under-represented minority faculty	
For women faculty	
For women faculty	

2. Which of these needs would you prioritize?

3. Which of the needs above would be secondary priorities?

4. Which of the needs above would be tertiary priorities?

5. What is the basis for the priorities you have specified above?

5.3. Worksheet to Identify Opportunities to Involve Faculty in Discussion and Planning

Please review any previous worksheets you have completed before filling out this next one.

A. Having thought this through, what changes would you like to see in mentoring and faculty development, and what are the most compelling arguments in favor of those changes?

B. On a 1 - 10 scale with 1 being "none of the senior faculty agree with my views expressed above" and with 10 being "nearly all of the senior faculty agree," how would your rate senior faculty agreement in the unit you lead? (Circle the appropriate rating.)

None Agree   1 2 3 4 5 6 7 8 9 10   *Nearly All Agree*

C. To the extent that your interest in improving mentoring services is *not* shared by senior faculty, why is this the case? Please list the main reasons for the disagreement here:

1.

2.

3.

4.

5.

D. Talk about your concerns with a trusted colleague and, together, identify actions that might address the concerns you have identified above.

1.

2.

3.

4.

5.

E. Consider whether any of the following approaches are relevant to reducing resistance to improving mentoring programs. Check as many as might be helpful.

Possible approach to getting buy-in	Helpful?
1. Ask a faculty group to study the matter and come up with a proposal.	
2. Educate faculty on new expectations from the provost, dean, or other leaders.	
3. Educate faculty about what other units on campus or at comparable institutions are doing.	
4. Make your case privately to key faculty leaders first and then, when you think they are persuaded, hold a general discussion.	
5. Bring in the dean or another senior leader to talk about the administration's perspective on the issue.	
6. Collect information confidentially from those groups who you think have important unmet needs, and share this information with senior faculty.	
7. Present your thinking formally to the faculty at a meeting.	
8. Ask early career faculty to speak with senior faculty about their needs and concerns.	
9. Show where funding for such a program could come in the budget.	
10. Show how any new mentoring effort could benefit senior faculty.	

11. Provide an option such that senior faculty who are not interested do not have to participate.	
12. Other helpful actions not listed above:	

F. If you think several of these actions might be useful, what is the correct sequence to take, in your view?

5.4. Checklist for Drafting an Effective Mentoring Policy for Your Unit

An effective mentoring policy statement may contain some or all of the following items. Use the list below as a guide to drafting a new statement or as the basis for improving your existing policy statement.

An effective mentoring policy statement:

1. References relevant literature on the efficacy of mentoring.

2. States how the policy complies with broader system, school, or campus policy.

3. Summarizes locally collected data on faculty mentoring needs and preferences.

4. Indicates how the program will benefit the unit, the faculty, and the students.

5. Clarifies the goals of the program and why these goals are relevant.

6. Describes the model of mentoring to be used (such as individual, committee, etc).

7. Specifies who is eligible to be mentored.

8. Specifies who is eligible to mentor and how they are chosen and qualified.

9. Identifies the roles and expectations of mentors, what is required, and what is optional.

10. Identifies the expectations of those being mentored and their duties under the plan.

11. Indicates the length of the mentoring relationships established, how they are monitored, and how problems are identified and solved.

12. Identifies staff and faculty members in the unit who will administer the program and their duties and relationships.

13. Identifies any incentives or recognition programs.

14. Indicates how effectiveness will be measured and what processes will be put in place for continual improvement.

5.5. Worksheet for Identifying Faculty Role Models and Mentors

To leverage the strengths of your faculty in developing the mentoring program, **list one or two faculty members** who are particularly good role models/mentors for each of the following important academic skills.

A. General professional skills	Who's very good at this?
Time management	
Using the summers well	
Work/life balance	
Managing conflict	
Communications	
B. Teaching	**Who's very good at this?**
Working with students	
Managing the classroom	

Preparing the syllabus	
Developing lectures and presentations	
Group and participative methods of teaching	
C. Research, writing, and publication	**Who's very good at this?**
Framing research questions	
Research design	
Proposal and grant writing	
Data gathering, analysis, and interpretation	
Writing articles for journals in the field	
Commenting on drafts	
Writing books	

D. Leadership and service	Who's very good at this?
Departmental leadership	
Leading faculty committees	
Working with faculty governance	
Managing and leading change	
Engaging with communities	
Working with alumni and other stakeholders outside the department	
Fundraising	
Engaging the major professional groups in the field	
Guiding faculty in the promotion/tenure processes	

E. Other relevant skills	Who's very good at this?
Other:	
Other:	
Other:	

In what ways could you use this knowledge of faculty strengths to build your unit's mentoring program? (See examples below.)

Examples

1. With the permission of those involved, create a document on faculty strengths and provide this document to faculty in the mentoring program. (E.g., "The following faculty have agreed to make themselves available for discussions in the relevant areas.")

2. Ask those faculty recognized as role models or potential mentors in a particular area to provide a

1-2 page "tip sheet" for new faculty members on that topic.

3. Ask recognized faculty leaders to do a short workshop in their area of expertise.

4. Involve faculty experts in a panel discussion for the benefit of those being mentored.

5.6. Checklist for Supporting Your Faculty Mentors and Mentees

We need to provide the following activity to better support mentors and mentees:	Yes/No?
1. Clear written expectations for mentors and mentees.	
2. Orientation session for mentors.	
3. Orientation session for mentees.	
4. Online FAQs about the mentoring program.	
5. Opportunities for mentors to discuss confidentially (among themselves) how the mentoring program is going.	
6. A point person for mentees/mentors to approach with any problems that arise.	
7. Written information on how to be a good mentor in general and/or in the specific role delineated by our program.	
8. Training session on how to be a good mentor (e.g., listening skills, advising skills, etc.).	
9. Written statement of promotion and tenure policies, standards, and processes.	

10. List of referral sources for problems that mentees may bring up that are outside the scope of your program (e.g., campus and community mental health and health services, research methods, statistical services, funding sources, teaching assistance, working with students, grading, etc.).	
11. Annual review and discussion of program effectiveness.	

5.7. List of Steps to Ensure the Program Leadership Role Is Adequately Supported

Use the following list to help you identify steps you need to take to make sure your mentoring programs are adequately resourced and supported over time.

1. Identify who/is directly accountable for the operation of your mentoring program.

   (If you are the dean or chair of a unit that is larger than about 15 faculty members, it probably makes sense to delegate the leadership of the mentoring effort to an associate dean or chair. In a very large unit, it probably makes sense to create a mentoring program director position.)

2. Identify the key duties of the leader of your mentoring program and put these duties in a written position description.

3. Actively recruit someone you think would be well suited to the job.

4. Stress the importance of the role to the individual recruited.

5. If the person needs assistance, recruit and establish a committee to assist that person.

6. Provide whatever incentives you have at your disposal that you think are appropriate (e.g., time release from a course, a work-study student to take over some repetitive duties to free up the program leader's time, additional stipend, research assistant, etc.).

7. Meet regularly during the first year to jointly assess how the mentoring program is operating.

8. If the program is large and a lot of documentation is required, provide a staff member to assist the program head.

9. Agree on the process for an annual evaluation of the program, at least for the first several years.

10. If you are head of a small unit or program, and you retain the management of the mentoring program yourself in your role as chair, dean, or institute head, then still take steps 2, 5, and 8 above.

11. Make raising funds to support mentoring and faculty development a priority in your work with alumni, if it is not so already.

5.8. Worksheet: What Funds can you Raise From Alumni to Support Faculty Development?

1. Consider the following list of funding needs and identify the most likely items alumni might be willing to fund if the importance of the mentoring program to your unit is made clear to them.

Item to fund	Would alumni support this? (Y/N)
A. Annual faculty mentoring award and recognition banquet	
B. Stipends for mentoring program head and staff	
C. Stipends for faculty mentoring	
D. Research leaves for faculty who need it most: junior, associate, full professors	
E. Course releases for faculty developing new instructional programs	
F. Funds to support faculty participation in professional meetings	
G. Research related travel funds	
H. Funds for research startup	
I. Assistance for proposal writing and support	
J. Graduate student assistance	

K. Post docs to assist in faculty research programs	
L. Special expertise training for faculty (e.g., research methods, presentation skills, teaching skills, laboratory management, etc.)	
M. Funds to support minority faculty recruitment, retention, and mentoring	

2. Look closely at the items you identified above as likeliest to earn donor support. What amount would it take to fund these services on an annual basis?

3. What case would you make to alumni or other donors that the services you have identified are really important to the unit, the campus, the students, or others?

4. Review past successes in raising funds from alumni. What ideas do those past successes suggest for whom you should reach out to, and how you would reach out to them?

5. What other units on your campus or what peer units on other campuses have been successful in earning donor support for mentoring programs? What are they doing that you might emulate?

6. What funding is absolutely needed to start and maintain your program? What existing funding can you reallocate from other areas while you work on securing new funding sources?

7. Is it possible to get additional funding from senior leadership on a temporary basis while you look for sustainable sources of external funding?

6. Tools, Tips, Checklists, and Other Resources For First-Time Mentors and Early-Career Faculty

NOTE TO THE READER

All of the material in Appendix B.6 has been adapted from resources the author originally assembled, or developed for new faculty mentors and mentees while he served as Leadership Coordinator at UNC's Center for Faculty Excellence.

6.1. What Makes a Good Mentor?

Good mentors are...	Which means:
Good listeners	They take the time to understand what is going on with the mentee before they offer advice and information.
Self-aware	They know what they can and cannot offer, and they observe and note how what they offer is being received by those they mentor.

Flexible	They are willing to adjust to the needs of mentees.
Good role models	They demonstrate good academic practices.
Transparent	They make their thinking explicit so mentees understand why they do what they do.
Positive guides	They recognize and compliment progress mentees make. They also provide constructive criticism and helpful advice. They pay attention to the timing of their comments and attempt to balance guidance, criticism, and praise.
Facilitators	They help mentees connect to others who share their interests and who can help them and provide resources.
People of integrity	They are honest in what they say and do, and they work for the good of those they mentor. They do not take advantage.

NOTE TO THE MENTEE

How good is your mentor? Nobody's perfect and you don't need your mentor to be perfect, but if you don't recognize your mentor at least somewhat in this list of descriptors, it might be time to have a discussion with your chair about how the mentoring relationship is going.

This list of the traits and qualities of good mentors was originally adapted from "Characteristics of Effective Mentors" by Nakamura, J., et al. "Characteristics of Effective Mentors," *Good Mentoring: Fostering Excellent Practice in Higher Education*, Jossey-Bass, 2009. This chapter was cited by Deb DeZure, Associate Provost for Faculty Development, Michigan State University, at her April 9, 2010 presentation for the Center for Faculty Excellence at UNC-Chapel Hill.

6.2. Seven Tips for First-Time Faculty Mentors

1. Make sure you fully understand the mentoring job you are being asked to do.

Each unit has a slightly different perspective on the mentoring task, informed by that unit's particular requirements and situation. Therefore:

- Read whatever is written down in your unit about the mentoring task.

- Next, have a talk with your chair, associate chair, dean, etc., to make sure what is written down is still current and is in fact the desired approach.

- Talk with a more experienced mentor in your unit about how mentoring usually goes. If mentoring is new to your unit, find an experienced mentor in a similar unit who can be a resource for you as you begin your career as a mentor.

2. Understand that you have something at stake here.

If you have been assigned a mentor role in your unit, then your unit leadership has placed its trust in you. There is no more critical function in the university then helping a faculty member (at any stage of the career) be creative, productive, and successful.

While each faculty member's success is ultimately his or her own responsibility, you have been given an important supporting role. How you perform that role in the estimation of your colleagues will be part of their evaluation of you as a colleague. If, after understanding what is expected, you do not think this is the time for you to be a mentor, it would be much better to say that up front, than to go forward with the job of mentor and do it poorly. If you do accept the assignment, then make sure you allocate the time and effort needed to do it well.

3. Understand that you have something to gain from the process

There are legitimate and natural rewards from being a mentor, as well as significant demands. These rewards include:

- Learning and intellectual stimulation from new faculty.

- Supporting the next generation of scholars.

- Helping your department or school retain and develop new talent.

- Growing as a person.

- Creating new and meaningful relationships.

Think about what you are hoping to gain from this process, but also be open to unexpected rewards and "aha" experiences.

4. Start the mentoring in an open, direct, and collaborative way

Unless there is a defined process in your unit for getting the mentor relationship started, here are some steps to follow:

1. Contact the person you are supposed to mentor and arrange a first meeting.

2. Share with them a bit about how you understand the mentoring process and how it should unfold. Explain the hoped-for benefits to the person being mentored. (You might also want to be clear about what mentoring is *not*.) If your unit has written materials that you can share before this first meeting, this can help focus the conversation.

3. Ask how what you have said fits with their expectations and what they think they might need at this stage of their faculty career.

4. Respond as appropriate. You may find that some of the things the person is interested in are areas you can help with, while others are outside the purview of the mentoring role or are issues about which you have little knowledge.

   In the case of the former, you can confirm that you can offer assistance; in the case of the latter, you can offer to make inquiries about who might be a resource.

   You do not have to meet all the faculty member's needs yourself. One of a mentor's important functions in helping the faculty member is to suggest other resources to support them.

5. Consistent with your units' guidelines for mentoring, discuss how you will work together. Make sure to address how often you will meet, what kind of contact between meetings is desired, who will initiate meetings, etc.

6. Close the meeting with a statement of the next steps.

7. Consider following up with a friendly email reveiwing the next steps.

5. Focus on being a supportive person

Focus on establishing yourself as a resourceful, approachable individual whose task is to help. One key to this is being clear about your job as a mentor, how your role works, and how this is intended to benefit the person being mentored.

Another key to this is being a good listener, taking the time to hear the person out and letting them know you have heard them. Listening and understanding is the core skill of mentoring and any helping relationship. Being a good listener in no way precludes your being directive or giving advice as needed by the person being mentored, but it will help you target that direction or advice effectively.

6. Be candid

Don't be afraid to say this is new to you as well, but couple that admission with a commitment to be as helpful as possible to the person being mentored—and to figure things out together when needed.

7. Follow through

Follow-through is an early test of the new mentor. Whatever next steps you identified during your initial meeting with the faculty member, you must follow through. If you do not follow through diligently, then you will be sending the signal that the mentoring relationship is more pro forma than real. This may set up problems down the road.

Similarly, if the person being mentored does not follow through, you need to call attention to that fact in a friendly, inquiring way. Failure to do so may also send the signal the relationship is more pro forma than real.

Also, lack of follow-through on the part of the person who is being mentored may be a sign that the person is having some problems and needs your involvement, whether they are willing to say so or not.

Conclusion: Now you are launched

In most cases, we hope, things will go smoothly, and you will be off to a good start and will be able to work through the mentoring process your unit has set up. The result will be that the individual being mentored has the support they need from you in your role as mentor.

6.3. Checklist to Help Determine Topics for Mentoring

The following checklist was inspired by the Mentor Form (2006) developed by Deborah DeZure, who was then Associate Provost for Faculty Development at Michigan State University.

Both mentors and mentees can make use of this worksheet:

- **Mentee**: Check the topics you are interested in. Your mentor may not be expert in all of these topics but may be able to connect you with other resources.

- **Mentor**: Check topics about which you could provide help. You may not be able to discuss all of these topics in depth, but you may be able to connect the mentee with those who have more information.

A. Topics related to *Expectations*	Mentee	Mentor
1. Performance expectations for renewal, tenure, and promotion		
2. Tenure or promotion stages, process, and activities		
3. Mentoring and how it works		

4. How to be a good citizen of the department (both *stated* and *unstated* expectations)		
5. General Do's and Don'ts for new faculty		
B. Topics related to *Working effectively*	**Mentee**	**Mentor**
1. How to set goals for the first year		
2. How to manage time the first year		
3. Working "smarter, not harder" in preparing teaching or launching research efforts		
4. Building connections on campus		
5. Maintaining a balanced life		
C. Topics related to *Teaching*	**Mentee**	**Mentor**
1. Issues in instruction in classroom, lab, or clinical settings		
2. Issues in teaching undergraduate, graduate, or doctoral students		
3. Issues related to online instruction or technology in the classroom		

	Mentee	Mentor
4. Grading issues		
5. Class preparation issues		
6. Syllabus preparation issues		
7. Identifying resources to help with teaching		
D. Topics related to *Research*	**Mentee**	**Mentor**
1. What is considered good research in this department?		
2. What are reasonable expectations for productivity?		
3. How do the new faculty member's interests in research fit in with the work of the department and faculty overall?		
4. How to connect with colleagues who share the new faculty member's interest		
5. Where to get help in planning and carrying out research programs?		
6. Going to workshops and conferences		
7. Getting the lab up and running		

8. Grant finding and writing assistance		
E. Topics related to *Service*	**Mentee**	**Mentor**
1. Supervising teaching or research assistants		
2. Navigating joint appointments		
3. Opportunities for public service and faculty engagement		
4. Connecting to others across campus/ Being a university citizen		
5. Other topic:		
F. More general topics	**Mentee**	**Mentor**
1. Cultural/social events and resources on campus and in the community		
2. Where to get advice about practical matters of living, commuting, shopping, schools, etc.		
3. Where to go if I have a serious medical, social, or legal issue to discuss that relates to me or my family		

6.4. What to Say to New Faculty Members

Mary Dean Sorcinelli, formerly an associate provost at the University of Massachusetts, is a national leader in research and writing about faculty development and mentoring. She has written an excellent piece titled "Top Ten Things New Faculty Would like to Hear from Colleagues," posted on the National Teaching and Learning Forum.

In general, her research supports the conclusion that tenure track faculty want three things generally (putting aside salary and benefits for the moment):

- A more comprehensible tenure system
- A stronger sense of community
- A balanced and integrated life

Accordingly, the three biggest enemies of the success of the new faculty member are: anxiety about evaluation, isolation, and overwork.

The effective mentor can help the new faculty member by emphasizing the following messages, paraphrased or quoted from Sorcinelli's article. It also might be a good idea for the person you are mentoring to read this list and then discuss it with you.

Here is what she recommended telling first-time faculty.

You are a winner.

You were hired because faculty in the department had confidence in you and your promise. They fully expect you to be successful, and they have an investment in your success. It's good to reach out to ask questions, make connections, get help, and partner with senior faculty.

Pace yourself.

You do not have to accomplish everything in the first year. Build a firm foundation for your teaching and research, and make a plan to show results by the second and third years. Give yourself time to get oriented and get started.

Figure out what matters and does not matter.

Consult widely in the department and get a variety of opinions as you work to create the profile of a successful faculty member in your mind.

Early on, this will probably mean concentrating on research and teaching. However, find a way to get involved with service that integrates you in the department and creates visibility for you in relation to scholarly work (e.g., by chairing a symposium or departmental seminar).

Some work—like your early research products—should be excellent; whereas, for other tasks, "good" may be good enough. Be sure you understand the priorities of your department.

Pay attention to your teaching.

This means being an effective teacher and getting help to do this. Work with the available assistance in your department and on campus (e.g., work with a Teaching and Learning Center). Find out what is considered good teaching in the department. Find out how much teaching counts toward your tenure or promotion (compared to research and service) and budget time accordingly.

Make a plan.

Make a plan with manageable goals and review that plan with your mentors, the chair, and others who advise you. Set out specific goals for the first, second, and third years. In making the plan, play to your strengths but match those strengths to the department's goals. If the department has a strategic plan and goals, be sure to read that document. If not, ask what the department's direction is and how you fit in. (Think about: Why were you hired? What were you hired to do?)

Think mentors, plural.

Even if you have a designated mentor, identify your own group of junior and senior professors who will help you in research, teaching, getting to know the campus, and the discipline. Include in your thinking faculty outside the department with whom you can discuss issues that are more sensitive in the department, as well as people outside the university who can give you a perspective on the discipline.

> *Note to the mentor: Suggest that the new faculty member ask you about who they might connect with; you may be able to make introductions in some cases.*

Connect to the faculty and the life of the department.

Be visible. Attend colloquia and get comments on your work from senior faculty. Invite people to observe and comment on your teaching. Attend department meetings. Find out how new faculty are expected to participate.

Set priorities and manage your time.

You have to multi-task, but you also need to be clear about what you have to get done in order to move your career forward. Put that first, then juggle the rest of your schedule. Some people block out a period of time each day for their priority work, even if it is just an hour. That may be worth trying. Find out what works for you.

Have a life.

Mary Dean Sorcinelli advises, "Take care of yourself and your life outside of work." This might mean regular exercise, time with friends, a night out, a short vacation trip, time with family, or time alone. The key is to maintain your energy and keep your spirits up. Being a tenure-track professor is very demanding—but it should not be depleting. The goal, after all, is to have a good and fulfilling life and career, not be eaten up by your work.

6.5. Helping New Faculty Members Think About the First Year

Robert Boice conducted a study of the characteristics of the most successful new faculty members, whom he called "quick starters." He then taught these approaches to faculty members who were having trouble adapting to their new role—and found that afterward they did better. So here are his techniques for success as a new faculty member, paraphrased from his article "Quick Starters: New Faculty who Succeed," which you can find in the "Effective Practices for Improving Teaching" issue of *New Directions in Teaching and Learning*, Michael Theall and Jennifer Franklin, eds., Jossey Bass, 1991, pp. 111-12.

> *Mentors: Use this list as a kick off for discussion with the new faculty member about getting started in their new role, and about how they are prioritizing their time.*

Quick starters, Boice says, develop "first factor bits." These include establishing from the beginning a balanced allocation of time across all tasks, doing what they can to make an acceptable first attempt, and working steadily to improve the product (teaching or writing) over time. Quick starters do not need to have their lectures completely written out. They are able to conduct writing and research in small blocks of daily time. They take time to network socially with others about research and teaching. They develop confidence and flexibility. They avoid defensive teaching and writing (i.e., teaching and writing with the motive of avoiding criticism). They adopt the following practices:

Teaching

While successful faculty members master the traditional lecture style of teaching, they also allow time for student involvement and encourage students, both verbally and nonverbally, to participate. (Recently, more schools have adopted "a flipped classroom model," in which students review lectures or other material before class and then use the class time itself for interactive learning. This model requires a different and perhaps more demanding preparation for the instructor, often involving use of new technologies. When shifting a traditional course to an active learning model, it makes sense to do so incrementally since this is often requires extra effort, such as: taping lectures, creating mini-on-line tutorials, and new in-class exercises.

Quick starters seek out teaching advice from colleagues and via reading and observing. They learn and use the tricks and tools that master teachers have developed. They use feedback from students and others to improve.

By the third semester, the quick starters in Boice's study had reduced the time spent on teaching preparation from 4 hours to 1.5 hours per classroom hour.

Attitudes

Quick starters have positive and accepting attitudes toward students, they do not complain about their colleagues, and they keep a sense of humor and enthusiasm.

Research productivity

In Boice's study, quick starters spent about four hours a week doing social networking relevant to their research and teaching interests. By the third semester, at least three hours per week were spent on academic writing. And they published at the level required by their campus for the tenure—one to two manuscripts per year.

Synergy between teaching and research

Finally, quick starters integrate their research and scholarly interests into undergraduate classes, which boosts their enthusiasm for teaching and aids in the recruitment of students as research assistants.

6.6. Practical Tips for Mentoring Faculty

This list of tips was prepared by Journalism Professor Ruth Walden, formerly the director of the UNC Center for Faculty Excellence, for her colleagues. I have edited her list slightly for this book.

Her tips include:

- Be in contact (in person, email, phone, etc.) at least once a month with your mentee. Meet in person two or three times per semester.

- At your first meeting, discuss what each of you expects from the mentoring relationship. Remember your mentee may have more than one mentor, so he or she may want you to focus on particular aspects of his or her professional development.

- Exchange CVs with your mentee to stimulate discussion about career paths and possibilities.

- Review your mentee's CV at least once a year.

- Assist your mentee to develop short- and long-range professional plans (e.g., a research or creative activity agenda or teaching development plan).

- Ask about and celebrate accomplishments. Encourage your mentee to inform the dean about major accomplishments (e.g., publications, awards, invitations, etc.) or do it for your mentee.

- Offer to read your mentee's manuscript drafts, syllabi, etc. Provide positive and constructive criticism and feedback.

- Use your knowledge and experience to help your mentee understand how the school or department and university operate.

- Help your mentee network in the school or department on campus and in the discipline. Introduce him or her to colleagues.

- Discuss annual performance reviews, third-year reviews, promotion and/or tenure reviews with the early career faculty member, e.g., how to prepare, what to expect. Volunteer to review drafts of the documents your mentee must submit for reviews.

- Assist early-career faculty in exploring the institutional and school culture (e.g., What is valued? What is rewarded?).

- Share knowledge of important university and professional events that your mentee should or might want to attend.

- Improve your skills as a mentor by attending mentoring workshops, reading about mentoring, and discussing mentorship with colleagues.

6.7. Sample Mentoring Agreement

After reviewing any relevant documents that may be provided by the unit to indicate the expectations for mentors and mentees, the mentor and mentee discuss each prompt below and then insert their shared understanding into each blank space on the mentoring agreement form to establish their agreement.

FACULTY MENTORING AGREEMENT
1. The goals of our mentoring relationship are:
2. The duration of this agreement is (months/years/career milestone):
3. This agreement is renewable on the following basis (e.g., annually):

4. The formal responsibilities (if any) of the mentor under this agreement, as defined by the program's sponsoring unit, are:

5(a). The *primary* informal responsibilities (i.e., offers to help) that are accepted by the mentor are as follows:

Example: The mentor agrees to serve as a [listener, advisor, or guide, or to provide contacts for or advocate for the mentee] with respect to [teaching, research, service, promotion and tenure, organizational culture and conflicts, protection of mentee's time, or other (specific) responsibilities].

... 5(b). The *secondary* informal responsibilities (i.e., offers to help) that are accepted by the mentor are as follows:

6. The responsibilities of the mentee under this agreement are as follows (e.g., keep mentor informed of progress and problems, make and implement plans, meet deadlines and follow up on agreements, etc.):

7. Our agreement about confidentiality is:

8. Circle one: The mentor will/will not share information about the mentee's progress with the chair or other departmental faculty who may be assessing the mentee's progress toward promotion or tenure.

will   /   will not

9. Circle one: We agree to meet on a [weekly, monthly, quarterly, other] basis.

weekly   monthly   quarterly   other: _____

... 9(b). Circle one: The mentor/mentee will plan and initiate the meetings.

mentor   /   mentee

10. The mentor will be available to the mentee between meetings on the following terms (e.g., specify the willingness to set up quick appointments, speed/responsiveness to email, etc.).

11. The mentee should not expect the mentor to be available under the following conditions. E.g., for conversations more than once a week, turnaround comments on documents with less than a week's lead time, for discussion of issues related to particular topics (research/teaching/conflicts in the department, personal issues/other).

12. Circle one and add contact information: The best way to reach the mentor is by:

Text

Email

Phone

Other

13. When either party sees a problem arise with the mentoring relationship, we will:

14. If one of us believes the mentoring relationship is not working effectively for any reason, and if joint discussion of the problem does not resolve it, we will: (e.g, terminate the relationship; speak to the department chair or head of the mentoring program, etc.)

15. Our agreements/expectations about socializing (if any) are:

16. Mentors and mentees will acknowledge progress and celebrate success by:

6.8. Developmental Survey: How Would You Assess Yourself as a Mentor?

This self-assessment for mentors is based on the findings of the article "*Nature*'s Guide for Mentors" by Adrian Lee, Carina Dennis, and Philip Campbell (*Nature*, June 13, 2007). The article provides a distillation of the views of 350 distinguished scientists.

Please use the following scale to respond to the items below:

A = This is already a strength of mine.

B = This is an area I need/want to develop further.

C = This is not an area I want to/need to work on.

Personal characteristics of a good mentor	Your rating (A, B, or C)
1. I show enthusiasm for the field.	
2. I respond sensitively when the mentee is struggling or confused, and I am both supportive and helpful.	
3. I understand and appreciate the mentee's career goals, work style, and personal traits, even if these are very different from my own.	

	Your rating (A, B, or C)
4. I show respect for the mentee in all communications and settings.	
5. I am supportive rather than competitive with the mentee as regards papers, presentations, ideas, and other opportunities.	
6. I enjoy teaching, mentoring, and advising, and I encourage an interest in teaching in the mentee.	
Effective mentoring practices	**Your rating (A, B, or C)**
1. I make myself available to the mentor.	
2. I show optimism and enthusiasm about the mentee's work and potential.	
3. I encourage learning from mistakes.	
4. I balance guidance (making suggestions) with coaching (questioning and exploring the mentee's ideas).	
5. I stay current on the latest findings and practices, modeling that for the mentee.	

6. I encourage the right level of risk in choice of projects for the mentee at this stage of their development.	
7. I model and encourage a balanced perspective on life and career.	
8. I am available for a long-term professional relationship and friendship.	
9. I recognize a mentee's progress and celebrate success.	
Areas of skill I can help the mentee with:	**Your rating (A, B, or C)**
1. Critical analysis of the literature in field.	
2. Writing for our field.	
3. Making oral presentations.	
4. Using my network to help the mentee build theirs.	
5. Encouraging travel and establishing wide-ranging contacts in the field.	
6. Giving advice on career decisions.	

6.9. Tips for Mentees for Finding Success Through Mentoring

The following list of 10 tips for faculty who are being mentoed was prepared by Journalism Professor Ruth Walden, formerly the director of the UNC Center for Faculty Excellence, for her colleagues. I have edited her list slightly for this book. Her 10 tips are:

1. Be proactive. Initiate contact with your mentor(s).

2. Give copies of your CV to your mentors and ask for copies of theirs. (Remember that your mentors often have been in academia for many years, so their CVs will be longer than yours. Be careful about making comparisons.)

3. Be willing to ask for help and advice. Recognize that your success is important not only to you but also to the School and University.

4. Be sure to share accomplishments with your mentors. Mentors are there to help you deal with problems and concerns but also want to share in your joys.

5. Write down questions as they occur to you and bring the list along to your meeting with your mentor.

6. Get to know your junior colleagues in the school and across campus. Remember the value of peer mentoring. Those who have been at the institution

a few years longer than you can provide you invaluable information and advice.

7. Take advantage of opportunities to speak about and present your work. That lets other people know what you are interested in and can help create partnerships and other opportunities.

8. Take advantage of the many faculty support services the institution offers.

9. Show initiative in planning your own career. Set short- and long-range goals for your teaching, research, and service. Share those goals with your mentors.

10. Be respectful of your mentor's time and other responsibilities. (Do not expect overnight turn-around on materials you ask your mentor to review.)

6.10. Tips for Mentees from Experienced Mentors

The following additional list of quick tips are based on an October 2013 panel discussion at UNC-CH of selected mentees who had experienced successful mentoring relationships.

What to know

Learn what is expected, how you are measuring up, and where you want to go:

- Know the structure of the mentoring program that is in place

- Know the tenure and promotion guidelines

- Continually refine your career goals and paths and have one or more back up plans

- Learn about the culture (what is rewarded and what is not)

- Learn your strengths and weaknesses, ask for feedback, self-assess relative to your goals, self-assess relative to your own expectations and unit requirements

- Clarify the help you need (e.g., do you need assistance with research, teaching, writing, publishing, counseling, acculturation, etc.)

- Ask the chair/mentor "What do I need to know?" and ask this early and often

What to do

Actively manage your progress and get the help you need:

- Create your support system

- Use any designated mentors appropriately

- Identify and use both challengers and supporters

- Have mentors both inside and outside of the unit

- Consider mentors and contacts at other universities

- Use mentors to help you say "no" to tasks that distract from priorities

- Build relationships with peers, compare notes, and get peer feedback

- Use writing groups, peer teaching support groups, etc.

- Do not get drawn into factional disputes

- Get extra training and coaching you need; don't burden your mentor with unnecessary tasks

How to find mentors

Seek mutual interest and compatibility:

- Identify people who are likely to share your interests

- Ask around; ask the chair

- Have preliminary conversations before asking another to mentor you

- Test interest and willingness

- Look for those who show interest and have an ability to listen

- Assess what a given person can provide

- Continue looking for others until you have built out your support system

General advice for relationship management

Pay attention to the process:

- Clarify the mentor's role—are they a supporter, advocate, evaluator, guide, etc.

- Don't be defensive—ask for critique; also ask for feedback on your strengths

- Get a second or third opinion if you have doubts

- Come prepared—and follow-up

- Be clear about boundaries

- Keep the mentor in the loop; tell them your successes

- Negotiate their preferences and yours (e.g., frequency of meeting)

- Read the chemistry of the relationship

- Understand the dynamics: inclusion, intimacy, control, dependency, mutuality

- If problems with the mentor arise, seek advice

6.11. The Work Plan: Sample Checklist for a New Faculty Member

For the best use of this checklist, fill in the *date completed by* for each activity that is relevant to your role—or mark a recurring daily or weekly time on your calendar for each activity. Also, note what unit expectations this task addresses.

A. Tasks related to my research goals	Relevant dates/times	Key expectations
1. Connect to faculty with similar interests.		
2. Establish a research agenda with a focused line of inquiry.		
3. Affirm importance of my line of inquiry with key members of the department.		

4. Submit _____ (add #) conference proposals.		
5. Submit ___ (add #) articles for publication.		
B. Writing preparation activities	**Relevant dates/times**	**Key expectations**
1. Send drafts of articles to ___ (add #) colleagues for feedback (e.g., one local, one national).		
2. Attend faculty development workshops on writing, research, and grants.		
3. Discuss conference proposal(s) with faculty colleagues.		

4. Submit conference proposal(s).		
5. Submit article.		
C. Grant activities	**Relevant dates/times**	**Key expectations**
1. Collect information about grant and fellowship opportunities campus-wide.		
2. Identify resources for summer funding and writing.		
3. Discuss ideas with advisors, select grants and fellowships that are worth the effort.		

4. Submit highest priority grants and fellowship applications.		
D. Teaching activities	**Relevant dates/times**	**Key expectations**
1. Seek out master teachers for advice on effective teaching and time management techniques.		
2. Prepare syllabus, order books.		
3. Limit preparation and grading time so that it does not crowd out above activities.		
4. Get feedback on course during each semester, conduct your own mid-term and end of semester evaluations and incorporate suggestions.		

E. Service activities	Relevant dates/times	Key expectations
Say no to activities for the first year, but attend meetings and social events		
In the second and third year, take on committee work that will integrate me into the department (e.g. admissions committee)		
Confirm service expectations with the chair		

Review your work plan with your mentors and advisors. Touch base on progress periodically.

This sample work plan is adapted from "Chapter 10: Creating Mentoring and Relationships and fostering Collegiality" in Estela Mara Bensimon, Kelly Ward, and Karla Sanders, *The Department Chair's Role in Developing New Faculty into Teachers and Scholars*, Anker Publishing, 2000.

6.12. On Being a Good Protégé

When he offered the following advice, David D. Perlmutter was a Professor and Associate Dean for Graduate Studies and Research in the William Allen White School of Journalism and Mass Communications at the University of Kansas. In the April 18, 2010 Issue of The Chronicle of Higher Education, *he gives the following advice to early career faculty who have mentors. His material is excerpted, summarized, and paraphrased below. The title of the piece is "Are You a Good Protégé?" This is a good piece for mentors to read as well.*

You can get good advice from people who may not possess all, or even most, of the qualities of the perfect mentor. For example, one person may have astute advice about research but not be a suitable confidant or a good listener. Perlmutter says, "The ideal advisor may be a composite of imperfect humans."

You should make an estimate of what a given advisor can and can't do for you, but you should never be afraid to ask for help—even if you are not sure the mentor can respond. If the mentor is effective, he or she will guide you to the appropriate resource. You never know until you ask. In fact, it is a good idea to have a conversation about expectations for the relationship, in terms of what each person is thinking the relationship can do or not do for the person being mentored.

Two areas in particular need attention: regulation of social closeness between the new faculty member and advisors and the frequency of help giving. He recommends being friendly (but not friends) with the mentor, and he recommends not getting socially entangled beyond the occasional cup of coffee and departmental social event. He also recommends that the new faculty member not be over-demanding (e.g., making daily requests for assistance); however, reading and commenting on a draft of a paper may be totally appropriate.

According to Perlmutter, "Being a good protégé also means learning to accept criticism gracefully. ...A useful mentor is one who is willing to give us bad news, but a proper protégé is one who is willing to hear it."

Both parties must be sensitive to the degree of independence the protégé wants (and needs) from the mentor. How closely linked are the research activities: joint or fully independent? If the faculty member is not doing independent research early on in the relationship, the chances for tenure are diminished.

Finally, you should accept that the protégé-mentor bond might simply fade away. This can happen when your mentor loses interest in research, becomes busy with other colleagues, or goes through a period of personal distraction. Politeness and kindness are called for, but there is no written contract that demands that you return to the same well for advice forever. Find others who are in a better position to help.

6.13. Assessing the Culture of Your Department and How You "Fit in"

This tool is for a faculty member's self-assessment. If completing this self-assessment raises questions of concern, consider discussing those concerns with a trusted mentor, or counselor, perhaps outside of your department.

The premise of this survey is that organizational culture is a real but difficult-to-assess dimension of academic units. One view is that the culture of an organization is largely a historical accident, and that all cultures have some arbitrary dimensions that are related to characteristics of the founders, the discipline, the institution, and the broader culture. The operative question is the degree to which you as a faculty member are a "good fit" with the culture, and more importantly, how you assess the environment as being a good organizational home in which to advance your career and live according to the values you think are important. The less the "fit" suits you, the more you will have to work to be successful in this culture and at some point, it may not be worth the effort. The better the fit, the more you are likely to have the chance to succeed on the basis of your accomplishments and talents.

Please consider the following questions. These questions reflect indirect ways of assessing an organization's culture. You may not be able to answer all of them, but some of them may cause you to hit on an important theme that will help with assessment of your department's culture.

Ultimately, this assessment might show how you are a good fit with the current unit or whether you need to change in some ways to fit better, work to change some things in the department, or whether you might consider finding a position in an academic unit or organization that better fits your values and preferences.

QUICK ASSESSMENT: DEPARTMENTAL CULTURE AND FIT
1. Is there someone whom members of your department identify as a "hero," perhaps a very respected past or present member of the department? What are the admired qualities of this person?
2. When people are proud of the department, what makes them so? When people are ashamed, what makes them so?
3. Is there anything distinctive about the way the department is laid out, where people's offices are, or what is used to decorate the building or the offices?

4. What, if anything, surprised you about your department when you first got there? What stories were told to you about the department? What stories do you tell others about the department?

5. What is distinctive about the way people in the department commun-icate in writing or the way the department communicates with others in writing?

6. What are the things (if any) that your department regularly does together as a group?

7. What would you say are your department's core values, beliefs, and norms?

8. To what extent are there multiple "subcultures" in your department (e.g., one for graduate students, one for staff, one for early career faculty, one for the more applied faculty, etc.)?

9. How similar or different are you from other members of the department (e.g., along gender, race, ethnicity, nationality, political, or age dimensions)? What difference, if any, does this make for how others see you and what they expect of you?

10. If this department were a club, what would its motto be? If this department had a mascot, what type of animal would it be, and why? If this department had a song, what would the song be?

11. To summarize: What are the core beliefs and values a faculty member "in good standing" in your department is supposed to hold? What are the most important things a faculty member in your department is expected to actually *do* to show they are true to these beliefs and values?

12. In what ways are you a good "fit" with this departmental culture in terms of what you do and think? In what ways might you be "out of step"?

13. If you have concerns about how well you "fit" with the department, whom can you approach with your concerns and get feedback? Are there some in the department with whom you can check out your concerns? Is there a resource outside the department you could consult?

This survey is based on the work of VJ Sathe in his article "Implications of Corporate Culture, A Manager's Guide to Action," 12, *Organizational Dynamics* (August, 1983).

6.14. Advice: How to Find the Right Mentor and How to Manage Your Mentor

The following advice is excerpted or paraphrased from panel discussions with award-winning mentors at UNC-CH.

How to Find Your Mentor

Seek out individuals who are likely to be truly helpful. I am very fortunate to be part of a formal mentoring program, but I still had to I look for a mentor. So, I made an assessment of those members of the faculty who were genuinely interested in me. I looked for people who could be a voice of reason when I was feeling stressed or overwhelmed and who could give me opportunities, like being the editor of journal. I look for people who would celebrate my successes but also would listen to me complain about my failures and problems—but then encourage me to move on and also give me ideas about how to move on.

Seek mentors who will support your interests. I especially look for what "lights up the new faculty member"—what they are passionate about studying—and I support them to do that. I would encourage you to look for mentors who are willing to do that for you. I would also encourage you to look for senior faculty who are at a point in their career where they can be generous and give you opportunities that earlier in their career they would have taken themselves.

Seek out diverse mentors. I think you can find mentors anywhere; they can be in other departments and at other schools. Consider choosing mentors who are different from you (e.g., different disciplinary orientation or style of thinking) who you can ask, "why do you think this?"

Get advice from others about who might be a good mentor. Often a discussion with your program or department chair can be helpful. The chair may suggest people with whom you share common interests. You might also seek advice from outside the department from relevant groups like the Teaching and Learning Center or the Association of Women Faculty.

Use work-related opportunities to assess potential mentors. Sometimes you can get mentoring from a joint project if you are working with a more senior person. You will need to discuss each other's interests in the project to make sure you bring complementary strengths and agree on division of labor and credit.

Use informational interviews to scope out potential mentors. Finding your mentor(s) can be a challenging process. A good way to proceed is simply to meet faculty in the department or who share your interests. Ask them to coffee, and get a sense of their interests in teaching and research. You can also tell them a little bit about your interests and experience. If they show interest in you and seem helpful, they might be good mentors. However, you don't have "to pop the question," *Will you be my mentor?* at the first meeting. You can take time to explore the relationship and see if your interests are common and you are somewhat compatible.

Pay attention to social cues. If someone seems to be too busy, they probably are; if you get the message that you are imposing on them, then they are probably not a good prospect. An ideal mentor is one who understands why it is to their advantage to make time for you, and who is in a position in their career where they can do this.

Build the relationship slowly. You don't have to ask for an open-ended mentoring commitment right away, but if you think a faculty member will be responsive, make a clear and specific request such as: read an article draft, observe teaching for one session, review the CV, talk over a specific problem, etc. In this way, both parties can see how it is working together before making a long-term commitment.

Do your homework. When choosing a mentor, I might ask where their former mentees are. Someone who keeps up with his or her mentees is likely to be a good mentor. Sometimes you will find you disagree with your mentor, and that is a tough situation, but a good mentor can tolerate that.

How to Manage Your Mentor

Stay in contact with your mentor. Follow up with your mentors and do what you commit to in your conversations with them. Regular communication is good. Keep the mentor posted and give them updates.

Do celebrate successes with your mentor. Keep them informed about your successes, so they can brag about you!

Ask for feedback and act on it. If your program does not already have a provision for annual feedback, ask for an annual comprehensive assessment of how you are proceeding toward your goals. Then respond effectively to areas that are identified for improvement. Also, get feedback about how specific classes, papers, or presentations could have been improved.

Share your success, and treat your failures as opportunities to learn. The earlier you confront deficits, the quicker you can turn them into strengths. Find people who can help you overcome problems in teaching or research methods. In one case, a new faculty member coming from a very formal graduate program did not know how to connect with students here and was receiving bad evaluations. The chair asked one of the best female teachers to work with her and she provided her with a few simple techniques to use in her classes (e.g., requiring students to meet with her early in the semester) that completely turned around her image with students.

Get help from your mentor in defining your service role. Sometimes early career faculty can use the mentor relationship to ward off taking on jobs that distract from your career focus. Some early career faculty, particularly women, may feel under a special obligation to help out in the department. Sometimes this can be detrimental to their career. The phrase "I have to speak to my mentor about this" can buy time for the new faculty member to genuinely seek advice about whether taking on this or that service task is really helpful for his or her career at this point. Ask your mentor or chair *how to say no* and *what to say yes to.*

Be willing to accept constructive criticism. If you bristle when criticized, then the mentor may be discouraged from giving you honest feedback. Getting honest feedback is one of the main reasons to have a mentor.

Be respectful of your mentor's time. Have an agenda for your meetings. Don't give mentors articles or papers to look at on a short turnaround basis. Work out some ground rules—when you are going to meet, how often you will connect, who will initiate, and when your busy times are. Be inquisitive about what is on the mentor's plate.

Do get help from your mentor, but don't ask your mentor to solve your problems, whether personal or professional. Everyone has a personal life, and personal problems can affect the quality and timeliness of work. You can share some personal problems with a mentor but perhaps only for context. Don't ask the mentor to help you directly with those issues, but he or she may be able to refer you to a counselor or other resource. The same is true with work-related problems. For example, don't ask your mentor to be your writing coach, he or she may be able to direct you to a resource on campus where you can get the more intensive coaching you might need.

Mentees should take responsibility for their own work and their own opinions. If they have questions about something the mentor says, they should express their thoughts but should not argue with the mentor. If you have doubts about your mentor's advice or feedback, then get a second opinion.

Don't make your mentor a parent figure. Don't surrender your own ability for critical thinking to your mentor. Mentees should not be overawed by their mentors. The main difference between mentor and mentee is age and experience, not some other mysterious quality. Mentees should also take time to evaluate the advice their mentors give them—even if that advice is 95% positive, there is reason to make your own assessment. For example, you can be overly influenced by your mentor's evaluation of colleagues. All faculty members have their own baggage, no matter how good they are in other ways. To get a balanced perspective, you might consider picking one mentor who is like you and one who is different on some dimension.

Beware of intra-departmental tensions playing out in the mentoring relationship. Sometimes mentoring relationships can be a venue for drama. They can express the pathology of the culture. Some departments have competing academic factions, so if a person in one "camp" mentors you, then you are viewed as part of the competing group. Mentors should not put new faculty in this situation. If you find yourself getting drawn into departmental conflicts, find neutral advisers inside or outside the department and take corrective action. Hopefully, you can find a way to have a frank, friendly discussion with your unit head and/or mentor about the situation as well.

Discuss the mentoring relationship. Ask how it is going. It's OK to say the relationship is not working for either party and to find another relationship.

Discuss the limits of confidentially and the reporting requirements your mentors have. Will your mentor be your advocate in that process or expected to provide an evaluative report? Understand what role your mentor will play in the tenure process. Whatever the situation is, discuss the best way to work together.

APPENDIX C: BIBLIOGRAPHY AND ADDITIONAL RESOURCES

1. Selected Studies of the Structure and Effectiveness of Early Career Faculty Mentoring Programs

Berk, Ronald A., et al. "Measuring the Effectiveness of Faculty Mentoring Relationships," *Academic Medicine,* vol. 80, no. 1, pp. 66-71, 2005, www.ncbi.nlm.nih.gov/pubmed/15618097

Eaton, Charissa K., et al. "Faculty Perception of Support to Do Their Job Well," (A Study of Teaching Faculty at Winona State University), *InSight: A Journal of Scholarly Teaching,* vol. 10, 2015, pp. 35-42, files.eric.ed.gov/fulltext/EJ1074049.pdf

Fountain, Joselynn, and Kathryn E. Newcomer. "Developing and Sustaining Effective Faculty Mentoring Programs," *Journal of Public Affairs Education*, vol. 22, no. 4, 2016, pp. 483–506, www.naspaa.org/JPAEMessenger/Article/vol22-4/05_Fountain%20Newcomer%2020160916.pdf

Ghosh, Rajashi. "Mentors Providing Challenge and Support: Integrating Concepts from Teacher Mentoring in Education and Organizational Mentoring in Business," *Human Resource Development Review*, SAGE Publications, vol. 12, no. 2, 2012, pp. 144–176, eric.ed.gov/?id=EJ1004341

Johnson, Brad W. "Why Mentoring Matters," *On Being a Mentor: A Guide for Higher Education Faculty*, NY and London, Psychology Press, 2006, pp. 3-17, www.rochester.edu/provost/assets/PDFs/futurefaculty/On BeingaMentor.pdf

Law, Anandi V., et al. "A Checklist for the Development of Faculty Mentorship Programs," *American Journal of Pharmaceutical Education*, vol. 78, no. 5, 2014, p. 98, www.ncbi.nlm.nih.gov/pubmed/24954938

Minter, Robert L. "The Paradox of Faculty Development," *Contemporary Issues in Education Research,* vol. 2, no. 4, Fourth Quarter 2009, pp. 65-70, clutejournals.com/index.php/CIER/article/view/1073

Mitchell D. Feldman, et al. "Does Mentoring Matter? Results from a Survey of Faculty Mentees at a Large Health Sciences University," *Medical Education Online,* 2010, vol. 15: 10.3402/meo.v15i0.5063, 2010, www.ncbi.nlm.nih.gov/pmc/articles/PMC2860862/

Sambunjak, Dario, et al. "Mentoring in Academic Medicine: A Systematic Review," *JAMA*, vol. 296, no. 9 (Reprinted), 2006, www.ncbi.nlm.nih.gov/pubmed/16954490

Straus, Sharon E., et al. "Characteristics of Successful and Failed Mentoring Relationships: A Qualitative Study Across Two Academic Health Centers," *Academic Medicine*, vol. 88, no. 1, January 2013, pp. 83-89, www.ncbi.nlm.nih.gov/pmc/articles/PMC3665769/

Trower, Cathy Ann. *Success on the Tenure Track: Five Keys to Faculty Job Satisfaction*, John Hopkins University Press, 2012.

2. Collected Guides for Early Career Mentors and Mentees in the Academy

A. Directed at Least Partially to Academic Leaders

"Fostering a Mentoring Community, A Guide for Department Heads," *The Carnegie Mellon Mentoring Series*, Eberly Center of Teaching Excellence, Carnegie Mellon University, 2005, www.cmu.edu/teaching/resources/MentoringFaculty/MentoringGuideDepartmentHeads.pdf

Bland, Carol J., et al. *Faculty Success Through Mentoring, A Guide for Mentors, Mentees and Leaders*, ACE Series on Higher Education, Roman and Littlefield Publishers, 2009.

Phillips, Susan L., and Susan T. Dennison. *Faculty Mentoring, A Practical Manual for Mentees, Mentors, Administrators and Faculty Developers*, Stylus, 2015.

Sorcinelli, M. D., and A. E. Austin. *Developing New and Junior Faculty: New Directions for Teaching and Learning, Number 50*, Jossey-Bass, 1992.

B. Directed Toward Mentees

Boice R. *Advice for New Faculty Members*. Allyn and Bacon, 2000.

Boice, R. *The New Faculty Member: Supporting and Fostering Professional Development*. Jossey-Bass, 1992.

Zerzan, Judy T., et al. "Making the Most of Mentors: A Guide for Mentees," *Academic Medicine*, vol. 84, no. 1,140-2, 2009, www.ncbi.nlm.nih.gov/pubmed/19116494

C. Directed Toward Mentors

"Mentors and Colleagues, A Guide for Junior Faculty Mentors and Colleagues," *The Carnegie Mellon Mentoring Series,* Eberly Center of Teaching Excellence, Carnegie Mellon University, 2003, www.cmu.edu/teaching/resources/MentoringFaculty/MentoringGuideJuniorFaculty.pdf

"Giving and Getting Career Advice, A Guide for Junior and Senior Faculty," Advance, University of Michigan, circa 2003, graduate.iupui.edu/doc/faculty-staff/mentoring-lit-2.pdf

Feldman, Mitchell D. "Faculty Mentoring Toolkit," *UCSF Faculty Mentoring Program*, The Regents of the University of California, 2017, academicaffairs.ucsf.edu/ccfl/media/UCSF_Faculty_Mentoring_Program_Toolkit.pdf

Shaw, Kathy, et al. "Shaping a career in academic medicine: Guidelines for mentor/mentee conversations" Advance Faculty Professional Development Program, Faculty Affairs and Professional Development, University of Pennsylvania School of Medicine, circa 2008, www.umassmed.edu/contentassets/a0dd6af107884e4991e9ca4b7062f296/mentor_guide.pdf

Waugh, Jessica. "Faculty Mentoring Guide," Edited by Carol Hampton, Virginia Commonwealth University, 2002, medschool.vcu.edu/media/medschool/documents/fmguide.pdf

3. Selected Accounts of Early Career Mentoring Programs in the Academy (arranged by institution)

Implementation Team for the Commission on Academic Excellence and Equity, *Final Report: Proposed University Wide Faculty Mentoring Policy and Program*, University of Buffalo, 2010, www.buffalo.edu/content/dam/www/provost/files/ITCAE E_Report_AA7FIN.pdf

Kohn, Harold. "A Mentoring Program to Help Junior Faculty Members Achieve Scholarship Success," *American Journal of Pharmaceutical Education,* vol. 78, no. 2, UNC-Chapel Hill, Eshelman School of Pharmacy, 2014, pp. 29, www.ncbi.nlm.nih.gov/pmc/articles/PMC3965137/

"Mentoring Plan," Department of Cell Biology and Physiology, School of Medicine, University of North Carolina at Chapel Hill, 2014, www.med.unc.edu/cellbiophysio/about-us/for-employees/mentoring-plan

"Faculty Mentoring Program," Department of Large Animal and Clinical Sciences, College of Veterinary Medicine, Michican State University, 2014, cvm.msu.edu/assets/documents/Faculty-and-Staff/LCS-Mentorship-Program-v.-Final-05.01.14.pdf

W.K. Kellogg Biological Station, "KBS Faculty Mentoring Plan," Michigan State University, 2016, www.kbs.msu.edu/wp-content/uploads/2017/01/KBS-Faculty-Mentoring-Plan_revised-Dec-2016_final.pdf

"Faculty Mentoring Practices at Penn," Office of the Provost, University of Pennsylvania, provost.upenn.edu/faculty/current/mentoring

Faculty Mentoring Subcommittee of the HHS Faculty Affairs Committee, "Faculty Mentoring Policy and Guidelines," College of Health and Human Sciences, Purdue University, 2014, www.purdue.edu/hhs/faculty/documents/Faculty_Mentoring_Guidelines-Spring_2014.pdf

Thomas, Rachel. "Exemplary Junior Faculty Mentoring Programs," Women's Faculty Forum (WFF), Yale University, 2005, cpb-us-e1.wpmucdn.com/blogs.cornell.edu/dist/8/6767/files/2016/01/Exemplary-Junior-Faculty-Mentoring-Programs-105ab08.pdf

4. Sources and Resources for Mid-Career Mentoring.

A. Understanding the Problem

Beauboeuf, Tamara, et al. "Our Fixation on Mid-Career Malaise," *The Chronicle of Higher Education*, 2017, www.chronicle.com/article/Our-Fixation-on-Midcareer/239476

Baldwin, Roger G., et al. "Mapping the Terrain of Mid-Career Faculty at A Research University, Implications for Faculty and Academic Leaders," *Change,* September-October 2008, pp. 46-55, www.tandfonline.com/doi/abs/10.3200/CHNG.40.5.46-55

June, Audrey Williams. "The Uncertain Path to Full Professor," *The Chronicle of Higher Education*, 2016, www.chronicle.com/article/The-Uncertain-Path-to-Full/235304

Misra, Joya, and Jennifer Lundquist. "Midcareer Melancholy," *Inside Higher Ed*, 2015, www.insidehighered.com/advice/2015/05/29/essay-frustrations-associate-professors

Wilson, Robin. "Why Are Associate Professors Some of the Unhappiest People in Academe?" *The Chronicle of Higher Education*, 2012, www.chronicle.com/article/Why-Are-Associate-Professors/132071

B. Directions for Change

Arshanapali, Bala. "Task Force Report on Faculty Development and Career Success Planning," Indiana University Northwest, circa 2012, www.iun.edu/aqip/docs/devcareerplanning.pdf

Canale, Anne Marie, et al. "Mid-Career Faculty Support: The Middle Years of the Academic Profession" The Wallace Center, Rochester Institute of Technology, 2013, www.rit.edu/academicaffairs/facultydevelopment/sites/rit.edu.academicaffairs.facultydevelopment/files/images/FCDS_Mid-CareerRpt.pdf

Flaherty, Colleen. "Midcareer Professors Need Love, Too," *Inside Higher Ed*, 2017, www.insidehighered.com/news/2017/01/26/research-midcareer-professors-makes-case-support-after-tenure

Jaschik, Scott. "Different Paths to Full Professor," *Inside Higher Ed*, 2010, tomprof.stanford.edu/posting/1007

Lees, N. Douglas, and Jane Williams. "Progressing Toward Creating a Campus Culture of Faculty Mentoring" *The Department Chair*, Winter, Wiley Learning, 2018, onlinelibrary.wiley.com/doi/abs/10.1002/dch.30179

Mathews, K. R. "Perspectives on Midcareer Faculty and Advice for Supporting Them," *The Collaborative on Academic Careers in Higher Education*, Harvard School of Education, 2014, scholar.harvard.edu/kmathews/publications/perspectives-midcareer-faculty-and-advice-supporting-them

Walker, Jeffrey T. "How to Manage the Move from Associate to Full Professor," *Journal of Criminal Justice Education*, vol. 27, no. 2, 2016, pp. 255-270, www.tandfonline.com/doi/abs/10.1080/10511253.2015.1129103?journalCode=rcje20

5. Sources and Resources for Senior Faculty Mentoring

A. Books, Articles, and Reports on the General Topic of Senior Faculty Development

Baldwin, Roger G., and Deborah G. Chang. "Reinforcing Our Strategies to Support Faculty in the Middle Years of Academic Life," *Liberal Education*, Fall 2006, files.eric.ed.gov/fulltext/EJ746034.pdf

Berberet, J., et al. "Planning for the Generational Turnover of the Faculty: Faculty Perceptions and Institutional Practices," *Recruitment, Retention, And Retirement in Higher Education: Building and Managing the Faculty of the Future,* R. Clark & J. Ma (Eds.), Cheltenham, UK: Elgar, 2005.

Bevevino, David, and David Attis. "Supporting the Productivity of Faculty After Tenure" University Leadership Council, The Advisory Board Company, Texas Christian University, 2012, cte.tcu.edu/wp-content/uploads/Supporting-Faculty-Productivity-After-Tenure_EAB.pdf

Bland, Carol J. and William H. Berquist. "Conclusions and Themes to Guide Approaches to the Vitality of Senior Faculty," *The Vitality of Senior Faculty Members: Snow on the Roof-*

-*Fire in the Furnace*. George Washington University Press, 1997.

Haines Seena L., and Nicholas G. Popovitch. "Engaging External Senior Faculty Members as Faculty Mentors," *American Journal of Pharmaceutical Education,* vol. 78, no. 5, 2014, p. 101, www.ajpe.org/doi/full/10.5688/ajpe785101

Fox, Robert A. "Mentoring in Mid-Career Faculty," American Speech and Hearing Association, 2014, www.asha.org/Articles/Mentoring-Mid-Career-Faculty/

June, Audrey Williams. "Most Professors Hate Post-Tenure Review. A Better Approach Might Look Like This," *Chronicle of Higher Education*, 2018, www.chronicle.com/article/Most-Professors-Hate/242483

"Report of the Task Force on Senior Faculty Development," Johns Hopkins University School of Medicine, 2017, medicine-matters.blogs.hopkinsmedicine.org/2017/11/senior-faculty-transition-program-sessions/

Rockquemore, Kerry Ann. "Rebrand Yourself," *Inside Higher Ed*, 2012, www.insidehighered.com/advice/2012/07/16/essay-how-mid-career-faculty-members-can-rebrand-themselves

B. Institution-Specific Programs and Websites that Serve Senior Faculty Members with Opportunities to Get Involved with Campus Leadership

Case Western Reserve

case.edu/facultydevelopment/career-path/faculty-leadership-development/

Iowa State University

www.provost.iastate.edu/faculty-and-staff-resources/development/fellowship

Michigan State University

msutoday.msu.edu/news/2017/msu-leaders-named-academic-leadership-program-fellows/

Northwestern University

www.northwestern.edu/provost/faculty-resources/career-development-leadership/ALP/fellows.html

Stanford University

facultydevelopment.stanford.edu/programs/leadership-development

University of California at Davis

academicaffairs.ucdavis.edu/faculty-leadership-academy

University of North Carolina at Chapel Hill

iah.unc.edu/faculty-resources/apply-for-a-fellowship/academic-
leadership-program-fellowship/

University of Illinois at Chicago

faculty.uic.edu/files/2016/11/FALP-Description.pdf

Virginia Tech University
advance.vt.edu/content/dam/advance_vt_edu/documents/
presentations/faculty_leadership_development_outcomes_pr
esentation.pdf

6. Sources and Resources for Implementing Faculty Mentoring Programs

A. Guides for Establishing Mentoring Programs in Universities, Book Chapters

Bland, Carol J., Tayler, et al. "Appendix A: Checklist for
Developing, Implementing and Assessing, Mentoring
Programs," *Faculty Success Through Mentoring, A Guide for
Mentors, Mentees and Leaders*, ACE Series on Higher
Education, Roman and Littlefield Publishers, 2009.

Phillips, Susan L., and Susan T. Dennison. "Guidelines for
Setting Up, Planning, and Facilitating a Mentoring Group,"
*Faculty Mentoring: A Practical Manual for Mentees, Mentors,
Administrators and Faculty Developers*, Stylus, 2015, p. 11-20

Phillips, Susan L., and Susan T. Dennison. "Advice for the
Director of a Faculty Mentoring Program," *Faculty Mentoring,
A Practical Manual for Mentees, Mentors, Administrators and
Faculty Developers*, Stylus, 2015, p. 41-46

B. Guides for Establishing Mentoring Programs for Faculty in Universities, Webpages

"Guide to Best Practices in Faculty Mentoring," Office of the
Provost, Columbia University, 2016,
provost.columbia.edu/sites/default/files/content/Mentoring
BestPractices.pdf

"Guidelines for Implementing Mentoring Arrangements,"
Brisbane, Australia: University of Queensland, circa 2004,
www.uq.edu.au/hupp/attachments/personnel/MentoringGu
idelines.pdf

Grove, Juliel, and Gao Huon. "How to Plan a Peer Mentoring
Program," A Users Guide, Sydney, Australia: UNSW, 2003,
www.wacampuscompact.org/retentionproject/onlineresourc
es/2011onlineresources/Mentoring%20Models/Peer%20Me
ntoring/How%20To%20Implement%20A%20Peer%20Men
toring%20Program_%20A%20User%27s%20Guide.pdf

Kiel, David. "Designing and Implementing a Mentoring
Program for Early Career Faculty," Center for Faculty
Excellence, University of North Carolina at Chapel Hill,
2010,
faopharmacy.unc.edu/files/2015/05/CFU_Mentoring_Desi
gn.pdf

"Michigan State University Faculty Mentoring Toolkit," *Resources
for Administrators and Faculty*, Michigan State University, circa
2012, www.adapp-advance.msu.edu/Faculty-Mentoring-
Toolkit-Resources%20for%20Unit%20Administrators

7. Sources and Resources for Supporting Full-Time, Non-tenure-track Faculty

A. Understanding the Problem

Kezar, Adrianna, et al. "The Imperative for Change: Understanding the Necessity of Changing Non-Tenure-Track Faculty Policies and Practices," Pullias Center for Higher Education, University of Southern California, 2014, pullias.usc.edu/delphi/resources/#make

Merritt Boyd, Alvin C. III, "Experiences and Perceptions of Full-Time, Non-Tenure-Track Faculty at a Four-Year University," *Fisher Digital Publications*, paper 254, St. John Fisher College, 2016, fisherpub.sjfc.edu/cgi/viewcontent.cgi?article=1256&context=education_etd

One Faculty Serving All Students, Coalition on the Academic Workforce, February 2010, www.academicworkforce.org/Research_reports.html

Waltman, Jean, et al. "Factors Contributing to Job Satisfaction and Dissatisfaction Among Non-Tenure-Track Faculty," *The Journal of Higher Education*, vol. 83, no. 3, 2012, www.tandfonline.com/doi/abs/10.1080/00221546.2012.11777250

B. Directions for Change

Seipel, Mathew T., and Lisa M. Larson. "Supporting Non-Tenure-Track Faculty Well-Being," *Journal of Career*

Assessment, vol. 26, no. 1, 2018, pp. 154-171,
journals.sagepub.com/doi/abs/10.1177/1069072716680046?
journalCode=jcaa

Simmons, Elizabeth H. "Supporting Academic Staff," *Inside
Higher Ed*, March 2, 2017,
www.insidehighered.com/advice/2017/03/02/how-senior-
academic-administrators-can-support-faculty-outside-tenure-
track-essay

For case studies of campus change. See the Delphi Project Path
to Change Archive: pullias.usc.edu/download/path-change-
campus-communities-worked-change-non-tenure-track-
policies-practices/

8. Gender, Mentoring, and Faculty Development

A. Understanding the Problem: Articles

Acker, Joan. "Hierarchies, Jobs, Bodies: A Theory of Gendered
Organizations," *Gender & Society*, vol. 4, no. 2, 1990, pp. 139-
58,
www3.kau.se/kurstorg/files/a/C10B963709d16168ABYyY1
4FAA27/Ack_Hierarchies.pdf

Carr, Phyllis L., et al. "Inadequate Progress for Women in
Academic Medicine: Findings from the National Faculty
Study." *Journal of Women's Health (Larchmt)*, Mar 1, 2015, vol.
24, no. 3, 2015, pp. 190–199,
www.researchgate.net/publication/272076943_Inadequate_P
rogress_for_Women_in_Academic_Medicine_Findings_fro
m_the_National_Faculty_Study

Flaherty, Colleen. "Relying on Women, Not Rewarding Them," *Inside Higher Ed*, 2017, www.insidehighered.com/news/2017/04/12/study-finds-female-professors-outperform-men-service-their-possible-professional

Flaherty, Colleen. "Dancing Backward in High Heels," *Inside Higher Ed*, 2018, www.insidehighered.com/news/2018/01/10/study-finds-female-professors-experience-more-work-demands-and-special-favor

Gumpertz, M, et al. "Retention and Promotion of Women and Underrepresented Minority Faculty in Science and Engineering at Four Large Land Grant Institutions" PLOS One, 2017, journals.plos.org/plosone/article?id=10.1371/journal.pone.0187285

Johnson, Heather L. "Pipelines, Pathways, and Institutional Leadership: An Update on the Status of Women in Higher Education," Washington, DC: American Council on Education, 2017, www.acenet.edu/news-room/Documents/Higher-Ed-Spotlight-Pipelines-Pathways-and-Institutional-Leadership-Status-of-Women.pdf

Ray, Victor. "Is Gender Bias an Intended Feature of Teaching Evaluations?" *Inside Higher Ed*, 2018, www.insidehighered.com/advice/2018/02/09/teaching-evaluations-are-often-used-confirm-worst-stereotypes-about-women-faculty

Weisshaar, Katharine. "Publish and Perish? An Assessment of Gender Gaps in Promotion to Tenure in Academia," *Social Forces*, vol. 96, issue 2, no. 1, 2017, pp. 529–560, https://academic.oup.com/sf/article-abstract/96/2/529/3897008?redirectedFrom=fulltext

Zonana, Kathy. "Pursuing Parity, A New Generation of Female Faculty is Gathering Data on Why There Should be More of Them," *Stanford Medicine,* Spring 2017, stanmed.stanford.edu/2017spring/women-faculty-use-data-to-seek-parity-in-academic-medicine.html

B. Understanding the Problem: Reports

Griffin, Kimberly. "Reconsidering the Pipeline Problem: Increasing Faculty Diversity," *ACE Blog,* Higher Education Today, 2016, www.higheredtoday.org/2016/02/10/reconsidering-the-pipeline-problem-increasing-faculty-diversity/

Hill, Catherine, et al. "Why So Few? Women in Science, Technology, Engineering, and Mathematics?" AAUW, 2010, www.aauw.org/research/why-so-few/

"Women Faculty at Northwestern, An Overview," Advisory Council on Women Faculty, Office of the Provost, Northwestern University, 2017, www.northwestern.edu/provost/faculty-resources/career-development-leadership/women-faculty/

C. Directions for Change

Brenda, Marina (editor). *Mentoring Away the Glass Ceiling in Academia, A Cultured Critique*, Rowman & Littlefield, 2015.

Carr, Phyllis L., et al. "Recruitment, Promotion and Retention of Women in Academic Medicine: How Institutions Are Addressing Gender Disparities," *Journal of Women's Health Issues*, vol. 27, no. 3, Jacob's Institute for Women's Health, 2017, pp. 374-381, www.ncbi.nlm.nih.gov/pubmed/28063849

Effective Policies and Programs for the Retention, and Advancement of Women in Academia," *Worklife Law*, UC Hastings College of Law, 2012, worklifelaw.org/publication/effective-policies-and-programs-for-retention-and-advancement-of-women-in-academia/

"Faculty Retention Toolkit," ADVANCE Center for Institutional Change, College of Engineering and the College

of Arts & Sciences, University of Washington, 2006,
https://advance.washington.edu/resources/docs/Faculty%2
0retention%20Toolkit.docx

Girdler, Susan, and Christin Colford. "Mentoring Junior Faculty
in the UNC School of Medicine," Presentation to the UNC-
CH School of Medicine Association of Educators, University
of North Carolina, 2017,
www.med.unc.edu/aoe/files/2017/12/Girdler-and-Colford-
AOE-November-2017.pdf

Lehfeldt, Elizabeth A. "#metoo in the Meantime: Small Steps
Women Can Take to Improve the Work Environment for
Female Colleagues," *Inside Higher Ed*, 2018,
www.insidehighered.com/advice/2018/05/18/small-steps-
women-academe-should-take-support-each-other-opinion

Smith, Kristin A., et al. "Seven Actionable Strategies for
Advancing Women in Science, Engineering, and Medicine,"
Cell Stem Cell, vol. 16, no. 3, 2015, pp. 221–224,
www.cell.com/cell-stem-cell/abstract/S1934-5909(15)00068-
5

Varkey, Prathibha, et al. "The positive impact of a facilitated
peer mentoring program on academic skills of women
faculty," *BMC Medical Education*, vol. 12, 2012, p. 14,
www.ncbi.nlm.nih.gov/pmc/articles/PMC3325854/

Voytko, M.L., et al. "Positive Value of a Women's Junior Faculty
Mentoring Program: A Mentor-Mentee Analysis," *Journal of
Women's Health (Larchmt)*, vol. 8, 2018, pp. 1045-1053,
www.ncbi.nlm.nih.gov/pubmed/29813008

Women Faculty Mentoring Program, University of Wisconsin,
https://secfac.wisc.edu/

9. Addressing the Development Needs and Concerns of Under-Represented Minority Faculty Members

A. Understanding the Problem

Mack, Dwayne A. "Sick and Tired of Being Sick and Tired," *Inside Higher Ed*, 2016, www.insidehighered.com/advice/2016/03/25/how-faculty-color-can-achieve-good-work-life-balance-academe-essay

Misra, Joya, and Jennifer Lundquist. "Diversity and the Ivory Ceiling: Midcareer Minority Faculty Members Face Particular Challenges," *Inside Higher Ed*, 2015, www.insidehighered.com/advice/2015/06/26/essay-diversity-issues-and-midcareer-faculty-members

Moore, Mignon R. "Women of Color in the Academy: Navigating Multiple Intersections and Multiple Hierarchies," *Social Problems*, vol. 64, no. 2, 2017, pp. 200–205, academic.oup.com/socpro/article/64/2/200/3231961

Moreno, Jose F., et al. "The Revolving Door for Underrepresented Minorities in Higher Education," James Irvine Foundation Campus Diversity Project, AACU, 2006, www.slcc.edu/inclusivity/docs/the-revolving-door-for-underrepresented-minority-faculty-in-higher-education.pdf

Toner, Mark. "Diversifying Diversity," ACE NET, 2016, www.acenet.edu/the-presidency/columns-and-features/Pages/Diversifying-Diversity.aspx

B. Directions for Change: Reports, Articles, and Book Chapters

"Faculty Diversity Training and Programs and Best Practices," *Draft Report of the University of Southern California Climate Committee of the Faculty Senate*, University of Southern California, November 10, 2016, academicsenate.usc.edu/files/2015/08/Climate-Committee-Faculty-Diversity-Best-Practices-11-10-16.pdf

"Addressing Generational Change with Senior Faculty Members," University Leadership Council, Educational Advisory Board, University of Massachusetts, 2012, www.umass.edu/provost/sites/default/files/uploads/Addressing%20Generational%20Change%20with%20Senior%20Faculty%20Members.pdf

Taylor, Orlando, et al. "Diversifying the Faculty," *Peer Review*, vol. 12, no. 3, AACU, 2010, www.aacu.org/publications-research/periodicals/diversifying-faculty

Williams, Damon A., and Katrina C. Wad-Golden. "Best Practices for Improving Faculty Diversity Recruitment and Retention," *The Chief Diversity Officer [CDO]: Strategy, Structure, and Change Management*, Stylus Publishing, 2013.

Zabrana, Ruth Enid, et al. "Don't Leave Us Behind: The Importance of Mentoring for Underrepresented Minority Faculty," *American Educational Research Journal*, vol. 52, no. 1, 2015, pp. 40-72, journals.sagepub.com/doi/abs/10.3102/0002831214563063

ABOUT THE AUTHOR

DAVID KIEL

For sixteen years between 2001 and 2017, Dr. Kiel was employed full and part-time at UNC-Chapel Hill where he developed faculty mentoring programs and served all 12 professional schools and the College of Arts and Sciences. He is the co-author of a previous book on professional and personal development published by McGraw-Hill in 2003. Trained as an organizational development and leadership specialist, he has published many articles on faculty leadership development, organizational change, and institutional innovation. He has been a presenter at national workshops and conferences on faculty development topics, and he consults with major universities on their faculty and leadership development programs.

While at the Center for Faculty Excellence (2010-16), he was the chief university-wide internal consultant on faculty mentoring. In that capacity advised departments and schools about how to create or improve mentoring programs for their faculty. He developed and presented public programs to assist new mentors learn about mentoring and to help mentees make the most of their mentoring relationships. He developed customized workshops for individual units that wanted to involve their faculty in improving and enriching their mentoring programs, and helped units evaluate and improve their programs. He conducted campus-wide surveys of mentoring practices and produced a study of campus best practices. He also reviewed and summarized the national mentoring best practice literature in various campus reports and presentations.

During his time at the Center for the Arts and Humanities (2001-9), he developed UNC's premier program for leadership development for midcareer and senior faculty and a program to assist new department Chairs in the College of Arts and Sciences. Those programs are still in operation. While at the Center for Faculty Excellence, in addition to working on mentoring development, he created professional development programs for early career faculty, for new faculty leaders, and for faculty innovators.

David studied organizational behavior in graduate school at Yale University and later received a Doctorate of Public Health from UNC in 1974. He did post doctoral studies there in Community Psychiatry and Health Administration from 1977-9. During 1975-85 Kiel taught masters level manage-ment courses at three state universities. From 1985-2000, he consulted with government agencies, non-profits, and small and large businesses. He has been a professional member of the NTL Institute Applied Behavioral Science for twenty years and has led that organization's research community of practice. Currently he serves as an Adjunct Clinical Associate Professor at the UNC-CH School of Social Work.

Made in the USA
Las Vegas, NV
26 September 2022

56001149R00319